IAN PAISLEY

VOICE OF PROTESTANT ULSTER

Tom Burne
17 Carrigmore
Carrigaline
Co Cork.

To my parents

IAN PAISLEY

VOICE OF PROTESTANT ULSTER

CLIFFORD SMYTH

SCOTTISH ACADEMIC PRESS LIMITED
EDINBURGH
1987

First published 1987 by Scottish Academic Press

Copyright © Scottish Academic Press

ISBN 07073 0499 7

British Library Cataloguing in Publication Data

Smyth, Clifford
    Ian Paisley: voice of Protestant Ulster.
    1. Paisley, Ian   2. Presbyterians—
    Northern Ireland—Biography   3. Clergy—
    Northern Ireland—Biography   4. Politicians
    —Northern Ireland—Biography
    I. Title
    941.6082′4′0924   BX9225.P.24

    ISBN 0–7073–0499–7

Typeset by Pindar (Scotland) Limited, Edinburgh
Printed and bound in Great Britain

Contents

Illustrations

vi

Abbreviations

CRA	Civil Rights Association
DULC	Democratic Unionist Loyalist Coalition
DUP	Democratic Unionist Party
EEC	European Economic Community
Free Church	Free Presbyterian Church of Ulster
INLA	Irish National Liberation Army
IRA	Irish Republican Army
MEP	Member of the European Parliament
MPA	Member of the Parliamentary Assembly
NILP	Northern Ireland Labour Party
NIO	Northern Ireland Office
OUP	Official Unionist Party

(The Party itself prefers to be known as the Ulster Unionist Party, but in a period of fragmentation, commentators found it necessary to refer to it as the Official Unionist Party to distinguish it from the others).

PM	Prime Minister
PR	Proportional Representation
RUC	Royal Ulster Constabulary
SAS	Special Air Service
SDLP	Social Democratic and Labour Party
SDP	Social Democratic Party
SPA	Scottish Protestant Action (Edinburgh)
SPL	Scottish Protestant League (Glasgow)
UCDC	Ulster Constitution Defence Committee
UDA	Ulster Defence Association
UDR	Ulster Defence Regiment
UDUP	Ulster Democratic Unionist Party

(This is the official title of the party, but it is generally known as the DUP).

UPA	Ulster Protestant Action
UPUP	Ulster Popular Unionist Party
UPV	Ulster Protestant Volunteers
USA	United States of America
UUP	Ulster Unionist Party

UUUC	United Ulster Unionist Council (or Coalition)
UUUM	United Ulster Unionist Movement (Original name of the organisation led by Ernest Baird; changed to UUUP when they started to put up candidates).
UUUP	United Ulster Unionist Party
UVF	Ulster Volunteer Force
UWC	Ulster Workers Council
VULC	Vanguard Unionist Loyalist Coalition
VUPP	Vanguard Unionist Progressive Party

Preface

The aim of this book is to explain how the revivalist preacher and politician, Dr Ian Paisley, broke the hold of the Ulster Unionist Party on the majority of voters in Northern Ireland, by forging a movement, the Ulster Democratic Unionist Party (DUP), which succeeded where similar alternative loyalist parties had failed in the past. Widely regarded as intransigent and bigoted, and lampooned in the media, Ian Paisley has worsted his critics by demonstrating a unique personal command over the affections and loyalty of hundreds of thousands of voters in the Province. Dr Paisley's influence is not limited to Northern Ireland; the Protestant preacher's family roots and theology lie in Scotland, where he has a small but vociferous personal following. In addition, his election to the European Parliamentary Assembly and Paisley's long association with leading fundamentalist preachers in the 'Bible belt' of the United States have brought international recognition to this most controversial of Northern Ireland politicians.

Ian Paisley's international notoriety rests on the impact which his style of politics has had on the situation in the Province. The DUP has tended to pull the more moderate Official Unionist Party to the right. The DUP's militancy contributed to the fall of the 1974 power sharing Northern Ireland Executive, and forestalled William Craig's Voluntary Coalition initiative in the Constitutional Convention of 1975. In the early 1980s, the DUP was more conciliatory and there were signs that the Party wished to assist the Conservative Government in its search for a political solution based on the concept of 'rolling devolution'. On November 15, 1985, the British Prime Minister, Margaret Thatcher, jointly signed an Anglo-Irish Agreement with the Irish Republic's Taoiseach, Dr Garrett Fitzgerald, at Hillsborough Castle. The Ulster loyalists, interpreting the Agreement as a betrayal and a concession to the violence of the Provisional IRA, asserted their right to equality of citizenship within the United Kingdom. Ian Paisley re-emerged to lead loyalist defiance of the sovereign will of Parliament, sustained by the seventeenth century Covenanters' conviction that the people are under no obligation to submit to the will of a government the actions of which are arbitrary and lacking in moral authority.

The book is based on an unpublished doctoral thesis, 'The Democratic Unionist Party: A Case Study in Political and Religious

ix

Convergence'. Additional research material has been incorporated in the book which, like the thesis, draws on personal experience of the events described. In particular, I was for four years (1972 to 1976) a DUP party member, and for a short time a public representative in both the Northern Ireland Assembly and the Constitutional Convention. In the Convention I was elected Honorary Secretary to the United Ulster Unionist Coalition with which the DUP was aligned at the time. Occasionally I have allowed personal reminiscences to intrude into the text of the book in order to illuminate incidents which otherwise would remain obscure.

Interviews played an important part in providing source material for both the thesis and the book, and I owe a considerable debt to all those who willingly gave of their time to illuminate aspects of Dr Paisley's story. Special thanks are due to a small number of those interviewed who gave particular assistance; they were: Rev. John Brown MA, Rev. George Hutton, Mr George Wylie, Mr J. G. MacLean of Edinburgh, Mr Frank Millar senior, MPA, and Mr Wallace Thompson, formerly DUP Finance Officer.

I have enjoyed considerable help, advice and encouragement from the outset. My thanks are especially due to Professor John Whyte, now of University College, Dublin, who made the initial invitation to me to undertake post-graduate research on the DUP at Queen's University. The Department of Education for Northern Ireland funded the work at Queen's which was supervised by Dr Sydney Elliott. Dr A. T. Q. Stewart offered important advice at the stage when the thesis was being rewritten for publication in book form. Rev. Wilbert Forker, Rev. Dr Robert Brown, and Mr Douglas Grant of the Scottish Academic Press all took a personal interest; and to all of those mentioned I owe a debt of gratitude.

Belfast is well served by good libraries and I should like to thank the librarians of Queen's University and at the Linenhall and Central Libraries for their unfailing courtesy and willingness to help.

Finally I should like to record my gratitude to my wife Anne; not only did Anne type the early drafts, and later the transcript for publication, but she intervened crucially, at one dark moment of frustration, to rescue the draft from the bin! Without Anne's unfailing support and enthusiasm the whole project might never have come to fruition.

CHAPTER I

Provocateur or Prophet

Ulster regionalism, or nationalism, can be traced back to the seventeenth century. It is rooted in the self-assurance of the seventeenth century Scottish Presbyterian 'Planters' in the former Gaelic kingdom of Ulster and the Anglo-Norman earldom of that name. This colonisation was a mass immigration which provided a new middle class and 'proletariat' – in fact, a whole new society – in Northern Ireland.

M. W. Heslinga
The Irish Border as a Cultural Divide

My mother was born on the 13th October, 1898. She was born into a Scots Covenanting home, in a place that was famous for revival, the place of Kilsyth, in the country of Scotland. I have her Bible with me, a Bible that she used during all her life, and on the front of the Bible she has a note, 'Redeemed August 2nd, 1914, Gospel Mission Hall, City of Edinburgh'.

Dr Ian R. K. Paisley
My Father and Mother

A twentieth century miracle

On 11 June 1979, the results of the first election to the European Parliamentary Assembly held in Northern Ireland were declared. Top of the poll came Rev. Ian Paisley, leader of the Democratic Unionist Party and a revivalist preacher, who had achieved international notoriety as a leader of Protestant opinion in Ulster. Gaining a total of 179,688 first preference votes, Paisley had surpassed John Hume, the highly articulate leader of the mainly Roman Catholic SDLP, and both the Official Unionist candidates. Harry West, the Unionist Party leader, was eliminated at the sixth stage under the Proportional Representation system of voting and only then was his colleague John Taylor deemed elected.

Besieged by pressmen in Belfast City Hall, Ian Paisley declared that this singular triumph was a 'twentieth century miracle'.[1] It was a phrase resonant with Paisley's confidence in the sovereignty of God, and an utterance typical of a man whose political outlook owed more to the principles of Scotland's seventeenth century Covenanters, than it did to any contemporary political philosophy. Not surprisingly many of Paisley's critics perceived him to be an anachronistic figure. The European election marked a significant stage in Paisley's rise as a major force in Ulster politics. This success underlined the achievement of the leader of the Democratic Unionist Party in engineering a political machine capable of out-distancing the Ulster Unionist Party at the polls. Since the inception of the Northern Ireland state the Ulster Unionist Party had, until the institution's prorogation, provided the ruling party in the Stormont Parliament and governed the Province, which had developed its own distinctive party system.

This election victory had been all the more remarkable because at the outset of his career, Ian Paisley had been an outsider, whose upbringing and early forays into politics seemed entirely inauspicious.

Ian Paisley was born in humble surroundings on 6 April 1926, in the ancient ecclesiastical capital of Ireland, the City of Armagh. His father Kyle, whose ancestors came originally from Scotland, was a Baptist preacher, and his mother, Isobel, was equally devout. Paisley has always spoken of his parents with evident emotion and affection. Two other children shared the Paisley home, an elder brother Harold, and sister Margaret. The family enjoyed little in the way of material blessing, though they claimed a rich spiritual heritage, which would have struck onlookers as puritanical in aspect. Family life was based on the Bible which was accepted reverently as God's revealed will to man.

It is evident from Ian Paisley's own writings that his father had a deep evangelical interest in winning sinners for Christ. That was not all, though, because Pastor Kyle Paisley was a member of the original Ulster Volunteer Force, an opponent of Irish Home Rule who believed that any government in Dublin would be dominated by the Roman Catholic hierarchy at Maynooth. Ian Paisley remarked later, 'What my father taught me, I imbibed and I believe it to this day'.

Isobel Paisley also made a profound impact on her younger son. Paisley attributed his coming to Jesus Christ to the prayers and ministry of his mother. Mrs Paisley was a very forceful character, despite her small stature, and Ian Paisley inherited something of his mother's abrasive dynamism.

After an entirely unremarkable scholastic career Ian Paisley entered the Christian ministry, his mind fired with enthusiasm for Protestantism and an 'old style religion' which already seemed outmoded to clergy who had progressed through mainstream theological colleges to enter the established denominations. Paisley's heroes were not the renowned theologians of modern times; his heroes were pre-eminently the great preachers of the Protestant tradition. He feasted on the works of C. H. Spurgeon, but none was held in higher personal esteem than the later Rev. W. P. Nicholson.

Nicholson led a number of religious crusades in central Scotland, but the greatest successes attended his ministry in Ulster in the 1920s. Paisley was to mould his preaching style on that of W. P. Nicholson. Professor Adam Loughridge, in an otherwise sympathetic treatment of Nicholson's ministry, provides an important clue as to why Paisley's political oratory was to cause so much offence to so many inside Northern Ireland and beyond. Loughridge has written of Nicholson noting that 'He was vulgar and rude and his language at times was ungracious as he indulged in personal abuse . . . to those who dared to criticise him. . . .'

On the centenary of Nicholson's birth, Paisley published a sermon he had preached about his mentor, Nicholson. He relates a story which explains why Paisley's confidence in the rightness of his cause made him almost impervious to criticism. Paisley states that W. P. Nicholson attended a morning service at which Paisley, then still only twenty, was the preacher. After Paisley had concluded his address Nicholson walked to the front of the church and said:

> I have one prayer I want to offer to this young man. I will pray that God will give him a tongue like an old cow. Go in, young man, to a butcher's shop and ask to see a cow's tongue. You will find it sharper than any file. God give you such a tongue. Make this church a converting shop and make this preacher a disturber of Hell and the Devil![2]

Rev. Ian Paisley later said of this incident: 'I well remember his standing there and uttering those words. I believe God answered his prayer, for my tongue has caused great trouble to Popes and Popery, Ecumenists and Ecumenism, Modernists and Modernism.'

By the age of twenty, Ian Paisley's Protestant fundamentalist roots had travelled deep. The young man revered the traditions of the Scots Covenanters and had mastered the techniques of American style revivalist preaching, but there had been little in his education to stimulate his critical faculties or to awaken the self-doubt that afflicts so many of Ian Paisley's contemporaries.

Parallel with Paisley's attempts to establish himself in an independent work as a revivalist preacher there had developed an awareness of the prevailing political situation in Northern Ireland.

Burgeoning political interest

In 1950 a Church of Ireland rector, Rev. James MacManaway, contested the Westminster parliamentary constituency of West Belfast. It was a time of political stagnation in Ulster. Despite the emergence of parties critical of the Ulster Unionists, the settled disposition of the majority of voters was to support the Party which had preserved the link with Great Britain and guided the Province into the post-war era. For their part, many of the Roman Catholics in the Province, who comprised one third of the population, supported the Irish Nationalist Party, though a proportion within the Nationalist population believed that only 'physical force men' with Thompson sub-machine guns in their hands could end the Partition of 'their country'. Rev. James MacManaway denounced such extreme Irish Republican sentiments; a gifted orator, the rector was a leading figure at Orange and Apprentice Boys processions.

Loyalist institutions like the Orange Order and the Apprentice Boys of Derry did more than celebrate by such processions important episodes in Irish and British history. These organisations inculcated through their rituals and folk traditions an alternative perception of Irish history to that of the Irish nationalists. The loyalist institutions also modified the tensions existing between the Protestant denominations in Ulster. Through a subtle inter-action with the Ulster Unionist Party, which accorded voting rights to Orange delegates, the loyalist institutions gave to Ulster politics its distinctive character.

It is hard to assess what impact Rev. James MacManaway's apparent success in combining the offices of Gospel preacher and politician had on the youthful Paisley but he was evidently impressed. Paisley worked actively for MacManaway throughout the election campaign. Others might find the dual role of preacher and politician incongruous and distasteful; Ian Paisley did not see any such contradiction.

On 17 March of the following year, the Free Presbyterian Church of Ulster was formed. The new sect, in a Province which proliferated with denominations large and small, was based around a group of disaffected Presbyterian elders at Lissara, near Crossgar in County Down. The Free Presbyterians also had a mission hall on the lower Ravenhill Road in Belfast to which Rev. Ian Paisley had been called as Pastor. The Belfast congregation comprised former members who had separated from the Ravenhill Road Presbyterian Church, and other locals of an evangelical persuasion who had no previous church connection. Soon this mission hall became known as the Ravenhill Road Free Presbyterian Church.

For a period of months a layman called Mr Lince fulfilled the office of 'Moderator' in the new Presbyterian sect, but finally in exasperation he turned to Paisley and said, 'Come on, Ian, you take the chair; after all, it's what you've wanted!' Once having established himself as Moderator of the Free Presbyterian Church, Paisley's attention turned to building up the 'work', and advancing the cause of militant Protestantism.

Though the Unionist Party dominated politics throughout Paisley's early years, there were loyalists who criticised the Party's administration in the Province. The loyalists opposed specific social and economic policies of the Stormont Government. Before the Second World War, the Local Optionists had campaigned on the temperance issue, while the Progressive Unionists called for a more radical approach to Ulster's social needs. Neither of these loyalist alternatives made much headway against the structure of Official Unionism.

Bridging the pre- and post-war eras were the Independent Unionists. Highly individualistic, the Independent Unionists at Stormont contained within their ranks an evangelical faction. Rev. Norman Porter, a Baptist, and Willie Wilton, an undertaker, jointly published a periodical entitled *The Ulster Protestant*! These evangelicals campaigned on issues of religious defence; aggressively Protestant, they were strongly critical of the Unionist Government's education policy, which allowed the Roman Catholic Church control of its own schools, and, they contended, threatened Ulster's Protestant ethos.

Rev. Norman Porter provides the link between the Independent Unionists and Ian Paisley's developing interest in building a political platform of his own. There is a measure of continuity between this evangelical faction of the Independent Unionists in the Stormont Parliament and the political movements which Paisley later initiated. Like the Scottish Protestant League in Glasgow and Scottish Protestant Action in Edinburgh, which enjoyed limited political success in central Scotland in the inter-war years, the Independent Unionists looked to the members of the Orange Institution for support. These inchoate factions adopted an ambiguous attitude towards Orangeism which still obtains in Paisleyite circles. While the Protestant zealots relied heavily on rank and file members of the Orange Order for electoral support, they were the first to accuse the leaders of Orangeism, whether in Scotland or Northern Ireland, of having compromised Protestant principles.

By the early fifties, Ian Paisley and Norman Porter had launched into a joint crusade under the banner of the National Union of Protestants. The two preachers conducted a series of revivalist meetings and as their association deepened it occurred to Rev. Ian Paisley that the moment might be opportune to invite Rev. Norman Porter to align himself with the ministry of the burgeoning Free Presbyterian sect. Perhaps Porter was more doctrinaire than Paisley, who had demonstrated a notably pragmatic approach to the minutiae of Protestant denominational theology, because the offer was spurned.

This rebuff reverberated throughout the National Union of Protestants which soon disintegrated in acrimony. The row proved to be the first in a series of disruptions between Rev. Ian Paisley and some of his closest associates which have punctuated the history of Paisleyism.

Porter may also have been unwilling to identify himself with a small Presbyterian sect which was coming under the increasing influence of American Protestant Fundamentalism, a trend which was reflected in the articles carried in the church magazine, *The Revivalist*.

Onlookers who were less familiar with the nuances of Protestant theology drew another conclusion: that Norman Porter harboured reservations about Ian Paisley's authoritarian personality and his arbitrary way of doing things. This characteristic was one which Paisley shared with the two Scottish Protestant protagonists, Alexander Ratcliffe of the Scottish Protestant League and the Edinburgh based leader of Scottish Protestant Action, Baillie John Cormack.

Paisley had also taken the initiative in attempting to recruit Porter into the growing ranks of Ulster Free Presbyterianism, indicating for the first time that the young Ravenhill Road evangelist had set his heart upon building a militant Protestant movement which accepted the style of leadership which he was prepared to offer.

Ulster Protestant Action: the catalyst

In 1956 Ulster Protestant Action was founded in reaction to a recent series of IRA cross-border raids. Ian Paisley joined a young lawyer, Desmond Boal, and his erstwhile associate Norman Porter at the inaugural meeting. Porter immediately withdrew, leaving Boal and Paisley with a clear field of influence.

The larger proportion of the UPA's membership consisted of working-class loyalists in Belfast, some of whom were also members of the Unionist Party. The importance of the UPA lies in the fact that throughout the decade of its history this loyalist organisation bridged the closing years of Lord Brookeborough's premiership and the years of reform associated with the administration of Captain Terence O'Neill. The UPA's incipient paramilitarism was to carry right through to June 1966, when the movement disintegrated in the aftermath of the Malvern Street murders committed in that month by loyalist paramilitaries of the UVF. The UPA can rightly be regarded as a potentially armed expression of extreme loyalism in Ulster which also sought to give political direction to working class loyalists during the years which preceded the current period of civil unrest.

The UPA's militancy appealed to Ian Paisley and his identification with the movement consolidated his friendship with Desmond Boal, bringing Paisley into contact with a group of the most politicised Protestants in Belfast.

For a decade Paisley's political development was to be strongly influenced by the inter-action between the militant working class loyalists in the UPA and his own followers who worshipped in the Ravenhill Road Free Church. Paisley's association with the UPA was only one of many intricate political and religious manoeuvrings undertaken by him during this period, but the impact of his involvement with the UPA is so crucial to the rise of Paisleyism that it is easier to understand future developments within the context of Ulster Protestant Action, rather than either the Free Presbyterian Church or the emergence of Protestant Unionism.

The UPA rapidly came to terms with the fact that the Stormont Government was successfully countering the IRA insurgency, so the loyalists decided to put paramilitarism on the back burner and create an alternative loyalist structure instead. Paisley was to the fore among those within the ranks who argued for such a role. The UPA moved on two fronts. There was a sustained attempt to influence patterns of employment in some Belfast factories to the exclusion of Roman Catholics, while simultaneously Desmond Boal was invited to draft a constitution which would give effect to the loyalists' aspirations.

The rules drawn up by Boal throw some light on the attitude of these activists to the Unionist political establishment in Northern Ireland in the late 1950s. The rules specifically debarred 'politicians' from membership of Protestant Action, and this clause underlines the widespread resentment among ordinary Unionist voters who believed that the Unionist Government used the Orange and other loyalist movements to its own advantage, merely paying lip service to Protestant principles.

In Northern Ireland this disenchantment with the Unionist establishment brought little comfort to the socialists because the loyalists' apprehension of Romanism, the resurgent IRA, and the claims of the Irish Republic had locked them in on the right, but across the north channel a similar disaffection with the Scottish Tory

Party, which was perceived to be soft on Romanism, had helped undermine the strength of the Orange working class Conservative vote. The Scottish Tories had not helped themselves by losing touch with those working class supporters whose patriotic fervour and cries of 'No Popery' were an embarrassment in our increasingly secular society.

No single individual emerged to lead the UPA. It is not clear whether Boal's Constitution favoured a committee system, but perhaps the explanation is to be found in the resistance which some of the loyalists mounted against Ian Paisley. Not everyone shared Paisley's commitment to temperance or his vehement anti-Catholicism which was becoming ever more strident as the preacher voiced his alarm at the ecumenical 'Romeward trend'.

Writing in his book *The 1859 Revival*, Paisley explained what he meant by this term, and Pastor Kyle Paisley's conviction that 'Home Rule was Rome Rule' re-emerges in his son's statement:

> The dark sinister shadow of our neighbouring Roman Catholic state, where religious liberty is slowly but surely being taken away, lies across our Province. The demands and aims of the Church of Rome are growing and as our Protestantism declines with the blight of modernistic apostasy, the ascendancy of that church is becoming more and more marked in our Ulster life.[3]

Acting on such beliefs, Paisley had aligned himself with those on the fringes of Unionism. This created tensions among the more pietistic of Paisley's Ravenhill Road congregation. Robert Clelland, formerly the Secretary of the Church, has described how the convergence of revivalist preaching with political action provoked dissent within the Free Church congregation. This was especially apparent in the Session of the Church where some elders rejected the theological stance of their Moderator on the acceptability of preaching the gospel one night and promoting loyalist politics the next. There was a walk-out by these pietistic office bearers which effectively consolidated the support for Paisley's style of politicised Protestantism among the remaining members of the congregation.

Paisley's difficulties in developing his parallel interests in the mission of the Church and politics helps to explain why he adopted a very cautious approach to the launching of the Protestant Unionist Party. According to Frank Millar senior, one time Secretary of the UPA, the term 'Protestant Unionist' was coined in Belfast in the 1930s. However, there are stronger grounds for stating that it was the UPA which revamped 'Protestant Unionism' as a 'scarecrow party' to frighten the Unionists of Glengall Street into adopting more right-wing policies in response to the IRA campaign and the propaganda of the Irish nationalists.

A decision was taken to contest the Stormont Parliamentary constituency of Iveagh in the general election of March 1958, and their candidate was a former Belfast councillor and superintendent of an independent gospel mission in Aughrim Street, Albert Duff. Iveagh was singled out as the testing ground for Protestant Unionism because the sitting member, Brian Maginess, was the Attorney General for Northern Ireland.

Duff criticised Brian Maginess on the grounds that the Official Unionist Cabinet Minister had 'tragically forgotten the deep Protestant conviction out of which the Unionist Party was born'. Duff articulated the belief of those loyalists who held that the convergence of Protestant interests with Unionism needed to be expressed in the political life of Northern Ireland. The election address of the Protestant Unionist candidate bore the impress of Ian Paisley, because Duff also warned the Unionist establishment of the dangers which the Protestant Unionists detected in a situation where 'more and more power is being given to the (Roman Catholic) hierarchy'.

Paisley's behind-the-scenes influence over Protestant Unionism was even speculated upon by a heckler in Hillsborough's main street square. According to Frank Millar senior, who had travelled down to the election meeting in Ian Paisley's Hillman car, the heckler, noting Paisley's 'mountainous' presence standing at the side of Albert Duff, shouted: 'If ever you get elected to Stormont you may take that big man there with you'. In fact Duff failed to win the Iveagh seat, but he was elected to Belfast City Council, together with another Protestant Unionist candidate, Charles McCullough, on 21 May 1958.

Initially, the membership of the Protestant Unionist Party comprised a handful of loyalists in Belfast who were associated with the UPA, but the emergence of the Party created tensions within Protestant Action, prompting a realignment which effectively consolidated Paisley's control over the Protestant Unionist Party. To achieve this, all the supporters of Paisley's political style were recruited into one branch of the UPA, known as the 'Premier' branch, which provided the nucleus for the development of Protestant Unionism. Paisley's success in capturing Protestant Unionism would become evident by 1964, but in the interval between the emergence of Protestant Unionism in 1958 and the elections to Belfast City Council in 1964, the loyalists in the UPA sank their differences because a by-election had been called in the intensely loyalist Belfast constituency of Shankill, following the retirement of Tommy Henderson, an Independent Unionist in the Stormont Parliament. Though Desmond Boal determined to contest the vacant seat as an Official Unionist rather than as a Protestant Unionist, Paisley found little difficulty in actively supporting Boal's candidature. Paisley explained that Boal was 'a man who puts Protestantism first – not like those who become Protestants and Orangemen when they are looking for nomination'.

Boal was returned for Shankill and took his seat on the Government benches at Stormont, and though his personal friendship with Ian Paisley was unaffected, it did mark a divergence in their political careers. Boal went on to establish a reputation for political radicalism 'when he voted with the Northern Ireland Labour Party on an economic censure motion',[4] and he even lost the Unionist Party whip for a time in 1961.

1962 marked the fiftieth anniversary of the signing of Ulster's Solemn League and Covenant. This document was of great importance, because it showed the strength of Ulster's opposition to Home Rule, and given the origins of the Province the decision to borrow the document's title straight from the pages of Scottish history seemed appropriate.

The Unionist Party and the Orange Institution organised a massive demonstration in commemoration of the anniversary to the Balmoral showgrounds in Belfast on the last Saturday in September, and the occasion gave the majority of the population in Northern Ireland an opportunity to reflect on the period of relative prosperity and peace which the Province had enjoyed since the austerity of the post-war era had ended. The IRA campaign in rural Ulster had petered out, the RUC and the part-timers of the Ulster Special Constabulary having successfully drawn the teeth of this attempt to end Partition by armed insurrection. Not everyone on the sidelines had cause to cheer, however, because apart from the Nationalist minority who sustained a deep sense of grievance over the partition of 'their country', there were other lonely figures watching the celebrations: they were Ian Paisley and his devoted followers. Paisley's predicament was the more acute because he had resigned from the Orange Institution on 20 September.

There has been speculation over Paisley's resignation. Marrinan, writing in *Paisley: Man of Wrath*, suggests that the resignation was a sequel to the UPA's protest against what the press had headlined as 'The Orange and Green Talks' held between Sir George Clark, Grand Master of the Orange Institution, and Senator James Lennon, leader of the Nationalist Party. This explanation is hardly possible, because these private discussions began on 17 October, weeks after Paisley's resignation had been forwarded from his Lodge, number 1069 in West Belfast.

Paisley had previously been a member of a lodge in East Belfast but following a fraught exchange with Rev. Warren Porter, a Presbyterian minister and fellow lodge member, Paisley transferred to Lodge 1069, only to resign completely in September.

Throughout these early years, Paisley's rough-hewn personality and anti-Romish zealotry had provoked discord on all sides and by the early 1960s he seemed almost totally isolated. Paisley had dabbled in alternative forms of fringe Unionism. He had resigned from the Orange Order which was a recognised route to political office and he had launched himself into a sustained preaching campaign across Ulster criticising the main Protestant denominations for their involvement in ecumenical dialogue. The revivalist preacher urged those who attended his gospel tent meetings that these Churches were on the road to Rome, and Paisley enunciated an alternative based on the Biblical doctrine of 'separation'. This doctrine of separation originated in the United States in the 1920s in opposition to liberal theology in the Protestant denominations. George Dollar in his history of Fundamentalism explains that 'separation . . . is the Biblical principle that the believer is to keep himself unspotted from the world . . . Ecclesiastical separation refers to an individual's separating himself from a church that endorses or condones apostacy. . . .'[5] Paisley's application of this doctrine proved to be of crucial importance to the growth of Ulster Free Presbyterianism.

Later that autumn Ian Paisley and some of his close associates set off for Rome to stage a demonstration at the opening of the Second Vatican Council. The episode attracted press publicity and gave the preacher on the Ravenhill Road the opportunity to present a florid account of his adventures to his congregation.

These endeavours were provoking increasing interest in the Province. At the time I was an apprentice quantity surveyor, and Paisley became a topic of conversation during coffee break at work. I recall the fascination shown in an account of one of Paisley's services given by one apprentice who had wandered into the Free Church one Sabbath evening. The preacher had become the talk of the town, but not all who attended his packed church remained sceptical: some 'got saved'!

Rev. Ian Paisley's protest in Rome in October 1962 presaged the change which was about to overtake Ulster. The Second Vatican Council helped to foster a new mood among Roman Catholics in Ireland, and this was also true of the nationalist minority in the North. In this changed climate bridge-building between the divided people of Ulster became a legitimate political task. And within six months of the commencement of the Second Vatican Council, Ulster had a politician with such a mission, in the person of its new Prime Minister, Captain Terence O'Neill, who succeeded Lord Brookeborough. It is hard to avoid the conclusion that O'Neill's personality alienated the new Prime Minister from his

Unionist grass-roots and that this change in the Unionist leadership worked to Paisley's advantage.

O'Neill had a sincere desire to promote a policy of reconciliation and though the Prime Minister's early gestures of goodwill set a precedent as far as Ulster Unionism was concerned, they did not intrude on contentious political issues.

The initial low-key approach adopted by O'Neill to the issue of community relations partly explains the next twist in the course which Paisley's erratic pilgrimage was following. In October 1964 a Westminster general election was called and Paisley declared his intention to work for the election of the Ulster Unionist Party candidate in the constituency of West Belfast, the barrister, Mr James Kilfedder.

A significant element of the UPA also threw their weight behind Kilfedder in an extremely bitter election campaign. Paisley exacerbated the situation by pointing out that the police were legally obliged to remove an Irish tricolour which had been unfurled outside the election headquarters of the Irish Republican candidate. Two days of rioting followed the RUC's attempt to remove the flag and thirty casualties were recorded as a result of these disturbances.

There had been a split in the anti-Unionist vote in West Belfast, while in reaction to the heightened tension, there was an increased turnout of Unionist voters. When the count closed on 15 October James Kilfedder emerged as the successful candidate with a majority of 6,000 votes. Kilfedder was reported as stating that without Paisley's help 'it could not have been done'.

Kilfedder's public acknowledgement of his debt to Paisley illustrates Paisley's opportunist tactics during this period. In the same year, 1964, the Protestant Unionists had contested four Belfast Corporation seats, and had managed to hold on to two seats. One of the unsuccessful Paisleyites was a Mr Noel Doherty, who had joined Rev. Ian Paisley's Church in 1956 and had become increasingly politicised through his association with Paisley. Another Protestant Unionist councillor was James McCarroll, who had been elected. Like Doherty, he also attended the Free Presbyterian Church.

In the interval between the Protestant Unionists' first sally into local government politics in Belfast in 1958 and the 1964 election, Protestant Unionism had fallen increasingly under the influence of Paisley himself and away from the control of the UPA, and this is borne out by the growing convergence of Protestant Unionism with Paisley's Ravenhill Road church through personalities like Doherty and McCarroll.

On 14 January 1965 Sean Lemass, the Taoiseach of the Irish Republic, paid an official visit to O'Neill at Stormont. Although the visit was generally well received O'Neill had kept the Parliamentary Unionist Party in the dark, and as the Party's policy had been that there could be no cordial relations with the Dublin government until the Irish Republic recognised Northern Ireland, a row ensued. One leading Unionist declared that 'it was an unwarrantable assumption of personal dictatorship by the Prime Minister to reverse that policy without the consent of the people who support his government'.

Paisley's reaction was intense and predictable. On 25 February he led a 'congress of processions' from the Protestant working-class districts of Belfast to the main door of the Unionist Party's Headquarters in Glengall Street. The Prime Minister was in the building attending a function and such was the ferocity of the crowd which Paisley had gathered around him that the RUC advised O'Neill to leave by another exit.

Before Paisley's vociferous demonstrators made their way home Councillor McCarroll informed the crowd that Rev. Ian Paisley might one day be Prime Minister. The suggestion was loudly cheered: Paisley's feud with the Unionist Prime Minister had assumed the aspect of a struggle which dominated Unionist politics between 1965 and 1969.

1966: The crisis foreshadowed

The following year, 1966, proved to be of critical importance for Rev. Ian Paisley and the Protestant Unionist Party. He began the new year with fervent Protestant resolution by staging an anti-ecumenical demonstration in Westminster Abbey: for the next six months Ian Paisley's activities kept his name in the headlines. In March he addressed a rally in Lisburn at which a Paisleyite organisation styling itself the 'Ulster Protestant Volunteers' made its first appearance. The movement, which was modelled on the Orange Order, wore red, white and blue sashes and paraded with flags and bands, and had been set up by the unsuccessful Protestant Unionist candidate, Noel Doherty. Doherty was a convinced Paisleyite who 'became dedicated to the movement', but though he enjoyed the confidence of Rev. Ian Paisley, Doherty's zeal for militant Protestantism would soon prove to be his undoing.

Considerable importance is to be attached to the emergence of the UPV. The organisation was constituted on a basis which would allow it to field Parliamentary candidates in the future. The Volunteers also provided Paisley with an alternative loyalist institution to Orangeism; but of greater significance was the fact that the UPV was later put to use as a movement of the streets, capable of staging counter-demonstrations.

/ encouraged Paisley to launch a newspaper, *The graph*, published by the Puritan Printing Company of .y was a director. Widely regarded as sectarian, the ıginally designed to get round the problems created for ugh the decision of the *Belfast Telegraph* not to carry any moı. ısley's advertisements. For a time the bi-weekly paper was personally edited by Paisley himself, but then Paisley passed the chore on to the managing editor of the printing company. The paper lacked official standing within Paisleyism because it was neither the official organ of the Free Presbyterian Church nor of Paisley's political movements, and Paisley's interest in the venture fluctuated over the years.

By the end of March, Great Britain was in the throes of another general election. Paisley and Boal decided to intervene behind the scenes in the constituency of West Belfast. By this time Boal and Paisley had turned against the sitting Unionist MP, James Kilfedder, whom they had supported in 1964; they wanted another candidate in his place. Frank Millar and Jean Coulter recall that some of the animosity towards Kilfedder arose from the suggestion that during his student days at Trinity College, Dublin, Kilfedder had joined Fine Gael. Despite their manoeuvrings, Kilfedder's nomination was secured and Boal and Paisley were rebuffed.

In the event, Kilfedder lost the West Belfast seat to a unity candidate, the Republican Labour politician, Gerry Fitt, who had a majority of 2,011votes. Jean Coulter, who was a Unionist official in the Party tally rooms, has insisted that the small Paisleyite element off the Donegall Road did not vote for Kilfedder, but whether there would have been sufficient strength of feeling among anti-Kilfedder loyalists to have cost him the seat is an open question. What is not in doubt is that the whole episode led inexorably to the final break-up of the UPA.

This came about as a result of the ill feeling amongst members of the UPA over Paisley's spoiling tactics. A letter was drawn up and signed by some members of the UPA and also by one Augustus Spence, brother of Kilfedder's election agent, William Spence. The thirteen signatories of this letter accused Paisley of treachery over the recent election campaign. The letter was duly forwarded to Paisley, but some weeks would elapse before the full repercussions of this incident would become known.

The fiftieth anniversary of the Easter Rising fell on 17 April and a popular front of pro-Republican groups announced that the event would be marked by a parade in the city. Paisley responded by declaring his intention to hold a counter-demonstration which would proceed to the Ulster Hall. There were no incidents despite the fact that at one point on their respective routes the parades passed within two hundred yards of each other. The authorities monitored Paisley's parade and the meeting where it was noted that in a welcoming speech to the crowd Paisley acknowledged the presence of a faction styling themselves 'the UVF'. Like the letter forwarded to Paisley by the UPA, the significance of Paisley's public acknowledgement of the existence of the UVF would take time to emerge.

In his preparations to counter the Irish Republican celebrations, which were accompanied by news stories in the press of a new IRA conspiracy, Paisley announced that he had formed yet another organ of Paisleyism, called the Ulster Constitution Defence Committee.

Tension in Belfast had hardly subsided when on 21 May a message sent to the press and authenticated by the 'Ulster Volunteer Force' threatened to execute known IRA members. Within a week the first victim of the 'men of violence', John Scullion, was seriously wounded on the Falls Road. Though Scullion died in hospital two weeks later the circumstances of his death remain shrouded in mystery.

Between Scullion's wounding and death, Rev. Ian Paisley had instigated the most notorious demonstration of his whole career. On 6 June he led a protest march to Church House, the headquarters of Irish Presbyterianism, where the annual General Assembly was in progress. Paisley's route passed through the Irish Nationalist district of Cromac Square where the march occasioned a riot which lasted late into the evening as stone-throwing youths battled with the RUC. This loyalist provocation was the first of two incidents that night, because when Paisley and his fellow demonstrators arrived at Church House the dignitaries of Irish Presbyterianism found that they had to run a gauntlet of Paisleyite abuse as they crossed Howard Street from Church House where the devotional proceedings had ended to the Presbyterian War Memorial Hostel where a supper had been provided for them.

Among the guests who had been subjected to jeers and cat calls were Lord Erskine, the Governor of Northern Ireland, and his wife, and Rev. Dr Alfred Martin, Moderator of the Presbyterian Church in Ireland at the time.

This 6 June demonstration became a *cause célèbre*. The protest at the Presbyterian General Assembly was an affront to the sensibilities of the dignitaries of the Presbyterian Church and at the same time the belligerency of Paisley's protest exposed the Unionist Government to the accusation that it had underestimated the threat which Paisley represented to the wellbeing and prosperity of Northern Ireland.

Jacques Ellul, the French sociologist, has noted that where there is a liberal outlook and a secularised society, then '. . . the socio-political discussion is less and less likely to touch on religion. In such an atmosphere, anyone who uses religion as a criterion tends to be regarded as divisive and sectarian, a disturber of civic unity.'[6] Paisley, the outsider, seemed determined to disturb the peace of the Province.

O'Neill did foresee the danger in the situation which Paisley had prompted, because the government attempted to mend its fences by offering a formal apology to the Presbyterian Church. O'Neill hit out at Paisley in a speech which contrasted the economic improvements in Ulster with the public image which Paisley's demonstrations had created: '. . . The spotlight of publicity now being turned upon us is not concerned with our buoyant economy or the votes of confidence which we have been given by companies like Rolls-Royce and Goodyear. It is concerned with the activities of a man who seems determined to make sure that the world will think of Ulster mainly as the place of the protest march and the insulting placard.'

Paisley apparently did not care what outsiders thought: God alone was his judge, though Paisley's lack of concern for British public opinion was not shared by O'Neill. In a speech in the Chamber at Stormont on 15 June, O'Neill returned to the attack: 'To those of us who remember the Thirties, the pattern is horribly familiar. The contempt for established authority; the crude and unthinking intolerance; the emphasis upon monster processions and rallies; the appeal to a perverted form of patriotism – each and every one of these things has its parallel in the rise of the Nazis to power.'

O'Neill's attempt to characterise Paisley as a fascist made little impression on the Unionist grass-roots, but O'Neill's vehement denunciations had little time to take effect. A serious incident had occurred in Malvern Street, off the Shankill Road, where a Roman Catholic, Peter Ward, was murdered in the early hours of 26 June. An extreme loyalist organisation which had revived the name of the Ulster Volunteer Force was believed to have been responsible for the crime, and a massive police hunt got under way.

Two nights after the Malvern Street murder, at an open air meeting in Holywood, Paisley rebutted any suggestion that he knew who the leaders of the UVF were or what the organisation was. Paisley referred to the letter which had attacked his role as a spoiler in the Kilfedder election campaign and he claimed, correctly as it turned out, that amongst those arrested for the Malvern Street murder were men who had been Ulster Unionist Party workers during the recent election in West Belfast.

Paisley's vindication of his own position at Holywood and the fact that the letter had fallen into the hands of the police brought about the final split in the UPA. The organisation disintegrated in a welter of bitter mutual recriminations between Paisley and his followers and the remainder of the UPA's Protestant working class supporters.

This aspect of the Malvern Street murder turned out to have a crucial bearing on the way Paisley's politics would develop in the future. The government continued to maintain that Paisley was compromised by the Malvern Street murder. He was thought to have knowledge of the existence of the UVF. Even more dramatically, and as the Prime Minister had alleged, Noel Doherty was heavily implicated in the affair, because he had acted as a contact between the Paisleyite UPV and the UVF. Furthermore, one of the defendants, Hugh Arnold McClean, had stated when charged with the murder: 'I am sorry I ever heard tell of that man Paisley or decided to follow him'.

The most damaging aspect was undoubtedly Noel Doherty's involvement, because he was so closely identified with Rev. Ian Paisley's organisation. Doherty was now arrested and charged with offences involving the transportation of explosives.

Paisley had realised what was likely to happen and had moved with lightning speed against Doherty. In order to minimise the damage to himself, Paisley, accompanied by the Vice-Chairman of the UCDC, had gone to Doherty's home, repossessed the UCDC minute book and summarily expelled Doherty from the movement he had helped to create. From now on Doherty would have to fend for himself, and after being found guilty of the offences he was jailed for two years.

Those authors who have discussed the Malvern Street murder in their books have closely followed Terence O'Neill's assessment of the event, but there are discrepancies in this extremely hostile version of the incident. As some of the prime movers in the UVF conspiracy had closer connections with the Orange Order in Belfast, and for that matter with the Unionist Party in West Belfast, than they had with Rev. Ian Paisley, it is incorrect to state as Michael Farrell does, that: 'the UVF was a small group of Paisley supporters who, alarmed at his denunciations of the Unionist sell-out, had set up an armed organisation. . . .'[7]

Furthermore, after the behind-the-scenes clash over Kilfedder's candidature in March, collaboration between Paisley's faction within Ulster Protestant Action and some of their fellow loyalist activists in North Belfast had been all but severed. The letter signed by the thirteen loyalist critics of Paisley's behaviour at the time of the election in West Belfast substantiates this.

Paisley's responsibilities in the affair turn on the fact that Noel Doherty was closely associated with him and that it is hard to resist the conclusion that Paisley was aware of the existence of the Ulster Volunteer Force but that he had chosen to ignore the fact that a group which he had publicly acknowledged at the rally in the Ulster Hall on

17 April was in all probability involved in the procurement of weapons.

Even more serious than this was Paisley's largely self-appointed role as the defender of Protestant Ulster, and the calling which he felt impelled to fulfil: that of alerting the Protestants of the Province to the ecumenical downgrade and the fatal betrayal of Ulster's interests which he considered to be implicit in the policies of Terence O'Neill. Paisley's future success depended on whether his fellow Ulstermen would come to regard him as a prophet who foresaw the dangers or a provocateur who stirred them up.

From the time when he had first shown an interest in politics, Ian Paisley had collaborated with other loyalist groupings. In the early days, he had worked on behalf of Official Unionist candidates like Rev. James MacManaway, and latterly, James Kilfedder, but as the years passed, his own particularist brand of political Protestantism had become more assertive and this development has to be taken in tandem with his increasing reputation as the voice of extreme Protestant religious sentiment in Northern Ireland. Ulster Protestant Action had served as a catalyst in Paisley's developing politicisation by providing him with an opportunity in 1958 to associate himself with the Protestant Unionist Party. He had succeeded in capturing Protestant Unionism, a fact obscured by those who date the emergence of the Protestant Unionist Party from the mid-sixties. This is significant because Paisley would proceed to take over the DUP in similar circumstances in 1973. Ian Paisley's career indicates that until 1966, he was still not totally committed to the idea of building the Protestant party into the political manifestation of his Protestant faith; however, with the disruption between Paisley and his supporters and Ulster Protestant Action, the complexion of the Protestant Unionist Party changed. The Free Presbyterian connection was consolidated, and this would be borne out by the candidates whom the Party would field in the Stormont general election of February 1969. A further consequence of the rupture between Ian Paisley and the UPA was a decline in Paisley's influence over loyalist activists on the fringes of Unionism in Belfast. This explains why the Protestant Unionist breakthrough, when it did come, occurred in rural constituencies outside the city.

These events in June 1966 marked an important stage in Paisley's development as a leader of Protestant opinion in the Province, because as a result of the General Assembly protest, he was sentenced to a term of imprisonment. O'Neill has argued in his autobiography that Paisley deliberately courted martyrdom; whether or not that was the case, there were indications that Paisley's support was growing. A survey carried out by Lancaster University and published that year 'showed that about 200,000 out of a potential 1,400,000 people in Northern Ireland supported Mr Paisley'.

Among those whose sympathies were aroused by Paisley's jail sentence was a young Protestant called William McCrea, who would eventually be returned as the MP for the Westminster constituency of Mid-Ulster in the 1983 general election. In his autobiography, Rev. William McCrea wrote of the impact which Paisley's imprisonment made upon him. McCrea referred to an incident when Rev. Ian Paisley preached at a gospel service near their family home: 'When . . . we used to hear controversy about Dr Paisley and later heard about his imprisonment in 1966, because of that afternoon when we had heard the gospel preached with power and conviction we found ourselves tending to take his side in the controversy'.[8]

Ian Paisley's enthusiasm for a style of Protestant religion which had many affinities with American Fundamentalism was reciprocated from across the Atlantic; Dr Bob Jones of Greenville, South Carolina, conferred an Honorary Doctorate on Ulster's Protestant leader following his release from prison on 19 October 1966.

The events of 1966 had proved to be a watershed in Ian Paisley's political career; the character of the Protestant Unionist Party was changing, his personal support as a leader of politicised Protestantism was growing, and Paisley had acquired an international reputation. Indeed, Patrick Marrinan has commented that at the time Paisley's 'life itself seemed to be a living protest'.[9]

The repercussions of the Malvern Street murder, and the Unionist Government's decision to proscribe the UVF, had increased the unease within the Official Unionist Party in Stormont at O'Neill's handling of the complex political situation in Northern Ireland. In September, Desmond Boal's name was associated with a 'conspiracy' to replace Terence O'Neill with another leader of the Unionist Government at Stormont who would be more amenable to Unionist backbench opinion. Nothing came of this attempt to replace the reforming Unionist Premier, but the episode illustrates the fact that while Boal eschewed Paisley's style of street politics and possessed an open mind on religious affairs, which suggests that he shared little of Paisley's zeal for Protestantism, he did share Paisley's antipathy towards Terence O'Neill.

Paisley now turned from the vagaries of political activism to religious outreach. In 1967 the twenty-first Free Presbyterian Church in Ulster was opened, while the income from Dr Paisley's own congregation increased by 100 per cent, reaching a figure of £34,616. Paisley's personal reputation as a controversial Protestant extremist also grew, and on 23 November Paisley participated in a televised debate from the Oxford Union. Norman St John Stevas, the

Conservative MP, opposed the motion 'That the Roman Catholic Church has no place in the Twentieth Century'. Ian Paisley, in proposing the motion, had caused consternation and affronted many of those present by producing a wafer used in the Eucharist. St John Stevas launched a vigorous rebuttal of 'the uncultured fundamentalism' of Paisley, carrying the House with him. Public opinion in England increasingly distanced itself from these manifestations of Paisleyism.

Some time later a similar debate was staged in the top floor refectory of Queen's University Students' Union building. The hall was packed with hundreds of people. I was a student at the time and was approached to chair this debate between the Jesuit priest, Father Corbishley, and the Free Church Moderator. A much less histrionic affair than the earlier one at the Oxford Union, this debate was largely good humoured; perhaps the Belfast audience realised that the hall contained an explosive mixture of barely concealed passions. And how right they were, for I later learned that one 'hard citizen' from the Shankill Road had carried a petrol bomb in her handbag into the building. It was a menacing portent of things to come.

The Civil Rights marches

It was inevitable, therefore, that when the Civil Rights movement took to the streets in 1968 as a means of publicising the grievances of the Roman Catholic minority in the Province and in order to campaign for reform of the Northern Ireland state, Paisley should find himself in the van of those who were determined to frustrate and harass the Civil Rights protesters. As had happened in the past, events outside Ireland had occasioned consequences entirely disproportionate to their apparent significance at the time. Vatican II had encouraged a new mood of self-confidence among Roman Catholics growing impatient with what they perceived to be the straitjacket of Ulster politics. More extreme Republicans, reflecting on the failure of the 1956–62 IRA campaign, noted in their journals that a new strategy was needed which would 'be the perfect blending of politics and violence at the most opportune time and under the most favourable circumstances'. The example of the Civil Rights Campaign in the United States was seized upon, and the techniques of non-violence applied to the complex and intensely parochial social structures of Northern Ireland.[10]

Simon Winchester has provided a good account of the manner in which journalists interpreted the political crisis which ensued and of the important role which the media played in bringing the allegations of the Civil Rights protesters before the public. There was, however, a sequel to the extra dimension which television reporting brought to the onset of Ulster's present 'Troubles'. Should Paisley choose to join battle with the Civil Rights demonstrators, then he would give a subtle televisual endorsement to the protesters' claims, because a downtrodden minority needed an ogre and Paisley had already been typecast for the part. Furthermore press interest in Paisley's response to the crisis would effectively enable Paisley to monopolise Protestant reaction to the Civil Rights campaign. Television crews working to a tight schedule sought out Paisley, while lesser known loyalist politicians were passed by.

Having established himself as the leader of extreme Protestant opinion in Ulster, Paisley was well placed to articulate and even monopolise reaction to the Civil Rights campaign. Although the larger proportion of Paisley's interest recently had been directed towards his gospel ministry, he had served notice early in May that his political motivation remained undiminished. In that month Paisley's 'O'Neill Must Go' campaign reached a new pitch of ferocity when O'Neill was subjected to a demonstration by five hundred loyalists during a visit to Craven Street Unionist Hall in Belfast.

As the summer of '68 wore on, the Civil Rights movement committed itself to further street protest as a means of securing its demands, and Paisley found himself drawn into a political struggle on two fronts. The Moderator of the Free Presbyterian Church continued his invective against the Unionist administration while simultaneously attempting to frustrate the Civil Rights movement in its declared intention to parade the banners of grievance and discrimination through the villages and towns of Ulster.

The rapidly developing crisis over Civil Rights brought about a realignment among Unionist politicians. Right wing loyalists, including the Unionist Minister of Home Affairs at the time, William Craig, the dissident Desmond Boal, and Paisley's Protestant Unionists, all interpreted the Civil Rights campaign as an attack on the Constitution of Northern Ireland and as an Irish Republican conspiracy. The liberal wing of the Unionist Party, led by Terence O'Neill, accepted that reform was needed, believing that once it had been secured, the agitation would die down.

Paisley gave physical weight to his belief in an Irish Republican insurrection when he and his supporters, wearing badges commemorating the gun-running exploits of the SS 'Clydevalley' in 1914 as a means of recognition, took over the centre of Armagh on Saturday, 30 November 1968. Their objective was to frustrate the Civil Rights protesters' intention to march through the town and as a result of this counter-demonstration Paisley would serve a second short term of imprisonment.

The Paisleyites sang hymns, built barricades and unfurled banners with the slogan 'CRA = IRA' upon them. Though Paisley's message that the Civil Rights movement was a 'front' for the IRA was crude and unsophisticated it did convey the loyalists' innate fear of the future inevitable course of the current agitation.

A. T. Q. Stewart, writing in *The Narrow Ground*, has argued that 'once the civil rights movement assumed a militant, and to all intents and purposes a sectarian, form, the entire escalation of the conflict was easily predictable'.[11] This is important; although the loyalist counter-demonstrators over-reacted to the tactical use of 'non-violence', they did so because they read the Civil Rights demonstrations in terms of their own folk memory.

There is an apocalyptic theme running through Orange songs which helped to colour the loyalists' perception that they were 'a Protestant island in a Catholic sea'. This feeling of being under threat was heightened by the emergence of a Catholic mass-movement demanding 'British standards' and enjoying sympathetic treatment by the media. Ian Paisley's role in opposing the Civil Rights demonstrations turned on his ability to voice such loyalist reaction. Paisley did not conjure up the reaction.

In the coming months Unionist electors would be able to contrast Paisley's prescient belief that the Civil Rights agitation would lead to an upsurge in IRA terrorism with the naïvety and self-doubt of a Unionist Government which sought to mollify those protesting in the streets by offering a limited package of social reforms.

The realignment among right wing Unionist politicians added to the mounting political pressure on O'Neill, who had become an encircled Prime Minister. O'Neill became all too conscious that the ground was slipping from under him; even his own backbenchers at Stormont had lost confidence in him. The final straw came on 3 February 1969, when twelve Unionist Party backbenchers met in Portadown. The 'arrogance' of this 'Portadown Parliament' provoked O'Neill into calling a snap general election.

The Protestant Unionist Party seized the opportunity which O'Neill's decision presented. Paisley, who had been imprisoned over the Armagh counter-demonstration, signed a bail bond, was released from prison and announced his intention to challenge the Unionist Prime Minister in his own constituency of the Bannside, County Antrim.

Of the six candidates fielded by the Protestant Unionists, three, including Rev. Ian Paisley himelf, were Free Presbyterian ministers, the other two being Rev. John Wylie and Rev. William Beattie. The Party concentrated its efforts in the four rural constituencies of the Bannside, North Antrim, South Antrim and Iveagh. Two Belfast constituencies were also contested. These constituencies were in the east of the city (Bloomfield and Victoria) which suggests that the Protestant Unionists avoided those areas of Belfast where Ulster Protestant Action had once operated.

The international press 'descended on Ulster' and the contest in the Bannside between Paisley and O'Neill became a bitter and bruising affair. As Paisley scrambled in and out of Wesley Adams' Land Rover to canvas votes in O'Neill's bailiwick, other supporters met in prayer in private houses or in Free Presbyterian churches to pray for God's blessing upon their Moderator's political mission. By contrast O'Neill's campaign lacked the populism and stamina which the leader of Protestant extremism was able to generate and when the vote was declared on Wednesday 26 February it was learned that O'Neill had narrowly beaten off the challenge from Paisley, his Unionist majority being only 1,414 votes.

The credibility of the Ulster Prime Minister had been undermined. Paisley had surmounted the fierce criticism heaped upon him by the Unionist Party and the media and the result indicated that O'Neill would probably be toppled whenever the next election was called in the Bannside. Though the Protestant Unionist Party had failed to win a single seat in the February general election, 1969 has correctly been interpreted as the year in which Protestant Unionism made the 'real breakthrough'. The Party, however, was associated with a minor Protestant sect, the Free Presbyterian Church, and it possessed a narrow political base; how could Protestant Unionism project itself in such a way as to garner votes from a mass of supporters who were not themselves Free Presbyterians? The answer lay in Ian Paisley's ability to articulate the sentiments of ordinary Ulster Protestants – that he became their 'voice' – and the fact that such people needed a 'voice', needed someone to speak up for them, was pressed in upon them from every side as the violence in Northern Ireland escalated and the constitutional position of the Province within the United Kingdom came increasingly under question.

A critical juncture was reached in August 1969, when the British Army moved into parts of Belfast after a period of sustained inter-communal rioting, and into Londonderry where the RUC had been unable to re-establish a presence in the area of the Bogside after forty-eight hours of continuous rioting which followed the traditional parade of the loyalist Apprentice Boys of Derry on 12 August.

The Home Secretary during the August crisis was James Callaghan. Callaghan's enthusiasm for reform and the attitude which he displayed eroded moderate Unionist opinion in the Province and marked another step in the onward march of Paisleyism. Multitudes of loyalists felt a deep unease about the manner in which the British

Army had been introduced into the streets of Londonderry and Belfast. These loyalists underwent a highly traumatic experience through having to come to terms with a seemingly 'unnatural' situation in which the military intervention was welcomed and applauded by the leading spokesmen of the Nationalist community while the troops took up a posture which suggested that the threat was expected to come from the Unionist population.

Later, Colonel Robin Evelegh in his seminal study *Peace Keeping in a Democratic Society* commented that the actions taken by the military when they took control of the streets in Northern Ireland in August 1969 'made a mighty breach in the doctrine of the rule of law and the constitution as a firm framework for the control of the military engaged in suppressing civil disorder'.[12]

Boal's increasing influence

Meanwhile, Callaghan and Chichester-Clark, Terence O'Neill's successor, agreed on a series of reforms which included new electoral laws and an enquiry by Lord Hunt into the functions of the RUC. Callaghan visited Ulster in mid-October and at the conclusion of his visit Boal made a vigorous criticism of the Callaghan-Chichester-Clark initiative. The underlying theme of Boal's criticism would be reiterated by right-wing Unionists, and rightly be regarded as a key statement of the loyalist position during this period:

> A more sober appraisal of the result of the Home Secretary's visit would show that lawlessness has been made respectable and sedition profitable. Not only have we apparently conceded the validity of slanderous allegations – sometimes scurrilous – but we have confirmed the principle that in this country if you want something, no matter how unreasonable, you simply throw stones and petrol bombs, and get it.

The comment typified right-wing attitudes at the time. Even though Desmond Boal was a radical Unionist politician with a highly informed social conscience, he interpreted the critical events of August 1969 as an Irish nationalist attempt to undermine the Province's constitutional position within the United Kingdom.

Boal enumerated two major points arising from the proposals of Callaghan and Chichester-Clark: firstly, the fallacy 'that there is validity in the allegations of the minority, and this, to put it modestly, has not been proved'; and secondly, 'that the people causing the trouble in this country will not be satisfied with any objective other than its destruction'.

The second part of Boal's statement in which he propounded his belief that the nationalists would not be satisfied until they had achieved their aim of a united Ireland would comprise an important element in the Unionists' rejection of power sharing. In the future the Unionist right would argue that a policy of power sharing was unacceptable because the SDLP would only endorse the concept on the understanding that it marked an interim stage in the process of bringing about the unification of Ireland.

As the pace of events quickened, the confidence of the Protestant Unionist Party in its ability to focus loyalist criticism on the Government and to defend the interests of the Protestant electorate increased significantly.

In April 1970 the Protestant Unionist Party seized the advantage offered by the retirement of Terence O'Neill and the prominent liberal Unionist Richard Ferguson from the Stormont Parliament. By-elections were called in the constituencies of the Bannside and South Antrim. W. D. Flackes, who regards the by-elections as 'probably the most vital in the history of the Stormont House of Commons',[13] noted that 'they were a test of Unionist feeling on the reforms carried through by the Chichester-Clark Government', and that 'they were a measure of the support for Mr Paisley'.

Dr Paisley stood against an Ulster Unionist, Dr B. Minford, in the Bannside, while Rev. William Beattie went forward in South Antrim. The convergence of militant Protestant religious interests with those of politics was emphasised when the Protestant Unionist Party formally endorsed the two clerical candidates. Other Free Presbyterian ministers must have asked themselves whether God would also call them into prominence as elected representatives of Paisley's Party. The results of the two by-elections, which were held on 16 April, inflicted further damage on the beleaguered Unionist Party. Paisley and Beattie both won their seats with majorities of 1,203 and 958 votes respectively.

Two months later, the whole electorate of Northern Ireland went to the polls in a Westminster general election. Again, Rev. Ian Paisley and Rev. William Beattie stood as candidates, but as a right-wing Unionist, James Molyneaux, was standing in South Antrim, Beattie allowed his name to go forward in North Belfast where he came third behind the NILP candidate and Stratton Mills, the sitting Unionist MP, who held the seat with a majority of 9,774 votes in a four-cornered contest. In North Antrim the Unionists did not fare so well; Henry Clark, the sitting Unionist MP, lost his seat to Dr Paisley by a margin of 2,679 votes.

Dr Paisley's election to Westminster marked another important stage in his political development, because Paisley was taken aback by the hostility which he at first encountered from Parliamentary colleagues who had only heard of Paisley through the media. The salutary effect which this experience had on Dr Paisley predisposed him to modify the more 'fanatical' features of his political crusade.

While Paisley's political consciousness matured, violence on the streets once again dominated the newspaper headlines. During the last weekend in June 1970, there were further serious disturbances in Belfast and Londonderry, which left five dead and two hundred civilians injured. The following day, Dr Patrick Hillery, the Minister for External Affairs in the Republic of Ireland, told the Foreign Secretary in the recently elected Conservative Government of Mr Edward Heath that the source of the conflict in the Province was 'the issue of a divided country'.

The escalation of street violence and the pressure for a change in Northern Ireland's status within the United Kingdom continued into 1971, by which time another Unionist Prime Minister, Major James Chichester-Clark, had been forced to resign. Brian Faulkner took over the Premiership of Northern Ireland on Tuesday, 23 March 1971. The Unionist Party's right wing and the Protestant Unionists were now locked into battle with a Prime Minister who was widely regarded as Unionism's most formidable politician of recent times.

The basis of a realignment of right-wing Unionists and Protestant Unionists had been inherent in their joint rejection of the Civil Rights movement as an extreme Irish Republican conspiracy. People had been educated by events, and the relative strengths of both the right wing of the Unionist Party and the Protestant Unionists had increased since 1969.

As the summer of 1971 came to a close, with the debris from the anti-internment riots still littering the streets and a further hardening of minority attitudes taking place, Jack Lynch, the Republic's Taoiseach, declared:

> As an immediate objective of political action, the Stormont Government should be replaced by an administration in which power and decision making will be equally shared between Unionist and non-Unionist. The Stormont regime, which has consistently repressed the non-Unionist population and bears responsibility for recurring violence in the Northern community must be brought to an end.[14]

Though the Republic's 'immediate objective' would soon be realised, the Unionist leadership failed to grasp this statement's importance. As the situation deteriorated, the necessity for some form of alliance between the right-wing Unionists and the Protestant Unionists seemed inescapable.

Dr Paisley's conciliatory mood was critical to the whole enterprise, and his mood reflected the political adjustments he had made as a result of his experiences at Westminster and probably as a natural reaction to the role he had played as a street demagogue and fomenter of street demonstrations during the initial phase of Civil Rights activism.

Furthermore Paisley's party, the Protestant Unionists, had been forced to come to terms with the ability of the Unionist right wing to mobilise loyalist sentiment into an increasingly powerful and effective political bloc. The basic element in this right-wing movement was the rank and file of the Orange Order, who had distanced themselves from the Unionist Government as their disillusionment with the manner in which the crisis was being handled grew. The hostility of the Orangemen towards the Unionist Government had been all too apparent at Dungiven on Sunday, 13 June when in defiance of the Government's ban on parades they clashed with troops, an incident which was indicative of the growing gulf between the Orange Order and Faulkner's Government. The Orange Order had been joined by two pressure groups formed in 1969. The West Ulster Unionist Council, led by Harry West, represented rural Unionist opinion west of the River Bann, and placed strong emphasis on the campaign to select hardline delegates to voting positions on the crucial committees of the Unionist Party. The other group was the Ulster Loyalist Association. Led by William Craig, this faction of Unionist opinion commanded the enthusiastic support of a considerable number of activists.

A series of meetings was agreed upon and representatives of the right wing of the Unionist Party and Dr Paisley attempted to hammer out a joint approach to the formation of a new political party.

Intense discussions ensued, and by early September, it appeared that William Craig, Rev. Bertie Dickinson of the West Ulster Unionist Council, Desmond Boal and Dr Paisley would reach an agreement. Would the 'Unionist Alliance' as this series of meetings in the Kensington Hotel was styled, build a bridge between right-wing Unionism and Paisleyism? Many right-wing Unionists remained sceptical. Their doubts turned on the political role that Ian Paisley had carried out. The 'big man' had voiced virulent criticisms of the Presbyterian Church and its membership of the World Council of Churches. Presbyterians on the right of the Unionist Party resented Paisley's sectarian outbursts and refused to align themselves with a Protestant leader whose words and actions were a source of acute embarrassment to them.

Others saw in Ian Paisley's authoritarian personality yet another obstacle to an agreed coalition of loyalties. By 1971 many Unionists had acquired first hand experience of Paisley's style through the loyalist infrastructure and they shared the opinion that Paisley was overly ambitious. Paisley had given ammunition to such critics a month earlier when in the course of an *Irish Times* interview the Protestant leader confided that he 'would not shirk the duty of becoming Prime Minister of Northern Ireland if the circumstances were such that the people of this country felt I was the right man'. Unionist reservations about Paisley's politics only added weight to the privately held conviction of many of the Glengall Street Party's members.

Whatever Paisley's personal desire for high political office might have been, he had a rival in William Craig, who had emerged as the acceptable face of right-wing Unionism.

Emergence of the Democratic Unionist Party

As the discussions reached a make or break stage, the personal friendship of Boal and Paisley took on a crucial significance. Boal signalled his willingness to collaborate with Paisley in forming a 'United Loyalist Party'. Craig and Dickinson had reservations but the talks continued. Then on the evening of 29 September, the Provisional IRA bombed the Four Step Inn on the Shankill Road. The terrorist outrage left two dead and twenty injured. Loyalist passions were inflamed. To defuse this tense situation Desmond Boal and Rev. Ian Paisley gave an announcement to the press that a new loyalist political initiative taking the form of a United Loyalist Party was about to be made.

This formal announcement about the formation of a 'United Loyalist Party' effectively presented Craig with a fait accompli. If Craig harboured reservations about Paisley's authoritarian attitude they were not public knowledge, unlike Craig's belief that the Unionist Party could be recaptured by the right. Boal and Paisley's premature statement concerning this proposed loyalist initiative now placed Craig in an invidious position. However, Craig only added to this confusion about his future intentions by issuing a statement published on 2 October in which he made the following ambiguous comment: 'It is the beginning of the end for the Unionist Party as now constituted'.

William Craig was one of a handful of Ulster politicians who could have aspired to Cabinet rank, had the political systems in Great Britain and Northern Ireland been more uniform. A profound change was taking place in the Ulster Unionist Party; numbers of the local gentry and upper classes who had provided the Party's leadership in previous years were disengaging from the political life of the Province. Politics was no longer considered 'respectable', and the field was left open to grass-roots activists mobilised by hardline politicians.

Boal and Paisley's somewhat premature announcement of a new loyalist party faced Craig with a dilemma. The public would interpret any positive decision by him to support the United Loyalist Party as an admission that Craig was participating in the initiative on Boal and Paisley's terms. This proved unacceptable to Craig who parted company with Boal and Paisley. Both factions were determined to maintain the Unionist cause and their right-wing orientation meant that there was still a fundamental alignment of attitude despite the personal rivalry and nuances of ideological emphasis which precluded the formation of a loyalist party based on a consensus between them.

Suspicion of the Ulster Unionist Party's right wing may also have encouraged Boal and Paisley to believe that there was little possibility of Craig's alignment with the proposed 'United Loyalist Party' and therefore nothing was to be gained by delaying the announcement of their political intentions. The announcement of some form of political palliative in the aftermath of a bomb outrage or of a period of sustained street violence was hardly without precedent in Ulster. Boal and Paisley probably thought that their statement would help defuse the situation on the Shankill Road by demonstrating that the loyalist politicians were doing something.

In the interval between the statement, issued on 29 September 1971, and the first formal meeting of the new Party on 30 October a number of leading loyalist activists pledged their support to the United Loyalist Party and amongst the first to do so were the Belfast Unionist Party Councillor, William Spence, and James Craig, a Unionist Councillor from Carrickfergus, who had been a regular attender at services in the Martyrs' Memorial Church. Craig and Spence were soon to be joined by Douglas Hutchinson, a delegate to the Central Armagh Unionist Association and a leading member of Paisley's Ulster Protestant Volunteers, and the Deputy Mayor of Enniskillen, Mr Robert Donaldson, who was also a member of the Unionist Party.

At Stormont on Tuesday, 5 October, the dissident Unionist Party MPs, Mr Desmond Boal and John McQuade, accompanied by the former Protestant Unionist members, Dr Paisley and Rev. William Beattie, took their places on the opposition benches which had been vacated by the SDLP following the introduction of internment. The new Opposition Party consisting of the four MPs would henceforth be known as the Democratic Unionist Party. Desmond Boal stated that the DUP 'would be right-wing in the sense of being strong on the Constitution, but to the left on social policies'.

The DUP represented a synthesis between the radicalism of Desmond Boal, and an Ulster variant of the politics of religious defence which the Protestant Unionist Party had been busily promoting. Though there was a strongly secular aspect to Boal's radicalism, Paisley attempted to accommodate himself to this secularising tendency in order to widen his political appeal which had become constricted as a result of Protestant Unionism's dependence on Free Presbyterianism and support drawn from rural constituencies. Boal's support for the new Party offered the prospect of renewed political expansion in Belfast. Paisley's willingness to collaborate in launching the DUP signified that he recognised the need to establish a Party with broader support.

This development in Paisley's political thinking was accompanied by a growing awareness that it was necessary to dilute the emphasis which the Protestant Unionist Party had placed on religious issues, and in particular Paisley's coarse and unsophisticated anti-Catholicism, typified in his campaigning denunciations of the Pope as 'old red socks'.

Boal's emphasis was significantly different; Boal wanted a Unionist Party which had a democratic infrastructure, and which would be more responsive to grass-roots opinion. And this is made clear in a statement published in the local press on 1 October. Having castigated the Unionist Government for its failure 'to provide security for its citizens in their persons and property', Boal turned the full force of his invective on the role of the Unionist Party 'which because of its political passivity and rigidity of structure, has failed lamentably to reflect the sentiments of its traditional supporters'.

Though the thinking of Boal and Paisley was dissimilar there was an underlying unity of purpose, in that both loyalist politicians saw the need to create a mass party. Paisley's willingness to curtail the Protestant emphasis in his political message made him more susceptible to the influence which Boal exerted in favour of a Party with a secular disposition. Although Boal and Paisley shared this objective of establishing a mass Party, their task was not so simply accomplished. Initially the new Party made little headway, and this is acknowledged by David Calvert, who has written that 'recruitment was slow and unspectacular'; nevertheless, the coalition built by Boal and Paisley did have the result of unifying divergent currents within the political backwaters of Ulster loyalism.

The loyalist tendencies which coalesced in the newly formed DUP were reflected in two geographically determined blocs of supporters. Boal was the leading Unionist dissident but he also personified the group of activists in Belfast which came over to the DUP. Sarah

Nelson has indicated that members of the Northern Ireland Labour Party joined the DUP. On the basis of her research into political attitudes Sarah Nelson concluded that 'the "socially discontented" formed only one section of Paisley's support, and were largely confined to Belfast'.[15] But dissident Unionism also found expression in rural Ulster and this was where the second bloc of supporters was located.

These supporters were in the main members of the Protestant Unionist Party's branches which Paisley had cajoled into joining the DUP. Apart from dissident Unionists like Donaldson and Hutchinson who had indicated their willingness to support the venture, two other fragments of loyalist opinion were mobilised by Paisley and either joined the DUP directly or came into the Party via the Protestant Unionist Party.

Sandy Spence, later Mayor of Ballymena, was a Pentecostalist who joined in response to Dr Paisley's gospel ministry in which he taught that it was a Christian's duty to be politically active. Spence represented a pietistic element within the Party which had never made any political commitment in the past but which forsook pietism and became politicised through Paisley's revivalist ministry.

James McClure of Coleraine was a member of an Orange splinter group, the Independent Orange Order, which was active and vocal in North Antrim. The Independent Orangemen were hostile to the link between the Ulster Unionist Party and the Loyal Orange Institution of Ireland and were therefore predisposed to accept Paisley's criticisms of the Unionist establishment. This independent Orange fragment contributed a number of key Party workers to the DUP, particularly in the Ballymoney area.

Though Paisley had broken with the Orange Order in Belfast in 1962, this had not cut him off from Orange support and not only did he succeed in mobilising Independent Orangemen but the vast majority of the DUP's membership also had Orange connections. They had either been members of the Orange Order like Paisley, Boal and Douglas Hutchinson, or they were still active members of the Loyal Orange Institution. The former NILP supporters who joined the DUP in Belfast may also have been Orangemen; it is certainly a matter for speculation, because a number of Belfast Orangemen have traditionally voted Labour. This Orange orientation among DUP supporters was a point of considerable significance because it emphasised the fact that Boal and Paisley were engaged in mobilising a mass party within a segment of the Province's population, which perceived itself to be traditional Unionist.

These fragments of loyalist opinion attended the first formal meeting of the DUP in the Ulster Hall on 30 October 1971. Dr Paisley made an historic speech which gained widespread publicity, because he accurately predicted that the British Government would prorogue Stormont and introduce Direct Rule. At the time Paisley's remarks were criticised as being highly speculative, but when Paisley's prophecy came true, his standing amongst the Unionist electorate was enhanced.

Curiously, the Unionist opponents of the DUP have never drawn political ammunition from the unquestionable fact that Paisley's neutral attitude to the impending abolition of Stormont probably helped to bring that constitutional change about. The British Government was being presented with evidence that Unionism was divided and that any loyalist opposition which did emerge would lack the belligerence and energy which Paisley could have promoted, had he felt strongly enough about defending the Stormont Parliament.

In the light of the fact that Paisley would later become a vociferous supporter of a devolved solution to the Northern Ireland crisis, his disenchantment with the Stormont Parliamentary system would appear to be quixotic. Perhaps Paisley's declared neutrality arose from the shrewd calculation that the prorogation of Stormont would rupture the Ulster Unionist Party's monopoly of loyalist electoral support and lead to a situation in which all the political parties would be placed on the same datum line. The advantage which accrued to the DUP as a consequence of this speech by Dr Paisley was never maximised, because internal confusion within the meeting over the form that the new Party would take blunted the point of his address.

The meeting speedily ran into difficulties over Boal and Paisley's arbitrary decision to call the new Party the Democratic Unionist Party. At the centre of the storm which developed lay three opposing points of view. Boal's commitment to a philosophy of secular humanism and Paisley's conciliatory mood have already been discussed, but there was a third opinion on the matter which reflected the unyielding sentiments of Protestant Unionists like Rev. John Wylie, who clung to the belief that by including the term 'Protestant' in the Party masthead, the Party was making a profound statement about religious doctrine and Christian principles.

The issue raised an acute personal dilemma for Paisley, because he had subtly shifted his ground. In contrast Boal and Wylie, though they differed widely, did at least approach the problem of what to call the Party from a position of principle. Paisley had discerned the need to moderate the overtly religious content of his political philosophy and furthermore he was in a conciliatory mood. Added to this, Paisley was determined to bring Boal along with him in the new venture. These two factors strongly influenced Paisley's decision to edit out the word 'Protestant' from the new Party's label.

The immediate problem, however, was how to avoid a vote taking place on the issue during the meeting, because Alan Lucas, Co-ordinating Secretary of the DUP at the time, has estimated that former members of the Protestant Unionist Party comprised 70 per cent of those in attendance while the remaining 30 per cent were dissident Unionists. These dissidents would have regarded the decision to retain the word 'Protestant' as a sign that the Protestant Unionists were unwilling to abide by the spirit of the pledge to create a 'Unionist Loyalist Party'. The problem was resolved through the expedient of appointing a committee charged with the responsibility of drawing up a constitution and rules to govern the future activities of the Party. Obviously such a committee was necessary and the controversy over the Party's name would remain in abeyance until the Rules Committee made its report. In the interim the masthead of the Party continued to be that of the DUP.

The debate over the change of name was only one aspect of the much more complex issue of the extent to which Boal's secular attitude and Paisley's moderation indicated that the formation of the DUP marked an important stage of development of a trend towards secularisation within Ulster Protestant extremism. However, there was an inherent difficulty: while Dr Paisley retained the Moderator-ship of the Free Presbyterian Church, and former Protestant Unionists relied upon Free Presbyterian clerics to give political direction on the lower tiers of the new Party's structure, the interior influence of the Free Presbyterian Church upon the Party would counter-balance Boal's personal commitment to a modern, secular and democratic image.

This failure to resolve the tensions between the secular humanism of Desmond Boal and Dr Paisley's determination to maintain a high religious profile created an atmosphere of confusion within the Party. This confusion was further accentuated by uncertainty over the manner in which the structure of the new Party was expected to develop.

The Party had adopted a loose structure at the Ulster Hall meeting on 30 October. The structure was to be based upon the six counties of Northern Ireland and the City of Belfast. A steering committee was set up, Desmond Boal accepted the office of Party Chairman, and it was agreed that the first task would be to assess the possible strength of the Party in each locality.

The meeting on 30 October had been long and wearisome, and the proposals for the Party's future development were far from precise. Neither Boal nor Paisley appreciated how dependent the whole venture was on the competence of the Party's local activists to build up the DUP through their own efforts. Boal was by inclination a highly self-contained individual who did not suffer fools gladly and Frank Millar senior has recorded his personal impression that Boal viewed his foray into politics as something of a 'hobby'; and it is doubtful whether Boal possessed either the administrative skill or the necessary patience which would be demanded of the new Party's joint leadership. Dr Paisley, by contrast, was weighed down with commitments to the fledgling denomination which he led, and he was committed to clearing the large debt on the Martyrs' Memorial Church which had been opened in 1969. As well as this, he had Stormont and Westminster constituencies to look after. These were sufficient reasons in themselves to explain why the new Party failed to take off; they provide justification for David Calvert's comment that '1972 was a bad year for the DUP'.

Vanguard poses problems for the DUP

The two issues of party philosophy and mobilisation were internal problems for the DUP which made little impact on the electorate at large. What was more crucial, and potentially demoralising, for the newly signed-up members of the DUP was the unpalatable truth that William Craig was succeeding in mobilising the majority of Unionist hardliners under the banner of his Ulster Vanguard Movement. Vanguard had been launched at a rally in the Apprentice Boys Memorial Hall, Londonderry, on 27 January 1972. The rally took place three days prior to the horrendous events of the following Sunday when thirteen Roman Catholic civilians were shot dead by soldiers of the First Battalion the Parachute Regiment reacting to skirmishing on the fringes of an illegal Civil Rights March. This serious incident made such an impact on the Conservative Government at Westminster that it led ineluctably to the prorogation of the Stormont Parliament and the imposition of Direct Rule in March 1972.

In addition, Paisley and Boal accentuated their problems by making radical political pronouncements on a wide range of issues. In their respective writings, Henry Kelly and Robert Fisk have made reference to the confusion which arose from this new direction in DUP policy. Kelly has stressed the leadership's opposition to internment and Paisley's conciliatory remarks on the impact that any changes in the Republic of Ireland's constitution might have on Protestant issues in Ulster as being the critical issues which explain why 'Paisley had very definitely confused his followers'. But Fisk puts his emphasis slightly differently. Fisk interpreted Paisley's call for total integration which the Doctor made on 12 May 1972 as being of significance. Like Kelly, Fisk also recognised that the suggestion by

Paisley 'that the idea of a united Ireland would not be so distasteful to Protestants if the Irish Republic disposed of its theocratic constitution' provoked incredulity amongst his personal following. In an interview published six months after Paisley's controversial remarks of December 1971, Boal pointed out that 'when the Rev. Ian Paisley suggested late last year that the people of the Republic should scrap their sectarian Constitution if they were serious about wanting a united Ireland, it caused quite a stir and was immediately interpreted as a willingness to talk about a Thirty-Two County Ireland. But the theocratic Constitution remains – and I believe will remain – essentially in its present form.'[16]

It was a comment with which Henry Kelly would have shared some sympathy. Kelly had written of the same episode: 'The arch-ogre of earlier days could say what he wanted, Dublin didn't seem to care. It was another missed opportunity'. Later in this interview in the *Irish Independent*, Boal provided a sophisticated and coherent explanation as to why Protestants in Northern Ireland found the Constitution of the Irish Republic so repugnant:

> When I say that the Constitution (of the Irish Republic) is theocratic I must not be taken as being opposed to Roman Catholicism as a theology. This I must emphasise very clearly. What I am saying is that I greatly fear the undue influence wielded by the Roman Catholic Church in the south in the political and social spheres. It can stultify social legislation, inhibit free debate in Parliament, prejudice the spontaneous expression of popular opinion, and pervert the course of democracy.

Jean Coulter has interpreted Paisley's willingness to forsake the bulwarks of loyalist intransigence for a more open-minded approach to the crisis as proof of Desmond Boal's influence over his thinking at the time. And information gleaned from the minutes of a DUP meeting held in Queen's University Students' Union on Monday 22 January 1973 largely substantiates Jean Coulter's view.

The meeting was addressed by Desmond Boal and like the interview in the *Irish Independent*, it gives a remarkable insight into the manner in which Boal's thinking about the Northern Ireland crisis had developed.

In the course of his address Boal asserted that the only thing that would govern 'England's' attitude to Northern Ireland was what would 'shut Northern Ireland up'. This remark was in line with his earlier analysis of the Government's document on constitutional proposals published in March 1973. At a meeting of DUP delegates held in Aughrim Street Mission Hall shortly after the publication of the document, Boal described the British Government's approach as one of 'inspired playing for time'. Later in the speech to the DUP branch at Queen's University, Boal acknowledged 'the irony of the fact that the proposal – of total integration – which would benefit the majority most is rejected by the majority'. Boal explained why the joint leadership of the DUP had supported total integration. It was, he said, likely to win the support of a section of the Roman Catholic community and was the policy which would guarantee the Unionist position and preserve the living standards of all. Unquestionably, though, the most provocative part of Boal's contribution that night came during a series of questions and answers when Boal, reflecting on the role of the Roman Catholic Church, remarked that the Church's influence in Northern Ireland was on the decline, and that he doubted whether the Roman Catholic Church wished to see a united Ireland. The meeting was stunned; the DUP students must have wondered whether they had invited a heretic into their midst. Boal's comment that he doubted whether the Roman Catholic Church had much interest in pursuing Irish unification was so much at variance with the public ministry of Dr Paisley, 'the leader of Ulster Protestantism', and the private sentiments of the majority of DUP members that it is hardly surprising that after Boal became a QC, on 26 January 1973, he lost interest in the 'hobby' of party politics, and resigned from the DUP in the following year.

Throughout the period of Paisley's collaboration with Boal, which was at its most intense from September 1971 to the early spring of 1973, Paisley had behaved in a conciliatory manner. He had played down his religious convictions, and abandoned his natural role as the populist spokesman of Ulster loyalism. The result had been disastrous for the Party. By the spring of 1973 Paisley had lost confidence in Boal's political judgment; what he needed was something to 'latch on to', a lever capable of lifting Paisley and Paisleyism out of the quicksand and back on to the commanding heights of loyalism which had been occupied by William Craig. Happily the British Government was at hand to provide Dr Paisley with the opportunity that he so desperately needed. Lawrence and Elliott have described in their detailed study of the Northern Ireland Border Poll the circumstances which lay behind the British Government's decision to conduct 'the first plebiscite in the history of the United Kingdom'[17] on 8 March 1973.

This was the day on which the plebiscite would establish whether the majority of the population wished 'to remain part of the United Kingdom' or not.

In the run-up to polling day Paisley launched himself pell-mell into garnering as many votes for the Union as possible. Paisley used the plebiscite to bring the DUP back in from the periphery of loyalist politics where the misunderstood and eccentric policies of Boal and Paisley had marooned it for nearly eighteen months. The issue of the Union was at the heart of the Province's existence and by presenting itself as a vigorous upholder of the Union the DUP began to attract attention and support in a way that had eluded the Party for months. Ernest Baird, a prominent member of Vanguard at the time, recalled the use that Paisley made of his Free Presbyterian churches, whose members served as auxiliaries to the DUP, adding strength to the Party's inchoate structure. As a consequence of this new sense of direction and public commitment to the fundamentals of loyalism the DUP 'gained increased support'.

The encouragement and success which Dr Paisley began to experience were not solely reflections of his single-mindedness, or the fervour of his Party workers, because William Craig, the leader of the Vanguard Movement, had through his own ineptitude raised questions about the soundness of his own political thinking.

A year earlier Craig's position appeared much more secure, after a series of Province-wide rallies, in the course of which Craig had been able to convene a crowd of between 60,000 and 90,000 loyalists in the Ormeau Park, Belfast. It was an impressive show of strength.

In the final analysis, however, there was little that could be achieved by one fragment of the Unionist population taking action on its own. Nevertheless, within the loyalist section of the Northern Ireland population, Vanguard had gained political prominence, and this was allied to the movement's close identification with the growing strength and menace of the loyalist paramilitaries.

Craig put all this in jeopardy by making the same mistake as Paisley, during a period of civil disorder and constitutional crisis, at a time when multitudes in Ulster were wondering whether life was still worth living, or whether, for that matter, there would be a life to live: he began to formulate an unsettling array of political ideas.

The significant feature of these policies was that they were in the main deviations from traditional Unionism. In the month of February 1973, Craig appeared to abandon democratic ideals when he called another of his one-day general strikes for Wednesday the seventh. The strike would be dependent for its success on loyalist paramilitary enforcers. This time there was an electricity blackout, accompanied by eight explosions, thirty-five malicious fires, twenty-seven civilian injuries, and two deaths. The episode was a disaster which bitterly divided Unionist opinion and was described in the *News Letter* as 'Ulster's Day of Shame'.

Six days later, on Monday 12 February, in a major speech in the Ulster Hall, Craig gave added credence to Paisley's charge that he favoured 'independence' by advocating that there should be 'an independent Dominion of Ulster'. And as if the Unionist population was not already satiated with political nostrums of one kind or another, just over a week later, information leaked out which linked the names of the SDLP politicians John Hume and Ivan Cooper to those of Craig and John Taylor, a former Unionist Cabinet minister. Apparently a private exchange of political views had taken place some weeks previously in John Taylor's home. The news led to further 'dismay and confusion' amongst the Unionist electorate. By this time, however, the electorate had other things on its mind, because the Border Poll was imminent. The plebiscite took place on 8 March 1973 and simply confirmed what was already known, that the majority in Northern Ireland wished to remain in the United Kingdom. (The figures were as follows: 591,820 or 57·5 per cent of the electorate cast their votes for continued membership of the UK, and 6,463 votes were cast indicating a preference to join the Republic of Ireland, 0·6 per cent.)

Just over three weeks later, on 30 March, Craig announced his intention to form a new party, which would be known as the Vanguard Unionist Progressive Party. Like the DUP some seven months before, the Vanguard Party soon encountered problems, because some prominent members of the Unionist Party who had indicated initial support, like John Taylor MP and Harry West MP, a former Minister of Agriculture, reneged. And a month after the announcement by Craig, Vanguard's two vice-chairmen, Rev. Martin Smyth, Grand Master of the Orange Order, and Austin Ardill, a right-wing Unionist, resigned from the movement. The Vanguard Unionist Progressive Party also experienced difficulties over the name which had been adopted as a means of expressing the new loyalist Party's commitment to 'non-sectarian and non-class' party politics. The name was eventually changed, and the new Party was simply known as the Vanguard Unionist Party.

The confusion over the basis of the Party's support amongst Unionist Party officials who were expected to follow Craig's example by resigning from the Unionist Party and affiliating to the new loyalist Party, was exacerbated by a costly decision taken by William Craig. On 8 April, Craig announced that the VUPP would not fight the first local government election in Northern Ireland since 1922 to be based on Proportional Representation. These elections were due to be held on 30 May. In all probability, Craig had calculated that early confusion about the new Party's role would not be helped by any bad publicity which might arise from the VUPP's poor showing in the local government poll.

Craig proposed to reserve the VUPP's strength for the election to the new seventy-eight member Assembly which would be held under

PR on 28 June. The new Northern Ireland Assembly had been set up by the British Government, which had declared its intention to support the emergence of a partnership government in its White Paper published early in the year, on 20 March 1973.

Craig's Vanguard Party, the DUP and the 'Anti-White Paper' Ulster Unionists were all committed to frustrating the willingness of the Faulkner-led Unionist Party, the Alliance Party and the SDLP actively to seek the power-sharing solution which the British Government favoured.

Would Dr Paisley also react by boycotting the forthcoming local government elections? At first it appeared likely; on Friday 27 April Dr Paisley declared that the DUP would not contest the local government elections. Fred Proctor, a DUP Councillor in Belfast City Hall, argued the case for the Party's official participation in the forthcoming local elections. Proctor won his point; Paisley relented, and the DUP officially contested the elections. This ensured that the DUP was able to put on what was, in effect, an electoral rehearsal, just four weeks before the more important Assembly elections, while the Vanguard Party was not. That, however, was not the end of the story. There was a great deal of confusion about which loyalist candidates were actually standing for which Party; some authorities have recorded that though the DUP put up thirty-nine candidates, unofficially the VUPP ran twenty-five candidates, while others contend that the DUP actually put up seventy-five candidates and omit any reference to the VUPP altogether.

As a consequence of the local government elections on 30 May, DUP headquarters was able to monitor the performance of its Party's candidates and this probably put the DUP in a stronger position than the VUPP to face the Assembly elections. However, it was a confusing election, and there is no consensus among the authorities about how many seats the DUP actually succeeded in winning. W. D. Flackes has settled for twenty-one gains by the DUP, while David Calvert, the Party historian, finally settled for thirteen seats won by the DUP.[18]

Though the rival DUP and VUPP parties were agreed that the unrest in the Province had been prompted by an Irish Republican conspiracy, supported the concept of majority rule and opposed the power-sharing philosophy of Brian Faulkner, the supporters of both parties were as antagonistic towards one another as Craig and Paisley were suspicious of each other.

Desmond Boal's position was much less certain because he had indicated to Ian Paisley that he would not seek election to the Assembly. This meant that the spotlight would concentrate on the joint leader with the higher political profile, Dr Paisley himself. With

Boal's influence on the decline, the Moderator of the Free Presbyterian Church of Ulster could not resist the temptation to stamp his personality on the Party in a manner similar to the way in which his authority permeates the Free Presbyterian Church. Paisley knew that there was nothing like electoral success to reinforce his political standing, and so with renewed confidence, he turned his mind to Thursday 28 June, polling day in the first election to a Northern Ireland Assembly.

Notes and References

[1] Dr Sydney Elliott, *Northern Ireland – the First Election to the European Parliament*, Belfast 1980, 54.

[2] Dr Ian R. K. Paisley, *Nicholson Centenary 1879 to 1976*, Belfast 1976, 23.

[3] Dr Ian R. K. Paisley, *The Fifty-Nine Revival: An Authentic History of the Great Ulster Awakening of 1859*, 4th edn, Belfast 1970, 202.

[4] John F. Harbinson, *The Ulster Unionist Party 1882–1973, Its Development and Organisation*, Belfast 1973, 191.

[5] George Dollar, *A History of Fundamentalism in America*, Greenville, South Carolina 1973, 385.

[6] Jacques Ellul, *The New Demons*, Oxford 1975, 30.

[7] Michael Farrell, *Northern Ireland – The Orange State*, London 1976, 236.

[8] Rev. William McCrea, *In His Pathway: The Story of the Rev. William McCrea*, London 1980, 26.

[9] Patrick Marrinan, *Paisley: Man of Wrath*, Tralee 1973, 149.

[10] Paul Arthur, *Government and Politics of Northern Ireland*, Harlow, Essex 1980, 99 et seq. See also Christopher Hewitt, 'Catholic grievances, Catholic nationalism and violence in Northern Ireland during the Civil Rights period: A reconsideration', *British Journal of Sociology*, Vol.32, No.3 (1981).

[11] A. T. Q. Stewart, *The Narrow Ground: Aspects of Ulster 1609–1969*, London 1977, 153.

[12] Robin Evelegh, *Peace-Keeping in a Democratic Society: The Lessons of Northern Ireland*, London 1978, 22.

[13] W. D. Flackes, *Northern Ireland: A Political Directory 1968–1979*, Dublin 1980, 164.

[14] Quoted in Richard Deutsch and Vivien Magowan, *Northern Ireland 1968–73: A Chronology of Events*, Vol. I, Belfast 1973, 119–120.

[15] Sarah Nelson, 'Ulster's Uncertain Defenders: A Study of Loyalists in Political Paramilitary and Community Organisations in Belfast 1969–1975', unpublished PhD thesis, University of Strathclyde, 236–241. (Now published in shortened form – Belfast 1984.)

[16] *The Irish Independent*, May 10, 1972.

[17] R. J. Lawrence and Sydney Elliott, *The Northern Ireland Border Poll 1973*, Cmnd. 5875 (January 1975), 1.

[18] David Calvert, *A Decade of the DUP*, Belfast 1981.

CHAPTER II

Pulpit and Hustings

The Christians are the salt of the earth and have a vital
responsibility to act as a strong preservative in the society in which
they are placed. Those Christians who refuse to fulfil their social
responsibilities are acting contrary to the plain teaching of
Scripture.

Ian R. K. Paisley
An Exposition of the Epistle to the Romans

The initial recruitment of political activists is important because it
demonstrates something of how the individual views politics and
how the collective party outlook may be shaped by the political
origins of its leadership.

Ian McAllister
The Northern Ireland Social Democratic and Labour Party

Internal tensions

With polling for the Northern Ireland Assembly now imminent,
the DUP election machine switched into top gear. From the outset
Ian Paisley has stressed the importance of election literature, posters
and the like. Soon the Puritan Printing Company vibrated to the
heavy tread of 'the big man' as Paisley bustled his way up the rickety
stairs of the cramped building with the latest draft of an election
address or poster slogan. DUP election agents inundated the printers
with enquiries as to when their posters would be ready: the
enthusiastic activists could barely wait to begin peppering the Ulster
countryside with loyalist placards. All of this frenetic activity on the
part of the DUP's supporters was largely inspired by Paisley himself,
who seemed to be able to live out two lives in the time span normally
allotted to one man: by turns the revivalist preacher in the pulpit

41

calling on sinners to repent and the politician at the hustings challenging the voters to save Ulster through the ballot box.

In contrast to all this feverish pre-election activity the party preparing to enter the fray was beset by substantially unresolved inner tensions. These tensions arose from Desmond Boal's determination to forge a political movement which was secular in character and sufficiently distanced from the outmoded style of Protestant Unionism to suit his own highly individualistic temperament. Ian Paisley had acquiesced in bringing about this change of political emphasis to be expressed in the DUP, but at the same time he continued to live out his dual commitment to evangelicalism and politicised Protestantism. Paisley's commitment to both the pulpit and the hustings now created an unusual kind of difficulty for the Party which is worth exploring. Dr Paisley in his role as Moderator of the Free Presbyterian Church of Ulster had at his back the organisational structure, discipline and finances of a vibrant and expanding religious sect. When the Moderator committed himself to Democratic Unionism he didn't stand alone: many laymen and ministers in his church came with him, and what needed to be resolved was whether the infrastructure of Dr Paisley's church organisation would be permitted to intrude upon the newly established and developing political organisation of the DUP in a way similar to the manner in which it had shaped Protestant Unionism.

The decision to drop the term 'Protestant' from the party masthead signalled a determination to present the public with an image of the DUP which had been sanitised of the more extreme manifestations of religion; but any attempt to differentiate the DUP from the Protestant Unionists encountered almost insuperable difficulties which turned on the role of Ian Paisley himself.

In the autumn of 1971 the Moderator of the Free Church was faced with a number of options. He could resign the ministry and devote himself single-mindedly to the promotion of this alternative loyalist cause, or he could see the Party safely over its launch, fade into the background and continue with his Gospel ministry. Ian Paisley chose neither of these options: instead he preferred, at whatever physical cost to himself, to maintain his dual role. Had Paisley taken the conscious decision to resign his clerical charge in the early 1970s and devote all his considerable energies to politics, then it seems highly likely that the DUP would have developed along different lines. Paisley's option provides an insight into the political culture of Northern Ireland, because there is no reason to dissent from Dr Edward Moxon-Browne's suggestion that 'it seems likely that Paisley's dual role as leader of a church and political party is one ingredient of his success'.[1] It is unlikely that the DUP without the additional support of Free Presbyterianism would have made the political breakthrough when it did.

The Free Presbyterian Church of Ulster provided Paisley with an auxiliary organisation which could be mobilised on specific occasions like that of the Border Poll in March 1973, or the South Belfast by-election in February 1982, to assist the Party in getting the electors to the polling booths. Rev. Ian Paisley's role as Moderator of the Free Presbyterian Church was instrumental in bringing about this association between the Free Presbyterian Church and the DUP which resulted in Dr Paisley's Church lining up behind the DUP party machine during elections.

Paisley's position, however, was not unique. There had long been a tradition in Ulster for Protestant clerics to assume the role of a political or military leader, and Rev. George Walker, Governor of Londonderry during the siege in 1688 and 1689, is a classic example. Two other clergymen whose record of loyalist and Orange activism has drawn comparison with the contemporary career of Ian Paisley were Rev. Dr Drew and Rev. 'Roaring' Hanna. What distinguished Paisley from the other Protestant clerics was the differing circumstances of the church institutions to which they belonged. The other clerics were invariably members either of the Presbyterian Church or the Church of Ireland, and they remained only members; they had influence, sometimes even great influence, but they never had control. Paisley was in a different category: his control and discipline over the Free Presbyterian Church were for all practical purposes complete and therefore the offices of Moderator and political leader carried more weight than in the cases of other Ulster clergymen in the past.

Paisley, though, was not alone in living out the roles of pastor and politician, because a number of the Free Presbyterian clergy emulated Paisley's style. This dual commitment on their part was conducted without all the attendant publicity that surrounded Paisley's career, and was invariably low-key, but given the limited scale of the DUP's organisation at the time the involvement of other Free Presbyterian ministers in the party apparatik would prove to be of considerable significance.

Alan Lucas recalls that Rev. Ivan Foster of Fermanagh, Rev. James McClelland of Londonderry and Rev. James Beggs (apart from being Dr Paisley's brother-in-law, Rev. James is his highly competent and unflappable election agent) took on important positions in the Party's infrastructure. Lucas also commented that out of fifteen appointments approved at the inaugural meeting only two positions went to dissident Unionists; apart from the appointment of Lucas himself, the only other former Unionist to gain a position was Oliver Gibson from Beragh in County Tyrone. The Free

Presbyterian and Protestant Unionist axis whose personnel were inevitably more cohesive and whose leading activists were already known to their supporters inevitably emerged as the dominant force within the new Party's structure.

A similar pattern was apparent in the City of Belfast which used the four Westminster constituencies as the basis of Party organisation. All eight members initially co-opted to the Belfast Executive Committee had a record of Free Presbyterian or Protestant Unionist affiliations. It was at this stage that Mr Peter Robinson (elected in May 1979 as DUP MP for East Belfast) was appointed as a representative from East Belfast. One respondent later recalled: 'Mr Robinson seemed very much on his own and arrived without coming from anywhere'. The other representative from East Belfast was Mrs Eileen Paisley, a Belfast City Councillor for the Protestant Unionists, and not unexpectedly the Executive tended to defer to the opinions of Mrs Paisley in the belief that she pursued projects which accorded with the wishes of her husband.

Another religious feature which was carried over from Protestant Unionism arose from the decision to begin each formal meeting of the Party, whether at Executive or branch level, with Bible reading and prayer.

Although the rural halls in which the DUP conducted its meetings were rented on the basis of what was available, early meetings of the Party Executive in Belfast occupied, at various stages, rooms above Wilton's Funeral Parlour on the Donegall Pass, and a suite of rooms in the Europa Hotel. In the light of this confusion about a suitable meeting place for the Belfast Executive of the DUP, it is not surprising that Sarah Nelson mused that 'there has been a certain esoteric quality about Paisleyite movements'[2] (sic). There was some little embarrassment as well, because on one memorable occasion a group of DUP members waiting for a meeting to be convened on an upper floor of the Europa Hotel was confronted by a scantily clad hostess, bearing the soubriquet of 'Penthouse Poppet', who enquired whether the serious-minded Protestant activists wanted 'something to drink'. The Party subsequently moved out of the hotel, which rented conference rooms at what turned out to be a prohibitive rate. However, the Party's regular use of the Aughrim Street Mission Hall off Sandy Row during the early period seemed to reinforce the religious dimension to the Party's development.

Free Presbyterian Churches also facilitated the fledgling party in the course of the announcements during services of worship when news of future DUP meetings and other relevant pieces of political information were conveyed to the congregations. This feature had been a long established facet of the ministry of Dr Paisley, who regularly broke into routine church announcements with a detailed account of the most recent political controversy and his Party's response to some new challenge from Ulster's encircling foes.

Secret Presbytery meetings

The Free Presbyterian Church is governed by a Presbytery, but the meetings of Presbytery have always been shrouded in mystery; this secrecy was encouraged by the Moderator himself. Paisley told the Free Presbyterian ministers and elders who attended these meetings that they were not even to tell their wives what went on. Although there was often humour in his voice, and anyone who was in the Big Man's company over a long period encountered this feature of Free Presbyterianism, the church has been remarkably successful in maintaining silence over its private decision-making processes. Rev. William McCrea, who is now an internationally established gospel recording artist, was the subject of a crisis meeting in Presbytery, but not a hint of this appears in his autobiography *In His Pathway*.[3] In earlier research work on the subject of Paisleyism, Cecil Harvey, a prominent Free Presbyterian who was entitled to attend these meetings, was asked about their political significance. Mr Harvey refused to answer any questions whatsoever pertaining to these Presbytery meetings. All the information on these meetings has been extremely difficult to come by, but it does throw more light on inner tensions between the Free Presbyterian Church and the DUP.

It appears that on at least four occasions and on dates which are not as yet ascertainable, the Presbytery of the Free Presbyterian Church took vital decisions, of a highly political nature, which had a direct bearing on whether the DUP would be able to select certain Free Presbyterian ministers as candidates for the Party, or not.

These Presbytery meetings were so secret that neither the paid-up grass-roots membership of the DUP, nor activists holding positions of responsibility within the Party, appreciated what was going on or the way in which decisions that were taken at these secret meetings influenced the development of the Party. As the lay membership of the Church does not have access to these meetings and whatever minutes that may be taken at the meetings are not open to inspection, it is not possible to state whether the Presbytery is able to moderate or influence the authoritarian trait in Dr Paisley's personality.

It is not, however, essential to establish whether the Presbytery is in effect the governing body of the Free Presbyterian Church or merely an instrument of Dr Paisley's 'will to power'.[4] Ignorance as to what goes on behind the closed doors of such secret meetings has been commented upon by those who have seceded from Paisley's church.

Former Free Presbyterians have cited 'the failure of the Church during its existence to produce a Constitution or Code of Practice for its members and officebearers, thus keeping them in ignorance of the true nature of the Church and of the rules, if any, for the regulation of its affairs'.[5]

The evidence is that on the eve of the first elections to the Northern Ireland Assembly in June 1973, a bitter wrangle broke out at one of these secret Presbytery meetings. The dispute arose because a leading Free Presbyterian minister, Rev. Alan Cairns, was adamant that the Presbytery should endorse the decision that only Dr Paisley and Rev. William Beattie would be permitted to go forward as DUP candidates at the election. Beattie's inclusion is to be explained by the fact that he had established himself as the Protestant Unionist MP for South Antrim and he had also acted as a deputy to Dr Paisley while the Free Presbyterian leader was in prison. Such a decision would have debarred three other Free Presbyterian ministers who, it was widely rumoured, were interested in becoming politicians. The ministers were Rev. James McClelland, Rev. Ivan Foster and Rev. William McCrea. The reason for refusing to allow these ministers the opportunity to seek political advancement was in all probability connected with Dr Paisley's desire to keep alive Desmond Boal's waning interest in the DUP and to avoid any unfavourable publicity.

The DUP would eventually field seventeen candidates in the Assembly elections, one of whom turned out to be Dr Paisley's wife, Eileen. Had the Presbytery approved of five Free Presbyterian ministers, including Dr Paisley and William Beattie, running for the Assembly, then over a quarter of the DUP's candidates would have been publicly associated with the Free Presbyterian Church.

It was a difficult situation and one curious aspect of the affair was the reluctance of the Presbytery meeting to consider John Calvin's pronouncements on the respective functions of the pastor and the politician contained in his 'Institutes of the Christian Religion'. After all, the Free Presbyterian Church claimed to be 'identical to our Presbyterian forefathers', and as the *New International Dictionary of the Christian Church* has defined it, 'Traditionally Presbyterianism is the general title given to the English-speaking, Reformed or Calvinistic churches coming out of the Reformation'.[6]

Calvin had argued that 'Christ wished to ban the ministers of His word from civil rule and earthly authority'. Calvin developed this theme and continued 'Christ means not only that the office of pastor is distinct from that of prince but also that the things are so different that they cannot come together as one man'.[7] How did the Free Presbyterian Church side-step John Calvin's injunction? According to Rev. George Hutton, the Free Presbyterians regarded Dr Paisley as 'God's man for the hour', which is taken to mean that God has providentially raised up Dr Paisley as a kind of prophet and guide to lead Ulster through these wilderness years. Rev. George Hutton amplified his point by explaining that to the Free Presbyterians at that Presbytery meeting Paisley 'was unique', and therefore Calvin's theology of the separate roles of the pastor and political representative was irrelevant. Ulster was different.

This incident at the secret meeting held in the spring of 1973 provides a further example of the equivocal manner in which Dr Paisley attempted to integrate his religious role as the outspoken Protestant preacher with his aspirations for political success. But the important issue here is that such a meeting could take place at all, and without Paisley's grass-roots support, the media or the DUP's political opponents learning anything about it. One interpretation of the Presbytery's decision suggests that Dr Paisley was able to use the authority of the courts of the Free Presbyterian Church to give a stamp of approval to his earlier political understanding with Desmond Boal, which resulted in the new Party's adoption of a much less aggressively Protestant posture. Another less malign interpretation, put forward by a leading Free Presbyterian, is that as all the ministers had at their ordination given a solemn undertaking to give themselves full-time to the Gospel ministry, they needed the approval of Presbytery before standing for election.

The effect of the Presbytery's decision, however, could not have been displeasing to Paisley himself. The DUP leader was taking into the election a Party with a more acceptable image. It is one thing, however, to launch a political movement and often quite another to win seats.

Electioneering technique

The electioneering methods employed by Dr Paisley have attracted considerable attention from the media. Every election fought by the DUP leader has been described and commented upon at length by both provincial and national newspapers. The *Irish Times*, in particular, has carried detailed and perceptive accounts of Dr Paisley's election campaigns. Television coverage of these events has also been extensive.

The campaign style of the DUP leader is best conveyed by the term 'barnstorming'; that is, Rev. Ian Paisley campaigns arduously and rapidly throughout the constituency holding open air political meetings in as many as three villages or rural hamlets a night. Paisley organises his election programmes like a military campaign, and an extremely demanding one at that. Amongst communities who have identified most strongly with the DUP, it is not thought unusual for party supporters to wait huddled together against the cold night air, as has happened at Carnalbana, near Larne, until after midnight awaiting the arrival of the DUP cavalcade, complete with flute band and party leader. Such political commitment makes an impression on the whole locality and demoralises the opposition, because opponents know that their party leaders lack the charisma which encourages such loyal support. At the same time, this evidence of enthusiastic endorsement bolsters Dr Paisley, assuring him of another political triumph.

The whole electioneering enterprise is tailor-made to expand the already larger-than-life impression created by Rev. Ian Paisley's physical appearance, and the impact upon these small communities is electrifying. Everyone soon realises that an election is being held, and the arrival of Dr Paisley and his entourage in the locality forces the ordinary voters to take sides, to state a preference and defend it in conversation with their neighbours. Requests from the DUP to the village Orange Lodge for the hire of their hall for electioneering purposes or an invitation to the local band to participate in election parades has often caused heated controversy and division within the local Protestant community. The aggressiveness of Dr Paisley's political programme and extravagant use of election posters and handouts ensure that the election becomes the main talking point in the constituency. Dr Paisley's physical commitment to the campaign, involving mornings and afternoons spent canvassing or 'door knocking' as the DUP terms it, and evenings parading routes, sometimes extending over nine miles in length, through housing estates and town centres, sets an example which DUP activists try to emulate. This has turned the DUP into a formidable political machine, feared by rival political parties, and the energy which the Party's membership devotes to each contest is not unreasonably described as having the hallmark of fanaticism. These experiences which have just been described have a particular relevance in Northern Ireland where, until 1969, a small number of constituencies had traditionally returned members to the Stormont Parliament without an electoral contest. This had been the case in the constituency of Bannside, where Rev. Ian Paisley first challenged the political supremacy of the Official Unionist Party by standing against the Prime Minister, Terence O'Neill.

In the late sixties, mobilising the voters therefore involved impressing them not only with the fact that an election was being held, but indicating through the vigour of the election campaign that the ruling Official Unionist Party could be displaced. Despite the fact that Rev. Ian Paisley succeeded in winning both the Bannside and later the Westminster constituency of North Antrim which incorporated the former Stormont constituency, and has continued to hold the seat for more than a decade, he has not significantly altered the electioneering methods which he adopted in the days of Protestant Unionism. The campaign technique which the DUP leader has used has traditionally been associated with Unionism and the Unionist Party and its most noteworthy feature is that it is outdated. However, Rev. Ian Paisley eschewed any suggestion that his entry into Ulster politics would be accompanied by an adoption of contemporary electioneering methods. This contrasts with the approach adopted by the SDLP, which rapidly established itself as a party dependent upon, and committed to, the promotion of its political platform through the most up-to-date methods of mass communication.

There are two main reasons why Rev. Ian Paisley chose to campaign in traditional style with bands, flags and marching ranks of committed supporters. In the first place one important thrust of his criticism was that the party of Terence O'Neill and Brian Faulkner had abandoned traditional Unionism; by campaigning in a manner which the older generations of Unionist electors had long associated with their own brand of politics, he encouraged the idea that a vote for Paisley was intrinsically a vote for loyalism, Unionism and Ulster. Furthermore, the use of the Union flag and fife and drum bands reminded spectators of the Orange Order's processions and loyal demonstrations, and this reinforced the impression that Rev. Ian Paisley sought to create, that he was the embodiment of Ulster's traditional political allegiance.

Secondly, this boisterous and very physical form of electioneering appealed to Rev. Ian Paisley's own personality. He was able to display his outstanding oratorical skills, to dominate his listeners, and to motivate his supporters. The methods which he adopted also attracted media and press attention which in the early days was far in excess of the interest that would have been shown in a more reticent political movement commanding similar minority support.

There was an implicit ruthlessness in this technique which found expression in the vehement language which Rev. Ian Paisley used to powerful effect at open air meetings. The speeches successfully created word pictures in the minds of those in attendance and Rev. Ian Paisley's skill lay in his ability to impress his audience with the veracity and passion of his political ideals despite the inadequacies of the public address system, the chill in the wind, the barking of dogs, the noise of nearby traffic and all the other distractions which competed with the DUP leader for the attention of the crowd. Few other politicians in Northern Ireland possess either the stamina or the mental agility to translate their political views into verbal cartoons which an outdoor audience can easily assimilate.

Political opponents lampooned by the DUP leader have often found themselves subjected to heckling at their own political meetings by the militant followers of Rev. Ian Paisley; these party activists have intuitively sensed the inherent ruthlessness in Rev. Ian Paisley's electioneering style and in order to prove their devotion and loyalty to the DUP have gone out of their way to be provocative in their verbal and sometimes physical assaults on rival Unionist politicians.

The personal attacks indulged in by Rev. Ian Paisley from the back of Wesley Adams' Landrover, which provided the DUP with a mobile and familiar political platform to electioneer from in all the major elections, had the effect of presenting the voters with a constant leadership contest; they were being asked to choose between Rev. Ian Paisley who provided evidence of his loyalism by his very demeanour and the symbols carried by his enthusiastic entourage, and a remote Unionist leader who had been ridiculed by Paisley.

The media appeared to regard Rev. Ian Paisley's histrionic electioneering as blatant exhibitionism, and film of the Protestant Unionist and, in the late 1970s, the DUP campaigns, was invariably hostile. Rev. Ian Paisley was represented by the media as the personification of 'Orange bigotry'. This television image was very damaging to the DUP leader outside the Province, but in Northern Ireland the reaction of many Unionist voters was quite the reverse.

The majority of the Unionist population believed that the media had been biased and unsympathetic both to the institutions of Ulster's administration and to the majority of the Province's citizens. The majority perceived that the media was broadly in support of the demand for civil rights and that television programmes invariably gave credence to the allegations about police (RUC) brutality, the Special Powers Act and discrimination made by the mainly Catholic civil rights protesters. Deep and widespread resentment was felt against television coverage of the first period of the troubles by many of the Unionist electorate who not unnaturally concluded that media hostility to Rev. Ian Paisley could only be interpreted as being confirmation of his claim to be the authentic articulation of a cause that was seen to be derided, demeaned and under threat.

The coverage and attention which television in particular gave to Rev. Ian Paisley also publicised the controversial political predictions which the DUP leader was wont to make. Claiming that he had contacts with access to privileged or secret information concerning the political intentions of his opponents, future government policy, internal decisions affecting the deployment of the RUC and other sensitive matters, Rev. Ian Paisley made startling claims which prophesied future developments in Northern Ireland.

These predictions were later shown to be largely accurate and this garnered more support for the DUP. Television coverage of this aspect of Rev. Ian Paisley's political technique served to build up his credibility as a leader.

Television was to benefit the DUP in two other important respects as well. Rev. Ian Paisley's aggressive, straight-from-the-shoulder style appealed to Northern Irish Unionists. The gruff, unvarnished and unaffected language gave expression to their own emotions and feelings, and an empathy was established between the DUP leader and many of the television viewers in the Province, who would have said that they were going to give their support to the DUP leader because 'he speaks out', that is, he articulated their own political ideals.

This analysis of television coverage has so far been confined to news-reel film and programme commentary, but when Rev. Ian Paisley came into the television studio he soon learned to adapt to what in effect was a one-to-one televised encounter with the elector and his family in their own home.

In studio coverage Rev. Ian Paisley softened his style; he attempted to impose his dominance and authority over both the presenter and any political opponents who may also have been participants, and in this he invariably achieved some success. There was intense local television reportage of the crisis in Northern Ireland until the Stormont Parliament was prorogued. During that period Rev. Ian Paisley polished and improved upon his studio image so that a clear distinction emerges between news film items on Rev. Ian Paisley and the projection of his persona which came across from intimate encounters in the television studio. Ian Paisley's emotional commitment, his deeply held religious convictions and his humour were all given ample expression and although many of these local television programmes were not necessarily scheduled or transmitted at election times, this aspect of the media's response to Rev. Ian Paisley helps to explain why he was able to establish himself as a major force in Ulster politics.

The electioneering technique adopted by the DUP also embraces aspects of a religious crusade. The manifestations of religious commitment are not readily accessible to the onlooker but there are strong indications that this is in fact the case.

Campaigning in the constituency of North Antrim is accompanied by a series of prayer meetings held either in private homes or the Ballymena Free Presbyterian Church. At such meetings God's blessing is called down upon the electoral campaign. Not all stalwart

DUP supporters will attend such religious meetings, but those who do fervently and sincerely believe that their prayer 'availeth much'.

This form of commitment inevitably encourages a far higher level of political involvement on the part of such DUP supporters. They regard campaigning with Rev. Ian Paisley as 'doing God's work'. This is because they accept that Rev. Ian Paisley has been raised up by God at this critical hour in Ulster's history. The religiously motivated activists have never been discouraged from holding such views by the DUP leader himself, and their willingness 'to go the second mile', to work extremely hard for the DUP leader, gives the DUP a considerable advantage over rival political parties because of the workload that each DUP activist is willing to bear in order to gain a political triumph.

Every election victory is interpreted in such circumstances as a special sign of God's blessing, and the growth of the DUP is believed to be a remarkable confirmation of God's blessing upon a Party which seeks to magnify His name and uphold the cause of Protestant Ulster.

Electoral reverses suffered by DUP candidates have never prompted the opposite reaction amongst the more spiritually minded Party activists: that the rejection of the candidate should be adjudged as the disapproval of the Almighty. This is a curious facet of the DUP activists' thinking; electoral victories signify God's blessing upon them, but political reverses are interpreted differently, as a challenge to redouble their efforts.

The campaign technique of Ian Paisley is inseparable from the political culture in which it has been employed. The traditional Unionist barnstorming technique which the DUP leader has used succeeded because the voters in the constituencies where these electoral tactics have been developed responded to and endorsed this style of demagogic persuasion.

Rev. John Brown, a retired History lecturer, has commented succinctly on three facets of the constituency of North Antrim which would have tended to frustrate an attempted breakthrough by a new political force.

These perceptive observations measure the complex factors which together contribute to voter appeal in one of the largest constituencies in the United Kingdom in relation to the talents and claims of a candidate who sought to unseat the sitting MP whose Party had held the constituency for over fifty years.

North Antrim divides into three diverse areas which correspond closely to the former Stormont constituencies of North Antrim, Bannside and Larne and, for a candidate to succeed electorally, the candidate needs to be well known in each of these areas. Dr Paisley therefore had a distinct advantage in being already well known through his itinerant evangelical crusades. These 'Gospel Campaigns' were further consolidated by the establishment of the Free Presbyterian Churches in the constituency. Dr Paisley's reputation became even more widely known after his spectacular Protestant Unionist campaign against the Northern Ireland Prime Minister, Terence O'Neill, in 1969.

Although there had been a tradition of radicalism in parts of North Antrim, Rev. John Brown insisted that this phenomenon was not straightforward, and it was suggested that in some districts the rural population were conservative because the local landlord was a Liberal, and that a further complication arose because of an undercurrent of opposition to some Church of Ireland rectors and those landowners who composed the Province's 'squirearchy'. The use of the descriptive term 'Presbyterian' in the titles adopted by the Doctor was held to have been of advantage to him as was Dr Paisley's denunciatory style of preaching and his loudly proclaimed opposition to 'sin'.

Some of those who voted Protestant Unionist and, in the 1970s, DUP, could under different contingent circumstances have been expected to vote Labour. These voters found the class snobbery of the ruling Unionist Party elite repugnant and they responded unfavourably to the claims of candidates with 'good breeding' and 'intelligence'. Those who have monitored Dr Paisley's electioneering technique have been impressed by his genial personal style which encourages constituents to invite him into their homes without feeling uncomfortable or ill at ease. Viewed in these intimate and often humble circumstances, supping tea and eating buttered scones, no one could doubt that Dr Paisley is a 'man of the people'. His ability to achieve such a rapport with the grass-roots Unionist voters is to be contrasted with the hesitancy, embarrassment and discomfort of the voters when the Unionist from the 'big house', Captain O'Neill or his ilk, arrived on their doorstep to canvass their support.

Finally, Rev. John Brown suggested that Dr Paisley held considerable sexual attraction for some female supporters of his political crusade. Ed Moloney, an *Irish Times* journalist, passed a similar comment on the sexual undertones in the observed reaction of some groups of women supporters after Moloney had attended the Carson Trail rallies.

These observations have dwelt exclusively on the electioneering technique of Dr Paisley. As the DUP has become established, other candidates have emerged who have modified those techniques which Dr Paisley has made his own.

The personality of other DUP candidates has been most important in determining whether they chose to model their own campaigns on

Dr Paisley's personal style or whether the candidates preferred to depend on Dr Paisley's name, endorsement and the dynamism of the local DUP electoral machine.

One of the more successful of the DUP's candidates, Peter Robinson, the Westminster MP for East Belfast, has relied much more heavily on the efficiency of the local party machine, because he does not possess the kind of extrovert personality that can easily adopt the flamboyant, semi-theatrical style of showmanship associated with the Party's leader.

Many of the other features of Dr Paisley's electioneering technique are common to all the DUP's candidates. These include the emphasis on door-to-door canvassing, and constituency-wide publicity through the use of thousands of posters and ruthless declamatory attacks on the DUP's rivals, gauged to attract publicity and notoriety. The energy of the Party's workers is not diminished because they are working for another candidate, because in their eyes the candidates act out the role of surrogates for Dr Paisley himself.

Dr Paisley has often likened forthcoming electoral contests to a 'crusade'. This is a term which is two-edged, suggesting a military struggle, or an evangelical religious meeting. These implications are not lost on the Party's workers and the word 'crusade' is itself entirely appropriate. Every election campaign embarked upon by the DUP and promoted by Dr Paisley has been undergirded by the internal conviction of many of the DUP's activists – and this has been publicly acknowledged by Dr Paisley – that the task which they and the Party had set themselves was to vindicate and uphold the Protestant cause. This religious motivation has given the DUP a powerful incentive which has more than compensated for the apparent advantages of traditional voting strength, political experience, years in office and media support, possessed by the dominant Unionist Party. Dr Paisley's unchallenged supremacy and authority over the DUP has been built upon his proven ability to win elections. Dr Paisley did the ground-work, and there is not a single candidate returned on behalf of the DUP who does not owe a significant (though unquantifiable) measure of the support he receives from the voters to the political skill, dexterity and tenacity of the DUP leader.

Sources of DUP support

Paisley's electioneering crusades did more than 'get people out', or mobilise the voters; such political campaigns also recruited more committed followers who were swept along by the tide of support into becoming party members.

Ian Paisley at an Orange March in Paisley, 1949.

Rev. Ian Paisley and Rev. John Wylie protest outside the
General Assembly of the Presbyterian Church in Ireland.

The author with Ian Paisley following his election to
the Northern Ireland Assembly in June 1974.

Assemblyman James Craig is helped down the steps of Stormont by
Ian Paisley following disruptive tactics against Brian Faulkner.

The dual role of Paisley as pastor and politician was reflected in the type of person mobilised by the Paisley crusade. The nature of Ian Paisley's support has been a source of controversy for years because those authorities who have written about Northern Ireland from a Marxist standpoint have over-emphasised Dr Paisley's role as the leader of Ulster's Protestant working-class. Such writers have tended to characterise the DUP as a Protestant working-class party, and this view of the type of supporter attracted by the DUP has been so all pervading that even Ian Paisley began to talk in terms of his leading the Protestant working-class himself! It is not difficult to understand why those writing about Ulster from a Marxist standpoint have adopted this position. In the first place many commentators are much more familiar with the situation in Belfast and the fact that Paisley's church is easily accessible and also situated in Belfast has tempted commentators into believing that all that they needed to know about the phenomenon of 'Paisley' could be gleaned by some research among the folk of Belfast's Shankill Road, and a visit or two to evening services in the Martyrs Memorial Church. Any attempted understanding of Paisleyism that is largely based on the political experience of Belfast suffers some distortion, because as the history of the Party indicates, a vital ingredient in the DUP's success has been the Party's strength in rural Ulster where the first political break-through was made.

Another problem arises from the reluctance of some commentators to come to terms with the powerful influences that religion can bring to bear in the shaping of an individual's political allegiance. It is difficult for academics who accept a secular or Marxist world-view to make an empathetic leap of faith which would enable them to grasp why humble and unsophisticated Ulster Protestants in the country-side around Dervock or the coastline at Glenarm accept what Dr Paisley says from the back of a Landrover as a faithful articulation of political reality. These supporters believe that Ian Paisley 'speaks the truth' in an age where the intelligentsia hold to a concept of truth which is based on relativism.

There are further constraints placed in the way of any attempt to construct a profile of DUP support which arise from what is termed 'the Northern Ireland problem'. Society in the Province is divided on sectarian and not on class lines. When the attempt is made to quantify the DUP's working-class appeal, that can only be understood as being an appeal to one section of the working-class in Northern Ireland: the Protestant working-class. The Protestant working-class in the Province cannot be perceived in terms of a bloc vote: the fractured nature of Northern Ireland society is evident within the

Protestant working-class which is sub-divided between urban and rural working-class.

The Protestant working-class also has divided loyalties and political preferences. All the Unionist parties have competed for their vote, and so, for that matter, have the moderate Alliance Party, the Northern Ireland Labour Party, and occasionally the Communist Party. The SDLP, while it is described in the media as 'the mainly Catholic party', also tries to gain votes from the Protestant electorate.

The DUP is not able to capture or mobilise a bloc Protestant working-class vote, for the reasons that have already been outlined. Furthermore, an attitude survey conducted by Professor Richard Rose in 1968 indicated that over half of those Protestants interviewed did not subscribe to the proposition that 'class conflict'[8] is central to an understanding of contemporary society in Northern Ireland. This lack of concern with class politics is an additional qualifying factor, which constricts the actual number of Protestant working-class votes available to the DUP. It is probable that a high proportion of Protestant working-class electors vote for the DUP not out of class loyalty but because of other issues which have salience for them – because the DUP has 'a strong leader', 'speaks with one voice', 'stands up for Ulster', and is 'against the IRA'.

The DUP may, through its electoral strategy, appeal directly to the concentrations of Protestant voters in working-class urban and rural Northern Ireland Housing Executive estates; and the Party is endorsed by a significant segment of the Protestant working-class, but further evidence can be adduced to support the conclusion that the DUP cannot be categorised simply as a working-class party. Moxon-Browne's *Nation, Class and Creed in Northern Ireland* sets out a profile of DUP support by social class as against Protestant religious affiliation which shows clearly that the DUP does recruit successfully across all social classes. The Party is, however, significantly under-represented in social class A and also unrepresented in social class B, but there is a marginally higher degree of support in the middle bands of the table – C1, C2 and D, and nearly twice the support in social group E. Moxon-Browne concluded that support for the DUP 'is found to some extent in the middle-class and in rural areas'.[9]

Professor Derek Birrell conducted a survey[10] which demonstrated the importance of the DUP's rural support, and indicated that the rural base of the DUP is more pronounced than that of any other Party in the Province. The picture which emerges is of a party recruiting support in the greater Belfast area but drawing strongly on a rural base among Ulster's farming community.

There is another significant group of activists mobilised by the DUP who are not readily accessible to survey research. This is a group consisting of those who joined the Party because they believed that supporting the DUP was 'doing God's work'. These are the activists who have become politicised out of a sense of Christian duty to uphold Protestantism and to campaign for high moral standards within society. These pietistic Party members have been identified by personal observation: Sandy Spence, a DUP Mayor of the town of Ballymena, and his DUP colleague on the Council, Maurice Mills, are representative of this type of pietistic activist.

The religious views of Spence and Mills were shaped by small Protestant sects other than Rev. Ian Paisley's Free Presbyterian Church, like the Pentecostalists, and the importance of this arises from the 'holiness doctrines' of these sects which invariably represent 'politics' as being of this world, carnal and unspiritual. Politics are shunned and a Christian's spirituality or godliness is questioned by other members of the sect if that Christian becomes politically involved. Spence and Mills and other devout Christians within the DUP 'take their stand in the political arena' because they believe it to be an extension of their Christian witness.

Though the DUP has been successful in recruiting across all social classes, the Party's voting strength is drawn almost exclusively from within the Protestant population of Ulster. This fact underlines a fascinating paradox which says much for the way in which 'Paisleyism' is perceived outside Northern Ireland.

In 1978 an Attitude Survey was published which included a table on 'religion and political party'. This indicated that while the DUP can muster 17·1 per cent support among Protestants, the Party only receives 0·3 per cent Roman Catholic support. This support for a Protestant party compares remarkably closely with 0·4 per cent of Protestant support for the SDLP. The SDLP makes a point of stressing that it is a 'non-sectarian party', but in reality the SDLP is no more successful in recruiting across the sectarian divide than the much more aggressively Protestant and 'sectarian' DUP is at attracting Catholic votes. The problem of the DUP arises from the fact that the SDLP's public image of non-sectarianism, moderation and tolerance has given this nationalist party a political standing outside Northern Ireland which the counter-productive political style of Rev. Ian Paisley and his supporters denies to the DUP.

Evolution of the Party Constitution

A Party committed to fighting elections and hoping to attract activist support could not survive on an *ad hoc* basis; a formal structure was essential, and at the inaugural meeting of the DUP in the Ulster Hall on 30 October 1971, it was agreed that the new Party would organise itself on the basis of the six counties of Northern Ireland. As a means of ensuring that the new Party would recruit right across the Province, a county structure had much to commend it, and the Orange Order was also organised on such a basis. However, a county structure imposed serious political limitations on the new Party because as a result of this decision, its organisation was not tied in sufficiently closely to the pattern of electoral boundaries in Ulster.

The inaugural meeting also agreed to appoint a committee to draw up draft proposals for a set of rules which would govern the Party's conduct. The meeting itself had been long and arduous, and it is not surprising, therefore, that the joint movers of the new Party, Desmond Boal and Ian Paisley, failed to communicate to the Rules Committee the extent to which their thinking about the new Party had matured beyond that of their supporters.

Boal and Paisley shared the aspiration that the new loyalist Party would be organised on such a basis that its structure would be closer to the democratic ideal than that of the Official Unionist Party.[11] This jointly held conviction that the new Party ought to be manifestly democratic in its structures and management had two sides to it. In the first instance Desmond Boal had fought a long battle inside the Unionist Party which focused increasingly on the premiership and policies of Captain Terence O'Neill as the political crisis in the Province worsened. In the course of this struggle with the leadership of his Party, Boal had become convinced that the Ulster Unionist Party was demonstrably undemocratic in its organisation and that in particular, the grass-roots supporters of the Party were unable to exercise their democratic rights effectively.

Boal's criticism of the Unionist Party's organisation was widely shared by other dissident Unionists who were dismayed by their Government's handling of the deepening political crisis in the Province. But in the struggle to reverse the Unionist Government's reforming policy commitments the dissidents were confronted by the fact that the structure of the Ulster Unionist Party strengthened the control which the leadership was able to wield over the Party. In the initial stages of the struggle between the moderate wing of the Unionist Party led by the Northern Ireland Premier, Terence O'Neill, and the right-wing Unionists, bloc voting by party appointees and even some of the wives of the Members of Parliament strengthened the hand of the Party's ruling elite against the rising chorus of dissent from among the grass-roots membership. An important part of Boal's case rested on the conviction that a new loyalist party should be guided by the desire to give its grass-roots supporters their place in the conduct of its internal affairs and in the development of party policy.

Paisley and Boal shared the belief that a loyalist party which was patently democratic in its organisation and in the place which it accorded to its rank and file membership would prove a sufficient inducement to attract the support of disillusioned loyalists. But there was another aspect to this task of forging a loyalist movement which conformed to Boal's democratic idealism. Not only did the Ulster Unionist Party's Constitution give a significant place to ex-officio members, peers and the wives of Members of Parliament on its major policy-making committees, but it also extended voting rights to other semi-autonomous bodies as well as to the Orange Order and other loyalist institutions. Did the joint commitment of Boal and Paisley to the concept of a thoroughly democratic Ulster loyalist party mean that the Orange Order would also be excluded from the organisational structures of the new movement?

Boal's principled approach to the creation of new democratic structures strongly suggests that he would have opposed any attempt to build a role for the Orange Order into the Party's organisation, but in fact the question was never seriously considered. There are a number of reasons why the members of the DUP committee charged with the task of drafting a constitution, and the party membership in general, were disinclined to give constitutional rights to the Orange Institution, or for that matter other less well known loyalist bodies like the Apprentice Boys of Derry, within the organisation of the DUP.

A major factor in shaping the party membership's attitude towards the Orange Order arose from the circumstances under which the DUP had been formed. Unlike the older Unionist Party which owed its origins, in part, to a meeting between 'seven Orangemen elected as MPs at Westminster in January 1886',[12] the DUP's formation had not been initiated by politicians who shared a prior membership of the Orange Order. In fact if anything there was a feeling of antipathy towards the Orange Institution on the part of some of the more militant members of the DUP, who held that the Orange Order had failed either to protect or to represent the interests of ordinary Orangemen and that the Order had been compromised by too close an association with the Ulster Unionist Party. Such sentiments re-echoed the criticisms which the breakaway Independent Orange Institution had levelled at the Orange Order at the turn of the century and this cannot be regarded as coincidental because from the beginning, Independent Orangemen in North Antrim had been attracted to the DUP.

A further consideration was the feeling that the Protestant principles of the Orange Institution had become corrupted as a consequence of the Orange Institution's close ties with the Official

Unionist Party. According to that line of thought, the Unionist Party had successfully neutralised Protestant militancy within the Orange Order by the use of patronage which ensured that prominent Orangemen received due rewards for their loyalty to the Unionist Party and the Northern Ireland Government. As the DUP's support has increased over the years so DUP sympathisers who are also Orangemen have become more persistent in their calls for the links between the Orange Institution and the Official Unionist Party to be broken.

The reluctance of the membership of the DUP to contemplate giving a prominent place to the loyal institutions within their newly formed organisation has added significance because as Harbinson has described in some detail in *The Ulster Unionist Party*, there has been widespread criticism of the link between the Orange Order and the Ulster Unionist Party among moderate Unionists and the spokesmen for the Roman Catholic minority in Northern Ireland over the years. The unwillingness of the DUP's supporters to give the Orange Order a role within their Party demonstrates that the controversial issue of the link between Orangeism and Unionism has not only encouraged Roman Catholics in Northern Ireland to regard the Ulster Unionist Party as being anti-Catholic in character, but has also given rise to a less well known view among militant Protestants that as a result of this link the Orange Institution has been tamed by the Glengall Street Party.

In the late autumn of 1972, the Rules Committee presented its draft proposals. The Rules made no reference to any future constitutional arrangement between the DUP and the Orange Institution, but in many other significant respects the draft proposals reaffirmed hardline Protestant attitudes; clearly the Rules Committee had failed to take cognisance of the fact that in the perceptions of both Boal and Paisley the DUP marked the emergence of a conciliatory approach on the leaders' part to Ulster politics.

The first proposal in the draft Rules stated that 'the name of the Association will be: The Ulster Protestant and Democratic Unionist Party'; and it was this proposal more than any other which prompted Ian Paisley peremptorily to set aside the draft proposals at a tense meeting of the DUP delegates held in Aughrim Street Mission Hall. Paisley correctly gauged that Boal would refuse to associate himself with an avowedly Protestant party and, recognising that the concept of a 'Protestant Party' could quickly become a matter of conscience with some of the DUP's militants, Paisley had moved rapidly to avert an unseemly internal wrangle.

Ian Paisley's rejection of the draft proposals was sufficient in itself to ensure that they sank without trace. The next phase in the evolution of the Party's constitutional structure began with the run-up to the Border Poll in March 1973. Rev. Ian Paisley threw himself into the political campaign prior to the referendum and by asserting himself in this way gave notice that his personal influence over the DUP was on the increase. Other significant indications that Paisley's personal control over the Party was becoming more pervasive followed later in the year because the minutes of the Executive Committee of the DUP noted that on 23 October 1973 a new committee was appointed to draw up a Constitution for the Party. The composition of this new Rules Committee suggests that this time the Committee would draft proposals which Paisley could confidently endorse.

The composition of this new Committee charged with drawing up a revised Constitution marked a further stage in Dr Paisley's emergence as the undisputed leader of the Party. Some weeks later this trend away from Boal's radical and idealistic approach to politics by the Party which he had helped to found was further confirmed by the decision taken by a meeting of party delegates in Ballymena on 3 November 1973. The delegates formally endorsed a decision handed down to them from the Party's Executive that the DUP would be reorganised 'along Imperial constituency boundaries', that is, on the basis of the twelve Northern Ireland Westminster constituencies at that time. The November delegates' meeting signified the abandonment of Boal's experiment in grass-roots democracy and marked the beginning of a new phase in which the Central Executive, led by Dr Paisley, would implement a plan for the reorganisation of the DUP.

Alan Lucas has suggested that some of the initial organisational difficulties experienced by the DUP could be attributed to an unwillingness on the part of either of the joint leaders to make a sufficient commitment to the administrative aspect of building the new Party. This is open to speculation, because Dr Paisley in particular has demonstrated outstanding talent in building up the ministry of the Free Presbyterian denomination. The difficulties experienced in establishing the new party were compounded because Boal and Paisley were both carried along by an idealistic aspiration towards a democratically organised party. This led them to underestimate how crucial the role of the leadership would be to the whole undertaking. An interesting point to be drawn from this early DUP experiment in inner-party democracy and grass-roots activism is that it tends to support Robert Michels' comments in *Political Parties* on 'the technical indispensability of leadership'[13] in the organisation of democratic parties and his even more controversial observation that 'every system of leadership is incompatible with the most essential postulates of democracy'.

By 1971 there were 8,000 adherents of the denomination and the Church had become widely distributed throughout the Province, and this rapid expansion of the Free Presbyterian Church continued throughout the seventies. The major driving forces behind the expansion and the church building programme were Dr Paisley's oratorical gifts, the zeal of fellow Free Presbyterian ministers and the enthusiasm of autonomous local groups who invited the Free Presbyterian Church to conduct missions in their particular localities. The Free Presbyterian Church grew, not in conformity to any overall strategy, but as a result of *ad hoc* arrangements entered into with local sympathisers and adherents who invited Rev. Ian Paisley to hold 'gospel campaigns' in their areas. If sufficient interest and indeed contention accompanied the campaign, which was usually staged in a large tent, then the local nucleus of supporters would take steps which would, in due time, lead to their being constituted as a Free Presbyterian congregation.

On rare occasions, Free Presbyterians attending Rev. Ian Paisley's own church on the Ravenhill Road left that church to set up a new work in their own localities. Finally, apart from the formation of churches as a result of vigorous and controversial 'gospel campaigns' in which the established Protestant denominations' membership of the World Council of Churches and involvement in the 'Romeward trend' were criticised and separation urged, old church buildings coming on to the market were purchased and a congregation of Free Presbyterians constituted in such buildings.

The growth of the sect was dependent upon the dynamism of Dr Paisley, the dedication of his Free Presbyterian ministers, the capacity to exploit any opportunities which presented themselves and the zealous enthusiasm of local autonomous groups. These features reappear in modified form in the development of the DUP. One of the reasons why the DUP failed to take off initially probably arose from Dr Paisley's assumption that the Party's development would be even closer to that of the Church than it proved to be.

How the emerging organisation handled dissent

As the DUP's infrastructure began to crystallise, a transparent fissure appeared between those committees or party organs which gave effect to Boal's enthusiasm for grass-roots democracy, and those committees which emphatically reflected a renewed willingness on Paisley's part to assert himself as leader of the Party. These committees were differentiated one from the other at the level of the Westminster Constituency Associations.

The leader of the Party had a right of access and could therefore make a personal contribution to the decision making process in all the party organs in the structure ranked above the Constituency Associations, but the Constituency Associations and seven other committees closely identified with grass-roots support were entitled to function autonomously. In effect the DUP's organisation reflected a two tier structure in which half the Party's committees reflected a high degree of leadership dependence and the other half enjoyed virtual autonomy according to the Party's constitution and rules.

While the leader does not need to be present at the various committees, the rules signify that he is the final arbiter of any policy decisions that such committees may make, and in the case of the Central Executive Committee, which is the most important committee in the Party's upper tier, there is constant reference to the leader to ensure that day-to-day party decisions meet with his wishes.

Furthermore, none of the organs on the upper tier can be taken over by a faction or dissident grouping within the Party's hierarchy. The Delegates Assembly and the Party Conference are both dependent upon the party officers for leadership and are unable to function without the presence of the officers, while even the policy subcommittees of the Central Executive Committee include the party officers as *ex-officio* members.

William Bleakes, who was a Central Executive member, stated that it was the policy subcommittees which formulated party policy, but the right conferred on the leader to attend such subcommittee meetings implied that in the event of the development of a policy which the leader regarded as unacceptable, he was well placed either to go to the subcommittee directly or to bide his time and achieve a reversal of the subcommittee's policy when it came before the Central Executive Committee. The probability is that before a policy emerged which the leader disliked the proposer of the controversial policy would have become isolated on the subcommittee.

Richard Rose in a detailed analysis of the political scene in Northern Ireland observed that the 'fragmentation of parties in Northern Ireland is extreme',[14] but he recognised that 'discord within the Protestant community does not occur between institutions but within them'. The DUP is a prominent example of what Rose termed 'the fragmentation of parties', but does the DUP reveal 'discord' within its own ranks?

In fact, between 1971 and 1981 the DUP was publicly acknowledged to be one of the, if not the, most unified political movement in Northern Ireland, and its party activists and spokesmen went to great lengths to ensure that the appearance of DUP solidarity was never in question.

Each of the DUP politicians has to balance his own desire for promotion within the ranks of the Party and his personal ambition against the demands that the authoritarian leadership style of Rev. Ian Paisley places upon him. In other words, aspiring political figures within the DUP have to establish their right to challenge for power in such a discreet way that the party functions and roles which are the essential concomitants of a leadership dependent party are not called into question.

The solution to this subtle political problem, namely how to advance ones own political prospects without antagonising the leader, has given added impetus to the autonomous political organs on the lower tier of the Party's structure. Among those who have established themselves as important local government public representatives are Rev. William Beattie on Lisburn Council, Rev. William McCrea on Magherafelt Council, Rev. Ivan Foster on Omagh Council, and Peter Robinson on Castlereagh Council. By 1982 each of these leading DUP personalities had been elected to the Northern Ireland Assembly. Robinson has also taken matters a step further by supporting the election of other DUP councillors on to Castlereagh District Council whose first allegiance is to Robinson rather than to Rev. Ian Paisley. In this way, Robinson appears to have created an independent political base within the DUP monolith, a bailiwick or fief which would protect his own position should he antagonise the DUP leader. Rev. William McCrea, in contrast, was frustrated in his early political ambitions by the ruling Presbytery of the Free Presbyterian Church of Ulster which refused to endorse him as a candidate for the Northern Ireland elections under the 1973 Act, but he doggedly pursued a political career and is now the Westminster MP for Mid-Ulster. Finally, Rev. William Beattie had initially been regarded as the natural successor to Rev. Ian Paisley, but Rev. William Beattie's political fortunes went into eclipse after a series of political miscalculations. These included his role in the Voluntary Coalition affair, his leadership of the Poleglass Housing Scheme protest, when he threatened that 30,000 Protestants would halt the Northern Ireland Housing Executive's plans to rehouse the Roman Catholics from West Belfast in Poleglass, and more recently his opposition to a circus performance on the Sabbath Day in Lisburn.

Each of these four aspiring DUP politicians had, then, his own reasons for seeing, in the Local Government Councillors Association and the Local Government Association, lower tier party caucuses in which his own qualities of leadership could be developed without the constant need to seek Rev. Ian Paisley's approval for whatever political actions the aspiring DUP politicians proposed to the Party's rank and file.

Discord does occur within the DUP but because of the emphasis Rev. Ian Paisley places upon personal allegiance to himself, all the Party's supporters either concur with all major policy decisions communicated from the leader or learn to manifest their objections to policy decisions in ways which do not call into question their ultimate loyalty to the leader and in forms that do not create public interest in the DUP's internal divisions.

The dissenting voices within the DUP have either to accept the limitations which the monolithic nature of their Party imposes on them or they have to resign. One such episode illustrates this problem for the dissentient very clearly and adds weight to the view that the DUP's Party Conference is so tightly controlled by the Party's Central Executive Committee that the Conference must be regarded as being a completely stage-managed operation.

In the summer of 1976, Newtownabbey branch of the DUP agreed that a committee of the branch should be empowered to submit a resolution or resolutions of the branch for the Party Conference scheduled for the following October. The resolution which finally emerged was progressive in tone and sought to elucidate whether the DUP would be willing to broaden its base, that is, to admit Roman Catholics into party membership, provided that such Roman Catholics would abide by the Rules of the Party. Those in Newtown-abbey branch who drew up the resolution were admirers of the politics of Desmond Boal, and they interpreted Boal's radical approach as being an attempt 'to get a broader-based Party'. Although the respondents felt that Peter Robinson sympathised with the gist of this radical resolution – for Robinson is reported as saying that he would have 'dearly loved to have seen the resolution discussed because it would have added a bit of beef to the Conference' – Rev. William Beattie, by contrast, who was chairman of South Antrim Constituency Association at the time, was violently opposed to the resolution which would have altered the Protestant character of the DUP.

A most acrimonious meeting was held in Ballymacash Orange Hall in which Rev. William Beattie seized control of the meeting and set the offending resolution aside. The treasurer of South Antrim at that time, Mr McCormick, privately remarked to the supporters of the discarded resolution that he 'thought that it was a very good proposal . . . but I can't vote against Rev. William Beattie'. According to the respondents, the meeting was so disorderly that one Free Presby-terian rose, left the meeting and severed his links with the DUP. In fact, not all South Antrim Free Presbyterians supported Rev. William Beattie's strenuous opposition to the resolution, but the whole episode was a traumatic watershed for the Newtownabbey supporters of the resolution. One of the supporters, Jack Campbell, was 'offended by the fact that the Party could not conduct a rational debate'.

The dissentients, therefore, whether in South Antrim or in other constituencies, discovered that the DUP leadership coped with controversy through heated private meetings during which the less flexible dissentients were forced out of the Party. In fact the animosity of those recalling the progressive resolution controversy was still deeply felt years after it occurred, and one spoke bitterly of 'Rev. Beattie's jackboot tactics' against Albert Hunter (who was a leading supporter of the resolution).

Further evidence that the DUP has experienced difficulty in coping with internal disagreements amongst its members became apparent during the winter of 1982 and the spring of 1983. Turmoil at branch level among DUP supporters in the constituencies of North Belfast and South Antrim attracted the attention of the local media. In North Belfast, Ted Ashby, a long established member of the Party, angered DUP supporters by attending an ecumenical service in St. Anne's Cathedral in his capacity as Deputy Lord Mayor. At the same time William Belshaw of Lisburn, a founder member of the DUP and a former Protestant Unionist, left the Party following a clash of personalities. In the short term these internal DUP wrangles damaged the general perception of the Party as a highly cohesive political movement 'speaking with one voice', but there were to be long term consequences as well, because one of the underlying causes of these divisions had been increasing tension and rivalries within each of the constituencies over the question of who would be best placed among DUP councillors to fight the approaching Westminster general election. These episodes attracted so much press interest because they occurred at the same time and on a scale which was far removed from earlier isolated instances of disruption in the ranks of the DUP.

The internal rivalries in North Belfast and South Antrim also suggest that the Party's machinery for settling disputes is far from adequate and that the method of selection of candidates, as it is set out in the Rules, did not enjoy the universal confidence of all the Party's members.

Dissent within the DUP is diffused, and those who articulate opposition to particular aspects of party policy invariably do so because they hold a position which gives their voice some weight, but the united front which the Party tries hard to present to the electorate at large conceals minor fissures within the party organisation. The way in which discord is handled within the DUP suggests that this united front which the DUP presents to all those outside the Party merges with the deferential attitudes of the Party's mass support toward the leader to forge a monolithic structure and this is often reinforced by the proximity of DUP party membership to membership of the Ulster Free Presbyterian Church.

This link between adherence to the Free Presbyterian Church and the holding of office within the DUP is stronger than an outside observer would be inclined to suppose. Wallace Thompson was asked to survey the denominational allegiance of committee members and DUP councillors for the year 1977. 1977 commended itself because the number of councillors was relatively small (there had been seventy-four elected) and Wallace Thompson was still on the administrative staff of the Party at that time.

The results of this survey of DUP councillors elected in 1977 were as follows: forty-seven were Free Presbyterian adherents, eight were adherents of other Protestant denominations, and twenty councillors were not known. In percentage terms, this means that 62·7 per cent of DUP councillors were Free Presbyterian adherents. Wallace Thompson also indicated that certain party committees had a very high percentage of Free Presbyterian adherents as members. Using the DUP Year Book, published in late 1978, Thompson cited the Finance and General Purposes Committee of the Party, which has eleven members, and with one exception they were all Free Presbyterian adherents. An even more dramatic example was provided by the Rules and Revision Committee, which was completely Free Presbyterian in composition.

The survey was then extended to include those DUP councillors elected in the 1981 local government elections. The results on this occasion showed that 49·6 per cent of DUP councillors were adherents of the Free Presbyterian Church, but that the religious affiliation of 38·3 per cent of the councillors was 'not known'. The conclusion to be drawn from this survey must also take account of the 1982 Assembly elections in which the DUP returned twenty-one elected members. Four of the DUP Assemblymen were Free Presbyterian ministers (including Dr Paisley himself) and a further fourteen DUP Assemblymen were Free Presbyterian adherents, while the religious affiliation of the three remaining DUP Assemblymen was not known. Evidently there is a strong correlation between adherence to the Free Presbyterian Church and party office in the DUP.

What emerges is the strong impression of a Party with a two tier structure. The committees closest to the grass roots function autonomously, while the committees with executive decision-making powers and responsibilities for the development of policy are leadership dependent, but in a manner which must strike the outsider as remarkable, the whole edifice is cemented together through a sense of loyalty to the leader and a religious affiliation to Free Presbyterianism which is shared by a high proportion of the Party's office-bearers and elected representatives.

Finance

One unforeseen consequence of the widely shared commitment to evangelical Protestantism within the DUP is that the Party has never been able to free itself from serious financial problems and in fact at times the financial commitments of the Party have so outstripped the DUP's available income as to create near panic amongst the Party's administrative staff and leadership.

This state of affairs appears at first to be incongruous, but it arises largely because of this relationship between the Free Presbyterian Church and the Party. In the first place, by the time the DUP came into existence in 1971, Rev. Ian Paisley had already gained a reputation as something of a financial wizard. Rev. Ian Paisley's ability to encourage the giving of vast sums of money to support the extension of the Free Presbyterian Church had already entered into Northern Ireland folk memory, and even local comedians and entertainers referred to the famous 'plastic buckets' which were used to collect the offering at Dr Paisley's 'Protestant Rallies' or gospel campaigns.

This image of the Free Presbyterian Church as a financially sound and expanding evangelical movement rebounded on the DUP. It was wrongly assumed from the very outset that the Party would in some sense be a recipient of the Free Presbyterian Church's financial largesse. In fact this has never been the case and the Party has had to survive financially without being able to call directly on the Free Presbyterian Church for aid to cover the Party's administrative and political commitments.

An added difficulty occurred in respect of those DUP activists who were also Free Presbyterians, because such activists believed that as they already made generous contributions to the 'Free Church' they were under less of an obligation to give equally generously to the Party.

From the point of view of the Party leader, Rev. Ian Paisley, the Party's financial predicament placed him in an embarrassing dilemma, because he could not acknowledge in public the actual state of the Party's finances without damaging his own image or ability to continue to attract considerable financial support. As a result the financial problems which press in upon the DUP are not public property and it is only the DUP activists and branches, upon which considerable financial demands are made, which are made aware of the Party's debts and encouraged to raise sums of money to cover the Party's expenses.

The second difficulty arises at this point because the Free Church's self-image is that of God-fearing and holy living citizens, and this has led to the imposition of doctrinal restraints on the way in which the DUP's membership is encouraged to raise financial support for the Party.

The Democratic Unionist Party has turned to the usual sources in order to build up its funds, finance its headquarters secretariat and publicise its aims and objectives. At branch level, every member pays an annual subscription, and each of the branches contributes to the central fund of the Imperial Constituency Association.

The Party has also had the support of wealthy benefactors, like Mr David Herron (formerly the Party treasurer), whose generosity and loyal support have more than once eased the Party out of financial difficulties. But individual commitments to the Party, no matter how generous, proved insufficient to meet the DUP's requirements. Additional funds had to be secured and Calvert has recorded in *A Decade of the DUP*,[15] two instances when special fund raising efforts separately raised sums of £12,000. Wallace Thompson, formerly the Party's Finance Officer, has described in an interview another occasion when he accompanied Dr Paisley on a Province-wide tour to raise extra funds to meet a financial emergency which the Party faced. Interestingly, Thompson alluded to the fact that not all the donations came from members of the Party. The circumstances in which these methods were employed suggest that the Party showed little foresight in coping with the financial demands which were made upon it.

Running a political party is expensive: the financial support of party members and the assistance of a few benefactors would hardly suffice to keep the party solvent and it is at this point that the tension between running a political party and maintaining a 'Protestant witness' emerges once again.

Evangelical Christians have a clearly defined position which rejects fund raising measures which involve raffles, ballots and methods which can be construed under the general head of games of chance or gambling. Dr Paisley has publicly decried other church organisations or institutions which rely on 'pea soup suppers and dandelion teas' to augment their bank accounts and meet day-to-day running expenses.

By late 1972, it became apparent that large public meetings were no longer appropriate, and as a sequel plastic buckets could not be used to collect financial contributions from those in attendance. The DUP found itself in growing financial difficulties, hardly a unique experience in the history of political parties. The question then arose as to how to meet the shortfall in income.

One school of thought articulated at Executive level by a chairman of the Bannside Democratic Unionist Association, Sandy Spence (Mayor of Ballymena), held closely to the line taken by Dr Paisley in his capacity as leader of the Free Presbyterian Church of Ulster, namely that all financial support should come as a response from loyal and faithful supporters to the needs of the situation. Sandy Spence did not go so far as to suggest that other means would be a form of 'compromise', but he inferred that it would be inappropriate for the DUP, considering the stand that it had taken, to adopt a 'worldly' method of raising funds.

The problem was that although Sandy Spence was not a Free Presbyterian, he was an Elim Pentecostal lay preacher; yet such was the nature of the DUP's crusade that he felt strongly that the Party could not demean itself by adopting fund raising methods in any way different from those used by the small independent evangelical churches, specifically freewill offerings.

Many of the Party activists from Ballymena, coincidentally a town renowned for the parsimony of its citizens, a veritable Aberdeen planted in North Antrim, saw that such a stance was impracticable. Not only would fund raising on a larger scale bring them into contact with an electorate much wider than the numbers represented by their own Party followers, but they admitted to a distinction between the circumstances which governed the activities of a church and its members and the activities of a political party. The Mid-Antrim branch went on to organise 'cake sales' which were a considerable financial success and also 'sacred music evenings'.

The 'sacred music evenings' were held in Orange Halls scattered across North Antrim, and they were chaired by leading personalities in the Party. The programme consisted of gospel groups, drawn from evangelical churches and usually invited by personal contact, who 'entertained' the audience with selections of sacred music, solo pieces and the like. The Party speaker then addressed the meeting in terms in keeping with the mood of the evening, after which supper was served. Initially, these evenings of sacred music drew large crowds and brought in much needed revenue, and they also carried in their wake the added advantage that quite a number of members of the audience were not followers of the Party. Thus they saw the DUP on favourable terms, recognised that its influence was growing in the Province and acquainted themselves with the local Party activists in that area.

Apparently, 'sacred music evenings' held the answer to the DUP's financial problems, and they had the seeming advantage that they did not offend against the consciences of those of the Party workers who would have preferred to rely on the giving of individuals than to hawk

Victory rally to Stormont. Ian Paisley (with twin sons) celebrates
the fall of the Northern Ireland Executive through Ulster Workers'
Council strike action.

May 1980: Paisley protesting at the presence of Charles Haughey at the
enthronement of the Archbishop of the Church of Ireland in Armagh.

August 1980: Paisley, in happy mood, at an Apprentice Boys'
March in Londonderry. The march passed off peacefully, but was
followed by rioting and bus-burning.

their Party wares in the market place in the same way as the 'worldly' political parties.

Two problems arose, though, both in their own way external to the DUP's immediate needs. Firstly, some Christians recognised that there were items on the programmes that were presented in a style which differed little from that of rock and roll and dance bands, in appearance, in musical beat, and in the mannerisms of the vocalists and musicians. Admittedly, the words had a Christian content, but, objectively, it was hard to restrain the opinion that these young people had found the best of both worlds, rock music and trendy clothes interfaced with godliness and spirituality. There were murmurs of discontent among the faithful. Secondly, the evenings of 'sacred music' proved such a valuable asset that far too many concerts were organised, and inevitably the audiences began to fall away.

Wallace Thompson, who was the Party's Finance Officer, said that there was another problem which could arise over these 'sacred music' evenings. Apparently, the gospel music artists had to be acceptable to the Free Presbyterian Church; if the artists were members of a church in the World Council of Churches they would be regarded as 'apostate' and barred from performing. The DUP was expected to comply with the Free Presbyterian Church's religious standards and taboos on such matters.

Of course, as Richard Rose has observed:

> A complaint that a party is short of money can mean any of several things. It can mean that the party's supporters are so few or so poor that they cannot pay for the politics they want. It can mean that although supporters have the money, the party cannot get them to give enough to the party. It can mean that the money is in one or another account of the party, but that the complainant lacks the influence within the organisation to have the funds transferred where he thinks they would do most good. Or it can mean that one man's idea of a political service is, in the minds of others, an unnecessary or undesirable luxury.[16]

Rose has analysed a number of features of this problem of party finance which are extremely relevant to the study of the DUP, but it would be useful to describe how the DUP spends the money that the Party receives before attempting to answer the question which Rose's observation suggests: are the DUP's financial problems perpetuated because the DUP's political ambitions far exceed the income which the Party's membership provides?

There are three main areas of expenditure for the DUP and, unlike the problems over raising money, these three areas are comparable with the necessary expenditure of most political parties.

Firstly the DUP has required substantial sums of money to fight elections, and there have been nine important elections during the first ten years of the DUP's existence. Although Dr Paisley and other candidates are expected to defray a proportion of the election expenses themselves, that proportion is variable, and is dependent on the financial strength of the constituency association; the principle, however, is that the candidate and the branches in the constituency have shared the cost of Westminster elections between them. Where, however, the DUP has been weak on the ground, the burden to be met by the candidate has been proportionately higher.

In North Antrim, for example, with seven branches, each branch was required to pay a levy of one seventh of the estimated cost of the election. The problem was, though, that while some branches like Bannside, Mid-Antrim and Ballymoney were able to raise more money than that levied, other branches like Larne and Carrickfergus had a poor record in respect of their contribution to the Constituency Association levy.

Although the DUP expected its candidates to assist in the payment of election expenses to Westminster, and to meet the considerably smaller cost of the expenses of local government elections, the election to the European Assembly in 1979 faced the DUP with expenses which exceeded the total DUP outlay in getting Rev. Ian Paisley elected for North Antrim over the past three Westminster elections. In the event the DUP spent £17,087 on the EEC election which, it has been stated, was 66·2 per cent of the legal maximum of £25,810·34. Rev. Ian Paisley's contribution to the expenses was stated as being a negligible £75·00, but the principle of the candidate's contribution to his election expenses was sustained. All the DUP's branches were expected to assist in defraying these expenses, which represented a considerable burden on Party funds.

Election expenses, therefore, are not financed out of a DUP central party fund as such; rather, the constituency associations, branches and candidates share both the responsibility and the burden of ensuring that the Party's electoral progress does not falter for want of funds. Nevertheless, raising money to fight elections has not proved to be an easy task and in the case of the 1974 elections the DUP in North Antrim remained in debt for some considerable time afterwards.

The two remaining areas of expenditure which the Party has to cover are headquarters administration and publicity.

The DUP opened its first headquarters in Belfast in August 1974, and in the following January the Central Executive of the Party accepted an estimate from the Finance Committee that it would cost £5,000–£6,000 to cover the salary of a fund raiser, together with the rent, rates and running costs of the Party offices. However, by June 1975, the Party was about £3,000 in debt which included £1,000 owed to one of the Party's financial backers, though the branches and Constituency (Imperial) Associations owed the central headquarters funds £1,800.

The difficulties the DUP experienced, firstly in raising money and secondly in successfully transferring money through the institutions of the Party, branches and Imperial Associations and into the central funds, were to remain a constant feature of Party finances until the end of the seventies, when the election of three DUP MPs and one MEP radically altered the Party's finances with the prospect of a considerable input from Parliamentary secretarial expenses.

In July 1978 the DUP moved to a new party headquarters suite of offices in East Belfast; by that year, one estimate concluded that the annual financial target for the DUP should be in the region of £35,000 to £40,000 per annum.

In other words, in a period of three years, which it must be noted were marked by a rapid increase in the annual rate of inflation throughout the United Kingdom, the DUP had increased its proposed annual target of expenditure sevenfold. It remains a fact, though, that such sums are dwarfed by the financial considerations of the British Labour or Conservative Parties which are 'multi-million pound activities'.

The third area in which the DUP has significant financial commitments is that of publicity. The DUP, and Rev. Ian Paisley in particular, have had frequent recourse to half-page and full-page advertisements in the Province's morning newspaper, the *News Letter*. Some of the advertisements have cost over £500 at a time, and although they are frequently accompanied by an appeal to the reader for funds, the resulting income has not always covered the cost of the advertisements.

The DUP regards these expensive forms of publicity as having a three-fold purpose: getting the Party message across, consolidating support, and bringing in further financial support. However, major political 'events' like the Carson Trail with its demonstrations, press advertisements and published booklets and pamphlets represents a considerable financial commitment to the DUP.

A further difficulty arises here because there is no public method of accounting for any money which is raised at rallies like that held by Paisley's 'Third Force' in Newtownards in 1981. And what happens to any money raised remains a closely guarded secret.

The detailed description of DUP Party finances which has just been adumbrated provides an appreciation of the manner in which the DUP differs from other political parties. The DUP has to raise finance to cover the three areas of election expenses, organisation and administration, and publicity; these requirements are compatible with the financial demands which are made upon any political party. In this respect the only significant difference is one of scale, in that the financial requirements of the DUP are, for all practical purposes, insignificant when compared with those of the major national parties in Great Britain. Furthermore, the information at the disposal of the researcher strongly indicates that the DUP experiences some difficulty in achieving a transfer of funds from the branches and constituency associations to the central headquarters. Rose's analysis states that this is common to political parties.

The failure of the DUP to formulate a sound financial policy contributed to the Party's financial difficulties throughout most of the seventies. A fundamental problem had arisen from the fact that the subscriptions of Party members and the levies imposed on inner-Party organs were insufficient to sustain the political ambitions of the Party's leaders. The DUP does, however, differ markedly from other political parties because the Party labours under a form of 'self-denying ordinance' whereby the doctrinal beliefs of the Free Presbyterian Church in Ulster dictate those forms of fund raising which the Party can legitimately endorse. This convergence of religious conviction with Party financial policy is most unusual. Apart from the restrictions placed on raising funds through ballots and games of chance, the widely held impression that the Free Presbyterian Church is financially sound militated against the DUP's independent claims on the Unionist population of Northern Ireland for financial support, thereby adding to the DUP's early financial difficulties.

Rose has commented that: 'like churches, parties are dependent upon many contributors supplementing cash gifts with an investment of time in voluntary work'. This is not only applicable to the DUP but is open to an even more specific application. That is, not only is the financing of the DUP comparable with the financing of other voluntary organisations like churches, but even more significantly, the religious motivations and techniques which the strict Protestant sects apply to fund raising have been adopted by the DUP. The consequence of this has been that the DUP, having denied itself the possibility of raising funds through the well established channels open to political parties, has resorted to whipping up semi-religious fervour at a number of set-piece meetings through the Party's history, during which Party members have pledged themselves to subscribe generously to Party funds. It is difficult to estimate whether this 'self-denying ordinance' has cut the DUP off from financial resources which it might otherwise have tapped. The likelihood is that financial support for the Party engendered by a feeling of commitment has more than made up for any loss the Party might have suffered as a result of separating itself from 'worldly' methods of financing.

The DUP's financial predicament may have been met, in part, by the influx of secretarial expenses for the three Westminster MPs and the European member. However, the underlying tension created by the Party's ambitions for further expansion will continue to tax the ingenuity of the party managers, because the limited financial resources provided by the party members and the self-imposed restrictions on methods of fund raising will continue to affect the means by which the DUP will try to finance its future operations.

Notes and References

1 Edward Moxon-Browne, *Nation, Class and Creed in Northern Ireland*, Aldershot 1983, 96.
2 Sarah Nelson, 'Ulster's Uncertain Defenders: A Study of Loyalists in Political, Paramilitary and Community Organisations in Belfast 1969–1975' (unpublished PhD thesis, University of Strathclyde), 118.
3 Rev. William McCrea, *In His Pathway: The Story of the Rev. William McCrea*, London 1980, 26.
4 Helmut Thielicke, *Theological Ethics*, Vol. II, Politics. The phrase 'will to power' is used as in Thielicke, page 130: 'The quest for power for its own sake, that power which enables him who has it to live and thrive at the expense of everybody else, undeterred by any authority which could serve as a norm for the use of power'. See also page 168: 'Even the man who has a blind and impulsive will to power – who in Nietzsche's sense enjoys power – and for whom power is an end in itself will always pretend that the power he seeks or wields is dedicated to a particular end'.
5 *Constitution of the Bible Presbyterian Church*, Larne 1980, Preface, item 6(6).
6 J. D. Douglas (Ed.), *The New International Dictionary of the Christian Church*, Exeter 1974. See Presbyterianism, p. 800.
7 J. T. McNeill (Ed.), John Calvin, *Institutes of the Christian Religion*, Philadelphia 1960, Book IV, Chapter XI, 8, page 1220.
8 Richard Rose, *Governing Without Consensus: An Irish Perspective*, London 1971, 505.
9 Moxon-Browne, *Nation, Class and Creed in N.I.*, 96.
10 Derek Birrell, 'Local Government Councillors in Northern Ireland', *Studies in Public Policy*, Number 83, Glasgow 1981 (University of Strathclyde Centre for the Study of Public Policy).
11 John F. Harbinson, *The Ulster Unionist Party 1882–1973: Its Development and Organisation*, Belfast 1973, 35–45.
12 W. D. Flackes, *Northern Ireland: A Political Directory 1968–79*, Dublin 1980, 103.
13 R. Michels, *Political Parties*, New York 1959, 400.
14 Richard Rose, *Governing Without Consensus*, London 1971, 219.
15 David Calvert, *A Decade of the DUP*, Belfast 1981, 9, 19.
16 Richard Rose, *The Problem of Party Government*, Harmondsworth 1976, 215.

CHAPTER III

Through Coalition
to Confrontation

> We can open a door which, because it has no handle on the other side, prevents our turning back and compels us to go on. What is past cannot be reversed and therefore acts as a switch or turning point which determines the way ahead and subjects it to a certain inevitability.
>
> Helmut Thielicke in
> *Politics: Theological Ethics Volume II*

> A conception of politics as 'the conciliation of divergent interests' had never taken root in Northern Ireland. It was much more simple to settle conflicting claims by traditional methods. It was also much more deadly.
>
> Paul Arthur
> *Government and Politics of Northern Ireland*

The political crisis promotes coalition building

The next five years would prove to be critical in the DUP's early history and they were to witness the translation of the Party from the periphery of faction-ridden Unionism to a position of signal importance within the Unionist spectrum. The political breakthrough depended partly upon Dr Paisley's ability to articulate the reactions of grass-roots Protestants in Ulster to the bewildering political changes which marked out the course of events in the Province. The Party's success, however, did not rest on Dr Paisley's personal achievements alone. The DUP was able to grasp two significant political opportunities which presented themselves and turn those openings to Party advantage. The first development was the formation of the Loyalist Coalition which committed both Bill Craig's

Vanguard Party and the DUP to a limited electoral pact, while the second event was the subsequent disintegration of the Vanguard Party following Craig's stubborn advocacy of a voluntary coalition in the Constitutional Convention to break the political deadlock.

The decision of the DUP to enter into coalition with Vanguard marked an important stage in the Party's development. The uncertainties over Party policy had by the Spring of 1973 given place to a new sense of direction. This was due to the emergence of Dr Paisley as the undisputed leader, and followed the departure of Desmond Boal. Boal's decision to leave politics presented Dr Paisley with the opportunity to capture the DUP for himself. This change of direction at the top had repercussions. The DUP appeared to be nothing more than a more media-conscious and politically responsive version of Protestant Unionism. Those dissident Official Unionists who had joined the DUP or United Loyalist Party and who regarded Desmond Boal as their political mentor had either accommodated themselves to the new situation or dropped out of active politics. The DUP was developing into a monolithic Party, gripped by an iron discipline, which gave Dr Paisley an important advantage over Craig, the leader of Vanguard, and Harry West of the Official Unionists. While Craig and West needed to consult their leading Party activists and arrive at a consensus on policy, Dr Paisley suffered no such inhibitions; he was in a much more powerful position. He could make vehement comments and take vital decisions without recourse to committee meetings or lengthy consultations. Dr Paisley knew that his followers would endorse any actions which he thought it necessary to take.

The DUP and the Vanguard Unionist Party[1] had reacted differently to the local government election held on Wednesday, 30 May 1973. Rev. Ian Paisley had been reluctant to authorise the Party to contest the local government election but he was prevailed upon to do so, and as a result the Democratic Unionists achieved some limited successes; but, more importantly, the Party had put its organisation to the test, the activists had 'knocked doors', and, as Rev. Ian Paisley never tired of telling his Party workers, in electioneering there is no substitute for knocking doors. The Vanguard Unionist Party had not participated in the local government elections because Bill Craig had staunchly refused to identify the Party with the Westminster-imposed electoral system of Proportional Representation. The Vanguard Unionist Party had also found that launching itself into the heavily congested political arena in Northern Ireland had precipitated a division in the ranks of its leadership, some of whom had preferred to continue their political activities within the Unionist Party. Furthermore, under Craig's leadership the Vanguard Party was intent on bringing together both the middle-class and working-class leadership of Unionist opinion in a common cause, and the vast crowds which had been mobilised at the various Vanguard rallies had infiltrated the public imagination in Northern Ireland: Vanguard was assumed to have captured the enthusiasm of the majority of loyalist voters. The rising tides of political fortune seemed to be running in Vanguard's favour.

The optimism of Vanguard was tempered by profound political considerations which dictated some form of alliance with the DUP. The security problem dominated the political situation and all Unionist parties reflected their concern at the continuing violence within the community in their public pronouncements. In the short period between polling day in the 1973 local government elections and nomination day for intending candidates to the new Assembly, five persons were murdered, twenty-three were injured, four bombs went off in the Province and there were also four minor explosions and two rocket attacks.

For its part the British Government intended to promote a devolved Assembly in Northern Ireland which would function on the basis of a power sharing executive. The partnership executive, it was anticipated, would comprise middle-of-the-road Unionists, the Alliance Party and the SDLP.

This confused situation was compounded by secret contacts between the government ministers responsible for the administration of the Province and various paramilitary groups, particularly the Provisional IRA. Distrust of the British Government's intentions was widespread throughout the Protestant electorate and these suspicions, far from being groundless or irrational, drew heavily on the experience of ordinary people confronted with a widespread breakdown of the social order and what was perceived as the willingness of Government spokesmen to question the value of the Union between Ulster and the rest of the United Kingdom.

These were the events which pushed Vanguard and the DUP together. The bitter recriminations which the activists in both loyalist fringe parties had heaped on each other were forgotten, and the subtle religious antagonisms between Vanguard and the DUP were veiled in a spirit of unity. Rev. Ian Paisley had built up his separatist Free Presbyterian denomination by a fervent crusade against membership of the World Council of Churches, and one of his prime targets had been the Presbyterian Church in Ireland. This frontal assault on the Irish Presbyterian Church had generated ill-feeling amongst Presbyterians; and the leadership of the Vanguard movement was almost exclusively Presbyterian, including at the time such worthies as Rev. Bertie Dickinson, Rev. Roy Magee and Rev. Martin Smyth. There was to be no settling of old scores, such was the gravity of the situation!

The re-introduction of P.R. to Northern Ireland also gave any loyalist coalition an internal, political logic, because there was a strong possibility that parties which encouraged their voters to transfer lower preferences to other candidates with similar political aims would improve their position overall. Though Bill Craig later discounted the suggestion that Proportional Representation was a major consideration in constructing the Coalition, it is hard to resist the conclusion that the implications of P.R. did exert some influence over Paisley and Craig's thinking. With the first elections to the newly set up Northern Ireland Assembly only a matter of weeks away, Rev. Ian Paisley and Bill Craig signed 'articles of agreement' committing both their respective parties to a limited electoral pact: Vanguard and the DUP would fight the elections as the United Loyalist Coalition.

There was no way of predicting the extent to which the horrendous events which had shaken the Province had disrupted traditional voting patterns. The United Loyalist Coalition was confronted by an intensely parochial electorate and every opportunity of getting the Coalition's message over had to be exploited. After the DUP and Vanguard had been refused a place in a pre-election television special, the two leaders took joint action which involved a threat to seek a High Court injunction to ensure that they received appropriate media coverage.

But thereafter, the campaigns of the Coalition partners diverged. Both Vanguard and the DUP published separate election manifestoes and their candidates campaigned separately, although some special pre-election parades and rallies were held at which Craig and Paisley appeared on the same political platform.

Initially the Loyalist Coalition had little effect on inter-party rivalries between Vanguard and the DUP, but as polling day neared and the common interest of both parties in maximising their potential vote assumed greater proportions, they tended to work more harmoniously together.

This collaboration between the Coalition partners has been qualified by leading Vanguard members who were taken aback at the ruthless way in which the DUP set about the task of winning seats. Marvyn Gowdy, one time secretary of the UUUC Committee in the Westminster constituency of South Belfast, related how the DUP in that constituency offered to provide workers at the largest polling stations on the Assembly election day. Too late, the naïve Vanguard partners in South Belfast discovered that the DUP Loyalist Coalition workers were using this 'helpful' offer to grab a seat for their own candidate.

Another Vanguard member, Reg Empey, was even more critical of the Coalition, and claimed that in his role as co-ordinator of the election campaign in Vanguard Headquarters, he saw little joint effort by the Parties, and came to the conclusion that there 'was virtually no co-operation between Vanguard and the DUP'. For this reason Empey regarded the undertaking as nothing more than 'a paper coalition drummed up for public consumption'.

Bombings and murderous attacks continued through the election campaign and the anxiety created by such incidents continued to be felt within the Official Unionist Party, which, mirroring the shattered and fragmented state of Ulster society, splintered again.

Brian Faulkner, the leader of the Official Unionists, was joined by thirty-eight other Unionist candidates who were 'pledged' to make the proposed Executive work and who accepted the principle of power sharing. However, some highly influential right-wing Unionists including Harry West, Captain Austin Ardill and John Taylor remained 'unpledged' and rejected Faulkner's leadership.

Polling day was on Thursday 28 June 1973. There was a 72·26 per cent turn-out of the 1,022,820 electors entitled to vote.

Vanguard had fielded twenty-four candidates while the DUP only put forward sixteen candidates but by the time the final count was completed Vanguard had succeeded in gaining only seven seats while the DUP had eight seats. The Loyalist Coalition partners had gained 20·16 per cent of the total votes cast.

Lawrence Elliott and Laver concluded in their analysis of the results that the Loyalist Coalition worked well in practice. Having examined 'the percentage of transfers that flowed between VULC and DULC when a candidate of both of the two groups was still in the running', they point out that 'on such occasions, a further 30 per cent of transfers went from VULC to DULC, and a further 26 per cent went from DULC to VULC. Thus, the VULC–DULC formed an extremely solid bloc. Almost two-thirds of its transfers stayed within the party of origin, and the greater part of the rest went to the other Coalition partner.'[2] Despite the success of the Coalition as an electoral pact, the DUP and Vanguard had put forward forty candidates of whom only fifteen were elected.

The confusion over Official Unionist candidates creates some difficulty in determining how many Unpledged Unionists went forward as candidates, but when the count was completed, ten unofficial Unpledged Unionists declared themselves to have been elected. Brian Faulkner was still the leader of the largest grouping of Unionists with twenty-two Assembly members, but Faulkner's position was extremely weak and it was evident that he had lost the support of the majority of Unionist voters.

On the eve of the first meeting of the new Assembly Dr Paisley and the DUP had established themselves as a powerful and cohesive minority within the broad spectrum of Unionism. The election enabled Dr Paisley to move in from the fringe of Unionist politics to the centre of the stage. This had been achieved because the Loyalist Coalition had answered the grass-roots demand for 'a united front' among the various strands of Unionism. Craig and Paisley had campaigned together and this partnership had reinforced support for both the leaders across a broad spectrum of loyalist voters – that is, the more extreme or hardline segment of the Unionist electorate.

The Coalition had provided Dr Paisley with a platform from which he proclaimed his commitment to Unionist unity. In the eyes of an increasing number of electors this brought him more into line with mainstream Unionism and invested him with a form of respectability by association. Any such impression gained by the voters would be confirmed six months later at the formation of the United Ulster Unionist Council, by which time Dr Paisley had established himself as leading political figure within the Province.

A number of factors contributed to this transformation from a politician of the 'lunatic fringe' to a credible and formidable spokesman for loyalism. Under pressure from Provisional IRA violence and faced with a possible threat to the constitutional position of the Province as an integral part of the United Kingdom, a significant proportion of the Unionist electorate had shifted to the right. These voters were moving from a position which would in all probability be classified as right-wing conservatism in Britain to an even more hardline attitude; simultaneously Dr Paisley, by abandoning the more virulently anti-Catholic brand of Protestant Unionism for the more pragmatic and sanitised image of the DUP, was moving from the extreme fringe of Unionist politics towards a more acceptable conservative stance on law and order and on the constitution, underpinned by a genuine, though well publicised, social conscience.

The structure of the DUP within the new Assembly tended to emphasise rather than detract from Dr Paisley's leadership.

Eight DUP Assembly members were returned of whom five had been prominent members of the Protestant Unionist Party and had contested either local government or Stormont Parliamentary elections as Protestant Unionists. Three members, Johnnie McQuade, James Craig and Ted Burns, had joined the DUP at the new Party's formation. Six of the DUP Assembly members had previous experience of local government, the only exceptions being Dr Paisley and Ted Burns, and four of the group continued to be active in local government after the May election 1973.

Another feature which was significant was the presence of Mrs Eileen Paisley, who had been elected for the constituency of East Belfast. Mrs Paisley had previously served for a period of six years on Belfast City Council. Dr Paisley's position as leader would not be challenged.

Throughout the election campaign Paisley and Craig had managed to convey their feelings of outrage to the electorate over the way in which the British Government had suspended Stormont and had failed to halt the Province's slide into conditions approaching civil war.

This indignation on the part of the Loyalist Coalition's members had already transmitted itself to Brian Faulkner who warned that there were those who would seek to 'sabotage' and 'wreck' the Assembly.

Confrontation in the Assembly

The Assembly opened on 31 July 1973, and it was the hope of Mr Whitelaw, the Secretary of State for Northern Ireland, that an accommodation would emerge upon which a power sharing Executive could be based.

The first meeting was highly acrimonious and fulfilled all Faulkner's dire predictions. Craig and Paisley led an orchestrated campaign to show that the Coalition had no intention of according legitimacy to the new institution. While Dr Paisley raised points of order, Craig stated exactly why the opponents of this political initiative refused to acknowledge the authority of the Assembly; Craig asserted, in an important statement, that 'the Constitution of Northern Ireland should not have been changed without the consent of the people of Northern Ireland, expressed through their Parliament. The Parliament of Northern Ireland has not given that consent and I do not believe that the people of Northern Ireland would have consented to this change in our Constitution.'[3]

At the time the media and press regarded the scenes with which the Assembly opened as 'disgraceful', while the Unionist and Alliance members who supported an accommodation with the Catholic SDLP through power sharing, played down the degree of support which the loyalist groupings could command. 32·66 per cent of all the votes cast had gone to right-wing Unionists (Unpledged Unionists, members of the Coalition or independent loyalists); it was therefore evident that a further split within the Faulkner Unionist grouping could only result in more gains for the right-wing Unionists.

The difficulties facing those who were committed to making the new initiative work were enormous. The parochial attitudes of

Northern Ireland demanded a massive campaign of political re-education to enable moderate politicians in a divided community to garner increased support.

Throughout the summer and autumn the attacks of the Provisional IRA continued, and incipient loyalist counter-terrorism added to the difficulties of the security forces, but the British Government exacerbated the situation by its arcane policy. Col. Robin Evelegh illustrates the problem with this little vignette:

> In the late summer of 1973 one battalion commander in Belfast was so infuriated by learning repeatedly through the clandestine informers whom he handled inside the terrorist organisations of secret negotiations with these organisations and proposals to them from the Northern Ireland Office that were kept hidden from him through official channels, that he set up in his own battalion a 'political intelligence' cell in a separate office with the task of discovering current British Government policy.[4]

Brian Faulkner pressed ahead with his intention to lead the Unionist Party into a power sharing Executive in the Assembly. While the Secretary of State, William Whitelaw, made every effort to ensure that an Executive would be formed, the key element would be the SDLP, and much of the political pressure was directed towards winning that Party's agreement. However, the SDLP wanted more than power sharing: they wanted some input from Dublin as well.

Dr Paisley, despite his abhorrence of the new initiative, was not adverse to using the Assembly 'to get his message across', and on 7 November 1973, he spoke in support of a loyalist motion calling on the Government to take sterner measures against terrorism. In his speech Dr Paisley claimed that loyalist opinion was being ignored by Mr Whitelaw.

By late autumn it was becoming clear that William Whitelaw was having some success and that an Executive incorporating the SDLP, the Alliance Party and the Pledged Unionists led by Brian Faulkner would be formed.

Within the Unionist Party the final battle between the right-wing (Unpledged) Unionists and the moderates was in progress. A crucial meeting of the Ulster Unionist Council was held in the Ulster Hall on 20 November, and Brian Faulkner's amendment advocating power sharing was adopted by a majority of only ten votes. Brian Faulkner was after all the Party leader and he ought to have had all the advantages of the Party machine at his disposal. The moderates were losing the struggle. Faulkner's near defeat was a further indication of the way in which grass-roots Unionist opinion had moved to the right under the 'corrosive effect of constitutional uncertainty', allied to continuing violence on the streets.

An important factor was the perseverance of the Unionist hard-liners who had waged a campaign to take over every elective office within the structure of the Unionist Party which became open to them. The right-wing Unionists had to contend with defections from within their own faction to parties further to the right, like Vanguard and the DUP. Despite such discouragement, they were determined to achieve their object by entirely constitutional means. Throughout their long campaign the right wing faced dogged opposition from the moderates who controlled the Party machine and were encouraged in their policies by the British Government and the media.

It might have been anticipated that the success of the right wing would have denied Paisley and the DUP any prospect of further recruitment from amongst the ranks of disillusioned Unionist voters. However, this was not to be because the struggle within the Official Unionist Party had not been fought to a final conclusion which enabled the DUP to make political capital out of the evident confusion in the ranks of the Glengall Street Party. Seeking to conciliate those moderate elements which chose to remain within the Glengall Street Party, the hardline Unionists made no public acknowledgement of the past failures of the Party, and this unwilling-ness to draw a sufficient distinction between the policy commitments and principles of the newly installed leadership and previous party leaders enabled Paisley and the DUP to tar both the right-wing and moderate Unionists alike with a catalogue of political crimes and shortcomings.

Another factor which ensured that the DUP would continue to make gains at the expense of the Unionist Party arose from the belief that the Unionist Party's ruling class had failed the loyalist people of Ulster. This resentment at the ineptitude of the Unionist political élite was widespread and found expression within other parties and factions besides the DUP. This was not the straightforward awaken-ing of class antagonism in which the loyalist working class as a bloc aligned itself with a specific party or political programme as some suggest, because two former members of Vanguard, Ernie Baird and Reg Empey, were extremely vigorous in their criticism of the Glengall Street élite but both were prosperous businessmen.

In the House of Commons on Thursday 22 November, William Whitelaw announced that an agreement to form an Executive in the Northern Ireland Assembly had been reached. Talks would soon take place on the subject of a proposed 'Council of Ireland'.

Dr Paisley, engaged in a series of preaching commitments in the United States of America, telegraphed a statement warning that a new loyalist grouping would be formed to defeat power sharing. However, both the British Prime Minister, Edward Heath, and Liam Cosgrave, the Republic of Ireland's Taoiseach, interpreted the new agreement as offering 'a real prospect of lasting peace'.

In the week that followed, Dr Paisley rejected an invitation from the Secretary of State to meet him for talks and was involved in the orchestration of further 'grave disorders' on the floor of the Assembly, from which DUP Assemblyman John McQuade was removed by order of the Speaker.

Such disorders, and there were more to follow, had two advantages from the point of view of the DUP. Firstly, the Assembly, which the DUP believed to be essentially undemocratic, was seen to be held in disrepute by a sizeable number of its own members. And, secondly, the DUP gained more publicity through the belligerence of its Assembly members.

Brian Faulkner scorned these antics and clung to the notion that this behaviour, which gained notoriety for the DUP, would lead to the rejection of such acts of civil disobedience by the Unionist population. Faulkner had, however, badly misjudged the situation.

Some loyalist workers[5] had already come to the conclusion that the attempts of the Loyalist Coalition to disrupt the Assembly were futile and would not materially affect the implementation of a programme of power sharing or other proposed constitutional innovations. These loyalist workers thought that Craig and Paisley were not being extreme enough, and they began to think in terms of a strike. Province-wide disruption would soon replace scenes of disorder in the Assembly.

While the formation of an Executive occupied the attention of moderate politicians, intense political activity within the Unionist and loyalist institutions brought results in early December.

The Unpledged Unionists formed themselves into the Ulster Unionist Assembly Party on 3 December, with Harry West as their leader, and later that evening the three parties held a meeting in the Ulster Hall.

Then, three days later, delegates from the Orange Order and other loyalist institutions, the DUP, Vanguard and the Unionist Party constituency associations reconvened at the same hall. The delegates voted to establish a wider coalition than that which had embraced Vanguard and the DUP: this new political formation was to be known as the United Ulster Unionist Council. The UUUC was to provide common leadership, which effectively required Craig, Paisley and West to operate as a triumvirate. Their immediate political task would be united opposition to power sharing.

This meeting was to have a crucial bearing on the development of loyalist politics in Ulster over the next four years. The UUUC joint steering committee, which now came into existence, would draft the manifesto of the UUUC and ratify candidates standing for the UUUC in future elections.

Although this united front received widespread acclaim from within the loyalist community, the media interpreted the formation of the UUUC as a triumph for Dr Paisley. On the following day the *Irish Times* headline noted: 'Paisley rallies loyalist groups'.[6]

As 1973 came to a close, Dr Paisley's efforts to conciliate rival loyalist parties and his militant tactics within the Assembly had increased his standing within the Unionist population. Paisley had gained acceptability as one of three joint leaders of the UUUC; but more, both the media and a large section of public opinion had read into this remarkable improvement in the DUP leader's fortunes the underlying message that Dr Paisley was the leader of right-wing Unionist opinion in the Province.

Dr Paisley had every reason to be confident, but a subtle distinction existed between the role of populist leader and that of Party leader! Dr Paisley might be recognised as the leader of Unionist opinion, but that did not imply that he would emerge as the leader of a new united Unionist party. Though journalists pressed the spokesmen of the UUUC about the prospects of the emergence of a new party, the reply was cautious, and it seemed that 'a new party, while desirable, would not be formed in the short term due to procedural difficulties'.

Austin Ardill, a leading Official Unionist who was determined to protect the rights and position of the Unpledged Unionists by blocking any encroachments from the DUP, emphasised that the UUUC was a 'coalition of equals'. Nevertheless it must have been galling for Official Unionist spokesmen to have to concede that Paisley and the DUP were now on an equal footing with them, though of course the same could equally well be said of Craig's Vanguard Party.

There was, however, a keenly felt expectation amongst those who supported the UUUC that they were helping to give birth to a new Party. This was particularly so of many of the activists who attended UUUC constituency meetings and the joint steering committee. There were still serious obstacles, though, which could well frustrate the creation of a united Party. The Unionist Party was suspicious and resentful of both Vanguard and the DUP, and Dr Paisley, in particular, was an object of caution and suspicion.

This attitude on the part of some leaders of the Unionist Party failed to comprehend the passionate commitment which Vanguard and the DUP had respectively made to the 'defence of Ulster'. The activists in the new Parties saw themselves as participants in the rebirth of 'traditional Unionism'. In their eyes the Unionist Party was gripped by a fatal complacency and inertia, reflected in an unwilling-ness to acknowledge those previous failures of policy which had brought Ulster to the brink of the precipice.

As 1973 came to a close, these undercurrents pulled in an opposite direction to the tide on the surface, which was running strongly in favour of coalition and unity.

The difficulties created by inter-party rivalries amongst the UUUC's constituent parts tended to conceal the structural changes which were taking place within each of the three parties.

The Official Unionists had suffered severely as a result of fragmentation during the Premiership of Terence O'Neill. At first, individual members had defected from the Party but with the rise of the DUP, and then when the Vanguard movement within the Unionist Party broke away to form a Party in its own right, the Unionists lost complete branches which switched allegiance and 'went over' to the Vanguard Unionist Party. The Unionists were constantly engaged in retrenchment, and in trying to hold on to their dwindling membership.

The circumstances for Vanguard and the DUP were the exact opposite to those the Unionists faced; instead of structural decay brought on by a flight of members away from the Party, Vanguard and the DUP had to cope with the vexations of forming a political party in the midst of a constitutional crisis.

Of the two Parties, the DUP was the more determined to build up its support. Added to this, Dr Paisley's personal ambitions and the Party's ideological commitment to the 'Protestant religion' made the emergence of a united Unionist Party appear remote.

On Sunday 9 December a ten page communique was issued bringing to a close fifty hours of talks at the Civil Service Staff College, Sunningdale. This was the culmination of tripartite talks opened by the Prime Minister, Edward Heath, between the parties to the newly constituted Northern Ireland Executive, the British Government and the Government of the Irish Republic.

The Government had originally indicated that all the parties in the Northern Ireland Assembly would be entitled to attend. The Irish Prime Minister, Liam Cosgrave, was opposed to the invitation to Dr Paisley and as a consequence the British Government, in the person of the new Secretary of State for Northern Ireland, Francis Pym, had informed Dr Paisley on 4 December that the loyalist representatives would not be welcome at the tripartite talks.

Rev. Martin Smyth, Grand Master of the Orange Order, described Francis Pym's action as 'a breach of faith', because the Government had originally declared its intention to consult with all the leaders of 'the elected representatives of Northern Ireland opinion'.

At Sunningdale, the structure of the proposed Council of Ireland was formalised. The SDLP, which had campaigned for this concession from the British Government and the moderate Unionists, had the satisfaction of seeing the 'Irish dimension' acquiring a momentum which could lead to significant constitutional changes in the relationship between Northern Ireland and the Irish Republic.

Although the Irish Government declared that 'there could be no change in the status of Northern Ireland until a majority' desired it, the loyalists pushed this proviso to one side and, seizing upon the proposed Council of Ireland, declared the proposals to be 'a sell-out'.

While Paisley, West and Craig made public their distaste for this further twist of the screw of constitutional change, the groupings soon to be known as the Ulster Workers Council took the fateful decision to call a Province-wide strike.

Dr Paisley claimed that 'Mr Faulkner and his Republican Unionists had been out-flanked, out-manoeuvred and out-witted', while Faulkner reciprocated by declaiming in regard to further rowdy scenes in the Assembly that 'it is absolutely diabolical that these people, led by a demon doctor, are holding the country to ransom like this'. On the following day, 13 December, Parliament voted to devolve power to the Northern Ireland Assembly, to take effect on 1 January 1974.

By mid-January, Dr Paisley was beginning to spell out not only detailed objections to the Sunningdale Agreement, but the outline of a programme of political and extra-parliamentary resistance. A 'Save Ulster' campaign got under way and on a united platform in Larne, the Doctor told his listeners that in a future Westminster election the UUUC might hold the balance of power. It was a highly prescient comment which would soon have an unexpected and sudden fulfilment. Then Paisley reiterated a constant criticism which Craig, Paisley and latterly West had made of the whole package of constitutional innovation in the Province by declaring: 'Tonight we are not really part of the United Kingdom, for the other parts have democracy, not the sham we have . . .' Dr Paisley had articulated a feeling common to the mass of Ulster Unionists that despite their desire to remain British, Britain rejected Ulster.

Opposition to the power sharing Executive

On 22 January 1974, the first meeting of the Northern Ireland Assembly to be held since the formation of the Executive was interrupted by renewed scenes of 'uproar and pandemonium'.

The RUC ejected a number of loyalists from the Chamber including Dr Paisley himself, and television coverage of these remarkable scenes occupied much of the available news space later that evening. The cameras focussed on James Craig, a DUP Assemblyman for North Antrim. James Craig suffered from a heart complaint and the stress and excitement of that day led to his collapse. Pictures of a worried Dr Paisley struggling with the police while trying to carry the limp figure of Craig from the Stormont Parliament building made a strong impression on the Unionist population. The visual message was coming across that the political situation was extremely grave and could rapidly pass beyond the control of the politicians.

Faulkner is reported as commenting that 'the loyalists had failed in their purpose, having managed to delay the business of the house for just over an hour'.

The carefully orchestrated events of that day, as Mr Faulkner correctly observed, had not succeeded in stopping the Assembly, but the Executive and the loyalists interpreted this conclusion very differently. The Executive thought that they could press on, overriding all opposition which they conceived was only attracting the opprobrium of all the moderate and decent people who wanted to see 'peace, order and good government' in Northern Ireland.

The vehemence with which the loyalists opposed the Executive can be gauged from a broadsheet[7] circulated by the Vanguard movement. The invective of the anonymous writer was directed at Brian Faulkner and those Unionists who supported power sharing. Faulkner was criticised for accepting the principle that the Westminster Parliament could set aside the will of the Unionist majority in the Province and legislate 'over their heads'.

The Vanguard pamphlet's apparent rejection of the sovereignty of the Westminster Parliament gave expression to the widespread belief shared by the DUP and other loyalists that the United Kingdom Parliament would impose new constitutional mechanisms on the Province which were geared towards the unification of Ireland and that the superficiality of the Government's adherence to democratic principles would outflank the Unionists' determination to maintain the Union.

The loyalist literature at the time accepted the Government's neutrality towards the Union as part of the natural order of things; what the Unionist polemicists could not stomach was the fact that Faulkner was not only prepared to go along with this situation but that he was willing to side-step his pledges to the Unionist Party in order to meet the British Government's requirements for the formation of a power sharing Executive.

In the atmosphere of violence and mistrust which prevailed at the time, Faulkner's inability to keep faith with his own political base undermined the credibility of the power sharing experiment. Many Unionists concluded that if Faulkner could go back on his commitments to the Party over the formation of an Executive he could not be trusted to keep Ulster out of a united Ireland.

The loyalist members in the Assembly were being brought to the conclusion that the tactic of disruption would not, by itself, achieve their intended objectives, the destruction of 'power sharing' and the abrogation of the Sunningdale agreement.

The pressure which attended events such as these provides a partial explanation for the next episode in the career of Dr Paisley. Mary Holland interviewed Dr Paisley for the television programme Weekend World, and when the item was broadcast Dr Paisley was heard to advocate a referendum which might open the way to independence for Ulster. Interference from Westminster had become an obstacle to progress and Paisley averred that 'if Ulstermen were left alone and were allowed to hammer out these things properly, a way could be found to get democracy going in this country in which all sections of the community can participate'.

This seemingly contradictory stance on independence brought a whoop of delight from Rory O'Brady of Provisional Sinn Fein who interpreted this call from Dr Paisley as endorsing Provisional Sinn Fein's policy of 'British withdrawal'.

In the next few days, Dr Paisley reinterpreted the broadcast, claimed that it gave a 'false impression of his views' and blamed this distortion of his position on the programme's producers who had edited a twenty minute interview to fit in with a three minute broadcast.

Dr Paisley and the DUP had developed into a formidable political force within the Unionist camp. They had the facility to make shrewd political calculations, the ability to develop an election strategy and the capacity to mobilise tens of thousands of loyalists at massed rallies in support of their cause, but all this spontaneous activity concealed the lack of a coherent analysis of the Northern Ireland problem. This lack of a firm theoretical base allied to Paisley's innate pragmatism occasionally tempted him, as in this case, to make sensational statements and offer solutions which it was beyond his competence to deliver.

While the population of Northern Ireland pondered these political developments, the political situation throughout the rest of the United Kingdom threatened to push the provincial turmoil of Ulster into the background.

The Prime Minister, Edward Heath, had become locked into battle with the coalminers. Britain was to experience the misery of the three day week, followed by the calling of a general election on 28 February 1974.

Not for the first time, events outside Ulster would bring about a realignment of political attitudes and set events within the Province on a different course.

The speed with which the election got under way benefited the UUUC because there was little opportunity for pre-election manoeuvring amongst the rival elements in the Loyalist Coalition. What rivalry did exist was held in check by the euphoria shown by the UUUC's leaders and their supporters when it was realised that the British Government had provided them with an unforeseen opportunity to validate their claim that there was widespread Unionist opposition to power sharing and the Sunningdale agreement.

The UUUC joint Steering Committee set about the sensitive task of endorsing candidates, although sitting MPs who subscribed to the UUUC received automatic endorsement. Bargains had to be entered into and deals struck in respect of the remaining seats and North Belfast was one constituency where rivalries within the UUUC nearly broke the surface.

The Faulknerite Unionists had every intention of holding North Belfast and hectic behind-the-scenes activity amongst the members of the UUUC soon indicated that the Coalition would challenge the Faulkner Party for the seat.

As the right-wing Unionists would not necessarily secure the support of all those activists who were entitled to nominate a candidate, Dr Paisley attempted to win over some of the nominating committee to the idea that James Craig, a DUP Assembly member from Carrickfergus, ought to be nominated. His suggestion was turned down flat.

A nomination meeting was held and John Carson, who had been active in loyalist circles in North Belfast for some years, was selected. Dr Paisley had still not resigned himself to the fact that the DUP would not be running the Coalition's candidate in the constituency, so he approached John Carson at the Stormont Parliament building and invited Carson to join the DUP.

This incident is important because it illustrates both Dr Paisley's freedom of action as Party leader and his opportunism. Paisley had no hesitation in approaching Carson and in making him an offer which could have endangered the UUUC Coalition. Given the mutual suspicions and ambitions of the Coalition's three parties, Dr Paisley's attempt to filch the constituency of North Belfast from under the noses of the right-wing Unionists could have been sufficient to wreck the UUUC. Reg Empey remarked that the issue of the distribution of seats between the Coalition partners was the most sensitive and potentially disruptive aspect of the UUUC tri-party alliance. Paisley's unsuccessful attempt to woo John Carson meant that the DUP was only able to field two of the UUUC's twelve candidates in the February election. Vanguard provided a further three candidates, while the remaining seven UUUC candidates were all members of the Unionist Party, led by Harry West.

The February election proved to be of historic importance. There was an extremely high turnout by the voters and the UUUC gained 50·8 per cent of the votes cast. The Coalition was able to claim that the power sharing Executive lacked a mandate from the majority of the Province's population. The result, however, was set to one side by both the newly elected Labour Government in Britain and the local power sharing Executive, who chose to take refuge in their belief that, given time, power sharing would be seen to work. The failure to acknowledge what was effectively a vote of no confidence in the Government's initiative encouraged the loyalists to press ahead with their plans to defeat the Sunningdale proposals by extra-parliamentary action.

The election represented another personal triumph for Dr Paisley who held his seat in North Antrim with a massively increased majority. The other DUP candidate, John McQuade, had little prospect of taking what was in effect a safe Republican seat in West Belfast, where the SDLP MP, Gerry Fitt, was returned once more. Although the DUP had only a small share in the overall triumph of the UUUC at the February election, Dr Paisley's personal standing had been further enhanced. It must therefore have come as a great personal shock to the DUP leader when within the space of three months, his political fortunes were to be eclipsed by the meteoric rise of the Ulster Workers Council.

On 14 May the Northern Ireland Assembly passed a vote in support of the Sunningdale proposals; the UWC responded by announcing that the workers in the power stations were coming out on strike. The strike lasted for fifteen days, and throughout this period of frenetic loyalist activity members of the DUP played a full and determined part in the day-to-day activities of the strikers, which included manning barricades, ensuring the supply of essential services, and monitoring the dispositions of the Army and the RUC. The involvement of so many of the DUP's membership during the course of the UWC strike failed to compensate for the absence of Dr Paisley who had flown off to Canada to attend the funeral of a close friend.

The UWC strike was a watershed in the contemporary history of Ulster because it brought about the collapse of the power sharing Executive, which resigned from office, and the strike also led to a detailed Government reappraisal of its Northern Ireland policy.

For a brief period of time the unity of purpose which the Unionists enjoyed gave them added leverage over their situation. The moral standing of the Northern Ireland Executive had been seriously undermined by the electoral successes of the UUUC in the February general election. Additional problems were caused for both the Executive and the Labour Government by the fact that the media appeared to adopt a neutral stance in respect of the stoppage and accorded UWC spokesmen like Jim Smyth ample opportunity to explain the strikers' case. The strike boosted the morale of the beleaguered Unionist electorate, but the loyalist politicians failed to analyse the implications of the strike which were that, provided the Unionists could articulate the moral basis of their position and sustain a united front, their capacity to influence events in the Province would be significantly increased.

Dr Paisley deduced from the constitutional stoppage the lesson that extra-parliamentary action such as a strike could succeed against the British Government. However, Paisley failed to appreciate the need to maintain a united loyalist approach and to ensure that future militancy would command the tacit sympathies of as wide a section of the public as possible.

The UWC leaders who had fronted the strike were 'unknowns'; unlike Paisley they did not have a previously flawed media image, and this had advanced their cause because the UWC leaders had not acquired a reputation for sectarianism. Whether Paisley, with his anti-Catholic image, could hope to direct a Province-wide strike without incurring the total hostility of the national press and provoking the Westminster Government into a more vigorous response would remain an open question for the next three years.

When the 1974 strike ended, Dr Paisley had to come to terms with the arrival on the political scene of a new group of working-class loyalist leaders who had a proven capacity for carefully considered, direct action.

This represented a set-back for the DUP, but it was only temporary because collectively the UWC leadership lacked political experience, while some individual members were not politically ambitious. Like Paisley, the UWC leadership had no detailed policy which could be expected to gain widespread acceptance, and this lack of a concrete programme suggests that the rapid recovery in Paisley's standing within the loyalist community rested on his impressive ability to articulate the aspirations, longings and fears of a substantial section of Unionist opinion.

Those fifteen days in May had made a deep impression on the DUP leader, and Paisley concluded that in other circumstances he could have been leader of the strike himself. And though some loyalist leaders concluded that another strike would not succeed, the 'constitutional stoppage' shaped Dr Paisley's thinking. In due time,

Paisley would commit himself, his Party, the UDA and Ernie Baird's UUUP to another strike and another battle of wills with the British Government.

It was the Secretary of State, Merlyn Rees, who had to respond to the immediate situation following the collapse of the power sharing Executive. Rees took the decision that a cooling-off period was needed, but by July 1974, he was in a position to announce that the Labour Government intended to set up an elected Constitutional Convention which it hoped would produce recommendations capable of achieving cross-community support.

There was another subterranean result of the UWC strike. The Government directed the intelligence services to monitor the activities of the loyalists. If there was to be another 'stoppage' the Government was determined that it should receive advance warning.

A month later the DUP announced the opening of a new Party headquarters in Belfast. The suite of offices was by no means impressive but the intention of the DUP to strengthen its Party organisation and administration was in conflict with the spirit of the UUUC Coalition. Was the DUP merely paying lip service to the widespread grass-roots Unionist desire for unity? Or did Dr Paisley's ambitions for his Party override every other consideration? Whatever the DUP's critics might say in answer to such crucial questions, it was the DUP's decision to establish an effective Party secretariat and organisation which helped to secure the Party's electoral successes over the next four years.

Violent disturbances had continued through the period, but in December 1974, an episode took place which provided a brief respite from the Provisional IRA's terrorist campaign, an incident which nevertheless created a deep sense of unease and suspicion within the Protestant segment of the community in Northern Ireland.

On 10 December, leading clerics in the four main Protestant denominations entered into talks with leaders of the Provisional IRA at Feakle,[8] County Clare. Rev. William Arlow, Associate Secretary of the Irish Council of Churches, had played an important role in establishing contact between the church leaders and the Provisionals, while the British Government had been kept informed of the intended talks through the British ambassador in Dublin. Though the talks were inconclusive, a Christmas truce did come into operation. In order to sustain the ceasefire, Merlyn Rees permitted his civil servants to enter into talks with Provisional Sinn Fein, and once again Rev. William Arlow played an important role as a go-between. By 9 January the IRA was able to announce an indefinite ceasefire.

Part of the agreement which established the ceasefire included the setting up of Sinn Fein run incident centres to monitor the situation and intervene in the event of any violent incident which threatened to disrupt the ceasefire. The incident centres aroused profound suspicions not only amongst the Protestant population but within the security forces as well. It was in response to this situation, in which it appeared that some form of secret diplomacy was under way, that Dr Paisley published 'A Call to the Protestants of Ulster'.[9] This statement, which was about 3,000 words in length, was widely published; it was also carried as a one page advertisement in the *News Letter*.

The statement by Dr Paisley made a profound impression on the Protestant leader's followers, and some devoted supporters in the Ballymena area projected that the statement was the prelude to Dr Paisley's taking up arms against the treacherous British Government. This illustrates the feelings of nervousness and high excitement which existed within Ulster Protestantism in January 1975.

With hindsight the 'Call to the Protestants of Ulster' is to be viewed as one of those histrionic gestures to which the leader of the DUP is prone. There was little that was new in the statement which explains why it attracted sparse attention, but it remains an important document because it consolidated support for Dr Paisley. The statement drew a parallel between the spiritual climate in Northern Ireland and political affairs. Rev. William Arlow's decision to enter into talks with the Provisional IRA was interpreted by Dr Paisley as evidence that 'Mr Arlow has drunk the heady wine of ecumenism so deeply that his mind is in a stupor and his eyes are blind to the plain, unadulterated facts'.

It was the ecumenical atmosphere which had encouraged Protestant church leaders to take on the role of negotiators with the Provisional IRA because, Dr Paisley argued, ecumenism had blinded these Protestant clerics to the true nature of the enemies of Ulster Protestantism. Dr Paisley then contrasted the 'desperate' plight of Ulster's Protestants with those values which Protestants sought to uphold. 'We are resisting revolution', Paisley declared.

The following two sub-sections of the document concisely restated his firm conviction that the Roman Catholic Church was the prime mover in a conspiracy to destroy Ulster: 'Ulster is the last bastion of Bible Protestantism in Europe and as such she stands the sole obstacle at this time against the great objective of the Roman See – a unified Roman Catholic Europe'.

This detailed and widely publicised attack on the Roman Catholic Church was moderated by an appeal to Protestants that 'no man should be persecuted for his religious views' and the assertion that in a country governed by the Protestant principle of 'liberty within the law and that law subordinated to the law of God . . . no Roman Catholic and indeed no man has anything to fear'.

The text was a distillation of all that Dr Paisley had been saying throughout the years in which he had become a focus for disruption and dissent, and the subject of intense media attention. The 'Call' ended by urging Ulster's Protestants to 'band ourselves together for the defence and preservation of our country'.

Ian Paisley's 'Call to the Protestants of Ulster' would have conveyed nothing to anyone living outside the Province who was merely curious or interested in the sad, tormented anguish of this 'place apart'.[10] The 'Call' is best understood as a parochial statement directed specifically at a Protestant audience within the population of Northern Ireland; the fervent religious beliefs of such folk were reinforced by Dr Paisley's identification with their independently-minded and defensive convictions. Dr Paisley's 'Call to the Protestants of Ulster' was in effect a quintessential expression of what has often been characterised as the Ulster Unionists' 'siege mentality'. The 'Call' made no attempt to communicate with a wider audience in the United Kingdom living in a secular society and the statement assumed that those who heeded the 'Call' would both comprehend the allusions to historic figures like Dr Henry Cooke and share the spiritual insights of its author.

In March the DUP started to consolidate its increasing support through the appointment of full-time staff to the Party Headquarters. Peter Robinson was one of those appointed and he quickly demonstrated a flair not only for administration and organisation but for inner-party wheeling and dealing.

The Steering Committee of the UUUC was empowered to ratify candidates being put forward for the imminent Convention election by the three parties in the Loyalist Coalition. The meetings were tense and time consuming as Vanguard, the DUP and the Official Unionists tried to obtain the most favourable allocation of seats for their respective parties. These internal difficulties were of little concern to the mass of loyalist voters, whose morale had been lifted by the formation of the Coalition and who placed their confidence in the shared leadership of Craig, Paisley and West.

The three personalities each reflected and represented one facet of the mosaic of Ulster Unionism. Harry West, a bluff farmer from County Fermanagh, was dedicated to rebuilding Unionist unity and to 'getting Stormont back'. He was the most moderate of the three leaders and represented a wing of the Unionist Party which was influenced by contemporary secular trends. West's politics were closest to those of O'Neill, Chichester-Clark and Faulkner. West denounced the disbandment of the Special Constabulary, opposed power sharing and Sunningdale, but he saw the need for compromise, and given the contingent political situation, West would probably have settled for a modified form of power sharing.

Craig was a much more enigmatic figure than West. Although he had attracted considerable popular support amongst loyalists and rapidly built up a dedicated coterie of personal followers Craig was not a great orator; certainly, as was demonstrated at a number of public rallies, he was no match for Paisley when it came to garnering popular support at some of the massive loyalist rallies held in the mid seventies.

Craig, like West, had little sympathy with those who stressed the religious dimension to the Ulster crisis, and his political stance is best described as that of contemporary progressive conservatism. Like West, Craig vehemently supported the return of parliamentary government to 'British Ulster', and his philosophy was endorsed by many who appreciated Craig's willingness to seek out 'expertise'. The Vanguard leader's readiness to build up a 'team' spirit within the activist ranks of the Vanguard movement was contrasted by Vanguard supporters with what they interpreted as the quasi-dictatorial leadership style of Dr Paisley.

For his own part, Dr Paisley must have had mixed feelings about this tripartite solution to the persistent search for an agreed leader, though the solution gave Paisley his place and put him on an equal footing with his rivals for the leadership of right-wing Unionist opinion. Both Craig and West had been Cabinet ministers in former Stormont Governments; now they affected to acknowledge in a public manner the meteoric rise to power of a man who had eschewed every recognised institutional route to power. It was this fact which pointed to the negative aspect of the UUUC's new-found troika-style leadership.

Throughout his Free Presbyterian ministry, those who chose to associate with Paisley invariably deferred to him, either because they acknowledged Paisley's position as a minister of the gospel or they looked up to him as a potential leader of nascent political Protestant-ism. As a result, Dr Paisley lacked the experience of working in partnership with men of equal status.

Now Dr Paisley was confronted with a significant personal challenge. Could he work in harmony with both Craig and West? The Unionist grass-roots had pinned their hopes on the UUUC, and the political dividends to be gained from a dynamic partnership of loyalist interests was incalculable. Amongst the UUUC's supporters the political will was there in abundance, but were Craig, Paisley and West possessed by a similar overriding desire to make the Coalition work? The Northern Ireland Convention election inaugurated a series of events which provided the answer.

Sixty-two Loyalist Coalition candidates contested the 1975 Northern Ireland Convention election. The DUP's share of the total number of UUUC candidates was eighteen, one more than that of the Vanguard Party; this left the Official Unionist Party with by far the largest representation in the field, twenty-seven candidates. W. D. Flackes has suggested that as only 65·8 per cent of the electorate exercised their right to vote, this 'indicated perhaps, a little election weariness, since this was the seventh poll in Northern Ireland in little more than two years'.[11]

When the count had been completed, the Coalition had gained 54·8 per cent of the vote and forty-seven seats, later to be augmented by that of an independent Unionist, Mr Frank Millar. The DUP's share in the overall Coalition victory amounted to twelve seats and a vote of 12·7 per cent. The DUP was the smallest partner in the Coalition because, though Vanguard had a smaller percentage vote overall, the Party had gained fourteen seats, while the Official Unionists had picked up nineteen seats. Nevertheless, the DUP was not displeased at its own performance.

Only four DUP Convention members lacked experience of Dr Paisley's leadership style, gained either through membership of the Protestant Unionist Party or the Northern Ireland Assembly, while only three of the elected DUP Convention members attended churches which were not affiliated to Dr Paisley's Ulster Free Presbyterian Church. The smallest partner in the UUUC Coalition was therefore likely to prove the most disciplined; and Dr Paisley had every reason to believe that of the three loyalist leaders, he was the only loyalist politician whose leadership would pass unquestioned and unchallenged.

The Northern Ireland Constitutional Convention

After the initial meeting of the Convention held under the chairmanship of Sir Robert Lowry, the Lord Chief Justice of Northern Ireland, an inter-party committee under the chairmanship of Dr Paisley was appointed to draft rules for the Convention.

The first serious altercations between the Coalition members and the SDLP occurred on this inter-party rules committee; nevertheless, as Dr Paisley later pointed out, the committee had been able to achieve unanimous agreement on some thirty-four occasions.

It was during the subsequent Convention debates on the draft rules that an air of unreality began to influence the atmosphere at the early sessions of the Convention. There were a number of reasons for this. The British Government had convened the election in late spring, and as the early summer approached the question of a summer recess or vacation arose. Once the dates for a summer recess had been agreed the natural tendency was for the members to assume that the real political negotiations could be put off until the late summer. Furthermore, members of the UUUC harboured the belief that if they exhibited moderation the British Government would be more amenable to majority opinion in Ulster.

Douglas Hutchinson was one DUP member who took advantage of this relaxed atmosphere during the first stage of the Convention. In the course of a series of debates on Rules for the Convention, Hutchinson made conciliatory speeches in which he declared that 'Planter and Gael can both live in the North of Ireland. We could settle our differences if there was less interference from Britain and from the South of Ireland.'

Hutchinson's statement expressed the sentiments of independently minded Ulstermen: those who wanted the Union with Great Britain but wanted it on their own terms. Some days later, Hutchinson urged: 'We want to build a new Ulster and a form of government in which we can all co-operate . . . When it is finished I hope we will have a new era of peace and prosperity. . . . Let us get down to building a new Jerusalem in Ulster's green and pleasant land.'

At first reading Hutchinson's florid speech seems to contrast sharply with the grim security situation which prevailed in the Province, but the DUP member's words were sincerely meant and they have been quoted in order to illustrate the cautiously optimistic mood which had surfaced in the Convention during June.

This optimism affected relationships between the SDLP and UUUC members as well as having concrete results within the Coalition. Encouraged by the electoral victory of the Coalition a serious discussion amongst UUUC members and leaders concerning the formation of a united party now got under way. Loyalists recognised that the creation of a new party would require patience and tenacity, but many of the Coalition's members believed that the will for unity was there and that the momentum for unity was increasing.

It was at this juncture that Dr Paisley convened one of the regular meetings of his Party in the Convention and produced a brief statement which set out the terms under which the DUP would have been willing to subscribe to the concept of a united Unionist party.[12] There were four conditions which Paisley stipulated as essential if the DUP were to agree to participate in the creation of a new Party. The most important condition insisted that 'there must be an adherence to basic Protestant principles by all those negotiating a new Party. There must be a recognition of moral standards in such areas as electioneering, fund-raising, procedure at meetings etc.'

This condition provides the most damaging evidence indicating a lack of enthusiasm for the cause of Unionist unity on the part of Dr Paisley. The statement that 'there must be an adherence to basic Protestant principles by all those negotiating a new Party' in effect provided Dr Paisley with a trap door which would have permitted him to escape from any proposed negotiations almost at will. Consider Paisley's position: he was Moderator of a dynamic and growing sect, the Ulster Free Presbyterian Church, he was acknowledged by the mass media as Ulster's most voluble Protestant spokesman, and his political standing in 1975 rested on a long and increasingly successful career as the unrivalled champion of political Protestantism in Northern Ireland. In such circumstances Dr Paisley would have been able to define what the 'basic Protestant principles' in this section implied. Anyone who dissented from this definition would by his own words and actions have branded himself as a 'Lundy' or 'compromiser'. The DUP was permeated by deeply religious overtones and this emphasis in the statement on 'Protestant principles' adds strength to the view that Boal's departure had encouraged Dr Paisley to regard the DUP as an extension of his own highly complex personality. As matters transpired, the DUP's policy statement was never put to the test because the Coalition was about to fall asunder. The episode, entirely unanticipated, which set in motion the eventual collapse of the partnership of the three Unionist parties turned on William Craig's tenacious advocacy of a 'Voluntary Coalition'[13] between the UUUC and the SDLP.

Craig's Voluntary Coalition proposal

Craig's commitment to a parliamentary system of government for Northern Ireland led him to the conclusion that the UUUC and the SDLP could well model a future joint administration on those coalition governments formed in Britain during the thirties and the Second World War. This solution bypassed the UUUC's opposition to what they termed 'enforced power sharing with Republicans'. Places would be provided for the SDLP in a future Cabinet of Northern Ireland on the basis of the well-established parliamentary principle that in times of emergency, rival parties could freely enter into coalition governments in order to secure the salvation of the nation and work for the common good of all.

One aspect of the work of the Convention had been a series of inter-party talks, and of these the most crucial had been the talks held between the UUUC and the SDLP. William Craig led the three-man UUUC negotiating team which also included Rev. William Beattie (DUP) and Austin Ardill (UUP). Craig determined to put the SDLP to the test in regard to his scheme for an emergency coalition. As Craig envisaged it, the proposed future Cabinet of Northern Ireland would be led by an Ulster Premier who would retain the power to 'hire and fire' his Cabinet colleagues.

An impasse was reached in these negotiations between the UUUC and the SDLP on 28 August. The Chairman of the Convention, Sir Robert Lowry, was approached and asked to examine the UUUC proposals and identify the extent to which they accorded with the UUUC manifesto. Sir Robert Lowry then met the SDLP and UUUC teams separately and produced a paper entitled 'The Voluntary Coalition Solution'.

It was Craig's contention that the SDLP should be required to respond to the proposal for a 'Voluntary Coalition' between the UUUC and themselves, and consequently inter-party talks should continue on this basis. Furthermore, Craig was very confident that he could retain the support of West and Paisley in his desire to force the SDLP to respond to his offer of an emergency coalition. Instead, Paisley withdrew his support and insisted that the talks must be halted and that no further discussion of a 'Voluntary Coalition' should take place.

Craig then found himself isolated from the majority of the UUUC's representatives who were marshalled behind Paisley. The leader of the DUP, now described as the potential 'supremo' of the UUUC in the press, opposed not only the idea that the UUUC could enter into a Voluntary Coalition with the SDLP, but even the much more elementary suggestion that the UUUC ought, at least, to explore the viability of such a solution.

This crisis burst upon the UUUC Coalition over the second weekend in September, and in the course of that weekend it is alleged that Dr Paisley shifted his position from that of personal endorsement of Craig and his Voluntary Coalition solution to outright rejection of both Craig and the possibility of achieving a political breakthrough. Is there any reason to believe that Paisley did renege on assurances which he had given to Craig? And if so, what could have been the motive behind Paisley's decision to revert to a hardline attitude?

The weight of evidence does point to Dr Paisley's abandonment of conciliation. In its place he reverted to his all-too-familiar role of belligerent defender of loyalist interests. Jim Molyneaux MP, referring to the conciliatory attitude which Paisley had adopted in the initial stages of the Convention, averred that Paisley had committed to paper detailed proposals which sought to meet some of the SDLP's demands. Craig has also asserted that Paisley was fully conversant with the implications of the Voluntary Coalition solution. Craig was particularly grieved about Paisley's role, for he remarked that Paisley had done 'an about turn and he hadn't the courtesy to give me advance notice'.

The evidence indicates that Paisley did abandon Craig, leaving him stranded up the garden path. The former members of Vanguard are of the unanimous view that this was a deliberate tactic by Paisley who foresaw that his *volte-face* would isolate Craig, destroy Vanguard and advance the particularist interests of the DUP.

This explanation appears to have little substance to it. While Paisley and the DUP did indeed reap great rewards as a direct result of the Voluntary Coalition debacle, there was no way of knowing on 8 September that William Craig would be sufficiently injudicious to remain up the garden path once he discovered that was the route he had taken. After all, Dr Paisley himself had never been so heavy footed as to exclude back-tracking from his political skills, and Bill Craig had proved equally adept in the past at side-stepping some of the more lethal pitfalls of Ulster politics. Craig's decision to pursue doggedly the Voluntary Coalition solution in the face of vehement opposition from within the ranks of Vanguard and the shocked hostility of all the members of the other two parties, is one of the most curious features of the whole episode. Perhaps Craig, inspired by coalition building among the loyalist parties, believed that such a strategy could be extended to include the SDLP.

Over that critical weekend, though, Paisley responded to the pressures upon him and changed his mind on a Voluntary Coalition. At the time I was secretary to the UUUC Convention Coalition and in personal conversation shortly after the affair, Peter Robinson stated that it was as a result of his own personal intervention that Paisley went back on his commitment to Craig's negotiating initiative. For his part, the Vanguard leader is of the opinion that hardliners from County Armagh met Dr Paisley at the Martyrs Memorial Church on the Sunday evening and prevailed upon the preacher to reject any tie-up with the SDLP.

Craig had committed himself to the Voluntary Coalition solution in such a wholesale way because he was personally convinced that this was the only way to get Stormont parliamentary government back; but Craig's vanity led him to underestimate the strength of opposition which the scheme would generate within the Loyalist Coalition; Craig's misreading of the situation was probably compounded by the response of the press and media which heralded Craig's proposal as a major breakthrough and inaccurately predicted widespread public support for Craig across the Province.

The Voluntary Coalition affair continued to promote confusion within the ranks of the UUUC for some weeks, and though Paisley's rejection of the proposal that the UUUC might explore the possibility of a Voluntary Coalition with the SDLP effectively brought to an end the inter-party talks between the SDLP and the UUUC it would be inaccurate to suggest that Paisley bears the sole responsibility for the manner in which these talks were aborted.

Enoch Powell, who had played little part in the earlier discussions of the UUUC Convention group, though his position as a UUUC Westminster MP entitled him to participate in any meetings which took place, now chose to intervene on the issue of a Voluntary Coalition. Powell's speech to UUUC Convention members 'played a major part in torpedoing the Craig plan'.[14] There is a danger in imagining that because the DUP was to make significant political gains as a result of the Voluntary Coalition debacle, Paisley offered the only opposition to Craig's scheme; this exaggerates the importance of Paisley's contribution to the whole affair, and fails to take into consideration the important political gains which the Ulster Unionist Party would be able to make in the event of the collapse of the Vanguard Party.

Not only did Powell's criticisms of the Voluntary Coalition weigh heavily with UUUC representatives but, as Craig later candidly acknowledged, elements within the Vanguard Party saw his commitment to such a radical solution as an opportunity to 'knife the leader in the back'. The whole affair was made more complex by an undercurrent of personal rivalries and jealousies which coursed underneath the surface of the UUUC Coalition. The Official Unionist Party also feared that they would be seen as following the dictate of Paisley and attempted a more cautious rejection of Craig's initiative, but they rejected it nevertheless because the mood of opposition to any tie up with the SDLP was too intense. Paisley was making all the running and the Unionists had little choice but to try and keep pace with him.

Once the Voluntary Coalition plan had been rejected attention focussed on the inevitable repercussions. The political careers of Craig and Rev. William Beattie were severely damaged by the whole affair, and those few members of Vanguard who stood by Craig also suffered a setback to their political progress. Beattie had become inextricably linked with Craig's misjudgement, not because he supported the Voluntary Coalition solution – Beattie aligned himself with Dr Paisley in rejecting the scheme – but Rev. William Beattie's misfortune arose from the fact that he had been less than candid in providing an explanation of his initial role in the whole affair. Beattie had failed to read the storm signals in time. This was a serious disability for a politician who was a member of a Party whose members prided themselves on their super-loyalty while sustaining themselves all the while with the belief that Ulster would be lost without them.

Within a few months, the Vanguard Party had collapsed and a new movement led by Ernest Baird emerged to take Vanguard's place in the UUUC Coalition, but Vanguard had been a buffer-party in the Coalition between the Official Unionist Party and the DUP, holding the incipient rivalries of the two parties in check. With Vanguard in disarray, the DUP pushed into the gap that had been left in the united Unionist front, leaving Baird's United Ulster Unionist Movement, as it was initially called, effectively isolated on the sidelines.

The Voluntary Coalition affair would in the fulness of time present the DUP with an irresistible temptation to challenge the Unionist Party's dominance of loyalist politics in the Province. Furthermore, Craig had been the only Unionist politician capable of fostering the kind of personal support and adulation which distinguished the followers of Dr Paisley from other loyalists. With Craig and the Vanguard Party driven into the wilderness, Paisley's personal position was correspondingly strengthened, but some months would pass before the full implications of what had occurred in the autumn of 1975 became clear, and in the meantime the rump of the UUUC Coalition would have to turn its attention to producing a majority Unionist report devoid of any accommodation with the SDLP. The high drama which had surrounded the Voluntary Coalition episode also ensured that the Report, when it did come, was an anti-climax.

In the meantime, the UUUC made strenuous attempts to recover from the crisis; Ernest Baird took over Craig's position in the tripartite leadership of the UUUC, and the Loyalist Coalition successfully steered its draft proposals through the Convention. Baird, who had a mercurial personality, lacked the political experience of Craig, or for that matter Paisley and West, and the new joint leadership was only a pale shadow of the style of leadership which had been given to the UUUC by Craig, Paisley and West between December 1973 and July 1975.

The Report of the Northern Ireland Convention was published in November 1975 and although the Convention met in early 1976, its task had been completed. However, the Voluntary Coalition affair influenced the manner in which the Report was received by the Labour Government at Westminster, and the Report was rejected by Parliament despite the fact that it had been supported by a majority of the Convention's members.

The British Government had pinned its hopes for an end to the crisis in Northern Ireland on the emergence of a power sharing agreement between the Unionists and the SDLP. Even without the Voluntary Coalition debacle a majority Report unilaterally voted through by the UUUC is almost certain to have proved unacceptable at Westminster. The only serious attempt to find an accommodation had cost William Craig his place in the UUUC and wrecked his Vanguard Party, but the irony was that the British Government may well have been unwilling to accept Craig's 'Voluntary Coalition' solution. Under pressure from the SDLP the Government would have diluted the powers of any future Prime Minister heading a Voluntary Coalition so that he would not have been able 'to hire and fire' at will as Craig had surmised he would. What is more, it is unlikely that the SDLP would have so readily acquiesced in the abandonment of the 'Irish Dimension' which never figured in the 'breakthrough' solution at all. With considerations such as these in mind, it seems highly unlikely that Craig's political career could have survived the kind of political pressure which British Governments had applied to reforming Unionist leaders in the recent past. The reward for the whisper of reconciliation was recrimination.

It is unreasonable to place all the responsibility for the collapse of the Voluntary Coalition solution on Dr Paisley and his Coalition partners in the Convention. Time and again throughout the Northern Ireland troubles, British Governments have shown an abiding reluctance to come to terms with the dilemma facing the Ulster Unionists, with the result that at crucial moments in the crisis the Government has demanded more of the Unionist leadership than they were able to deliver. Craig now followed Faulkner, Chichester-Clark and Captain Terence O'Neill into political exile; perhaps the British Government would have little alternative but to come to terms with 'the demon Doctor' himself, the personification of Ulster grass-roots sentiment.

Dr Paisley and the DUP gave enthusiastic support to the Convention Report and adherence to this document became an article of faith for the three Unionist parties in the Coalition; the vexed problem was how to achieve the implementation of the Report when the Westminster Parliament had determined to set the Report's findings to one side. Dr Paisley thought that the answer might lie in some form of direct action, but the Official Unionist Party was much more cautious. It is probable that the Unionists regretted being stampeded into a hasty rejection of Craig's tentative proposal and they began to distance themselves from the DUP; those Unionists who had always been most critical of Dr Paisley deduced that their personal assessment of the rival Unionist leader had been vindicated. By the spring of 1976 underlying tensions between the parties to the UUUC Coalition began to increase and cordiality gave way to political intrigue.

Direct action planned

With the Vanguard buffer removed, the incipient distrust between the loyalist faction represented by Paisley and Baird and the rival Unionist Party began to increase.

The Unionist Party was predisposed to seek a redress of the political situation by constitutional means. This involved the OUP in an attempt to rebuild its shattered party infrastructure while its elected Members of Parliament argued Ulster's case on the floor of the House of Commons.

The disintegration of Vanguard had brought home to the DUP members in the Assembly the inherent differences in the structure and discipline of the DUP when contrasted either with Vanguard or the Unionist Party; James McClure, a DUP Assemblyman from County Londonderry, had remarked in conversation with me that the DUP was not like other parties, subject to divisions and splits. I pointed out to McClure that the explanation arose from the fact that activists who broke with the DUP would not only suffer political isolation but be denounced as religious heretics as well. It was a prescient remark!

With their rivals in the Unionist Party adopting a cautious and unadventurous approach to Direct Rule, Paisley and Baird proceeded with their plans for direct action. In a welter of publicity Paisley and Baird launched a United Unionist Action Council which was intended to band the three parties together in an unspecified form of militant action.

To give added muscle to the Action Council's aims of ending Direct Rule and achieving the implementation of the Convention Report, the DUP began to give consideration to the role of the loyalist paramilitaries. In June 1976, Peter Robinson, who was professional party secretary at the time, spoke to me in my capacity as a DUP member of the advisability of establishing a DUP paramilitary force.

My response was to warn that such a proposal was fraught with difficulties: organising a paramilitary force would have placed the DUP in a dilemma. If the paramilitary force were to be led by DUP party members, this would have diverted experienced activists from their political role. The alternative would be to recruit a DUP paramilitary force with its own self-generating leadership but this posed the very real risk that the men with the guns might attempt to enforce alternative political policies on the leadership of the Party.

Nothing came of Robinson's proposal in 1976, but the DUP's belief in the merit of a 'Third Force' composed of loyal Ulstermen, dedicated to the defence of Ulster, took on more tangible shape later.

Paisley and Robinson came up with an alternative: to win over the Ulster Defence Association to the programme of militancy being advocated by the Action Council. The ensuing dialogue with the loyalist paramilitaries was conducted secretively. Andy Tyrie, the leader of the UDA, did attend some Action Council meetings, but much of the contact between Tyrie and the DUP was made over the telephone. Peter Robinson worked assiduously to establish strong links with the UDA in East Belfast, and this relationship would later enable Robinson to mobilise the UDA for his successful Westminster election bid in East Belfast.

There was an underlying difficulty in this association between the DUP leadership and the UDA. The more spiritually minded and God-fearing DUP supporters in North Antrim regarded the UDA with distaste. The UDA's well established links with sectarian murder and illegal drinking clubs and the policy of Independence pursued by this, the largest of Ulster's various paramilitary groupings, would have given rise to profound misgivings about Dr Paisley's new-found allies. The less that was known in Ballymena, the DUP's 'holy city', the better.

At the same time as these contacts were being established with the UDA, another paramilitary formation was coming into its own. Known as the Ulster Service Corps, this was an organisation with its roots in rural Ulster and drawing heavily on members who had previously served in the disbanded Ulster Special Constabulary or 'B' Men. The Ulster Service Corps' intention was to stage vigilante road checks in an effort to disrupt the Provisional IRA's campaign of terrorism, but such activity would inevitably bring them into confrontation with the Crown forces. Five Ulster Service Corps members from County Armagh were charged by the police after operating an illegal road check and their impending trial provided a *cause célèbre* around which Paisley and Baird could galvanise support for their intended confrontation with the Government.

As the DUP, UUUM and the loyalist paramilitaries began to establish a common interest in direct action, the Unionist Party became more convinced of the folly of this new political venture. The difference in emphasis between the militant demands of Baird and his DUP colleagues and the moderate stance of Harry West and Rev. Martin Smyth burst into the open at a joint meeting between the Action Council members and the Unionist Party politicians.

West had deep reservations about whether direct action would prove effective but the lack of definition in the phrase 'direct action' also caused him concern. Rev. Martin Smyth was even more blunt, and he stated that the Unionist Party didn't have the heart for subversive action.

It was apparent that ideological divisions between the Ulster Unionists and the other parties to the Coalition were creating a widening gulf between the Coalition's groupings. Nevertheless the pretence of Unionist unity would continue to be maintained in public for another twelve months. This crumbling façade of Unionist unity was further undermined in July when Austin Ardill and Rev. Martin Smyth held secret talks with Paddy Devlin and John Hume of the SDLP.

On 4 June Dr Paisley again demonstrated his ability to get hold of, and publicise, sensitive information when he vigorously denounced this unilateral political initiative taken by one of the Coalition parties. Rev. Martin Smyth, like other Unionist Party leaders who had incurred the anger of Dr Paisley in the past, was then subjected to vehement heckling at a demonstration of the Royal Black Institution in the village of Scarva, and this form of abuse could hardly have been calculated to maintain a spirit of cordiality between these two loyalist personalities.

A few weeks after this incident the former Premier of Northern Ireland and leader of the ill-starred Northern Ireland Executive, Brian Faulkner, announced his decision to quit politics. 'Protestant Ulster' was fast becoming a land of lost leaders. Faulkner subsequently remarked that 'power sharing had cost him his political life'.[15] Faulkner's decision to 'opt out' robbed the moderate wing of Unionism of an effective and articulate politician, and his decision indirectly strengthened the position of the DUP, because by resigning Faulkner had signalled that moderate Unionists could not hold the elusive centre ground in Ulster politics.

In early September Roy Mason, a former Secretary for Defence, took over from Merlyn Rees as the Secretary of State for Northern Ireland. Mason's stolid no-nonsense Yorkshire approach, his experience of army procedures, and his reluctance to get involved in experimental solutions, won him a high measure of respect from many ordinary Ulster folk, but the Action Council had committed itself to direct action and there was to be no going back.

These were days of frenetic activity, much of which seemed to go on beneath the surface of events. Rumours abounded, and it was during these planning stages of intended 'direct action' that my association with the DUP came to an abrupt and unexpected end. Perhaps because of my cautious approach to paramilitary adventures, of which I had had some experience in the past – at one time I had been approached to join Gusty Spence's UVF, an invitation which I declined – the DUP leadership concluded that I was not to be trusted. There was a hastily convened and quite irregular meeting in Dr Paisley's 'Parsonage' and I gained a first hand insight into the DUP's methods of Party discipline.

Though Provisional IRA terrorism continued on a reduced scale in early 1977, the effectiveness of the security forces fell far short of that being demanded by the Action Council whose intention to cause disruption had developed a momentum of its own.

The cause of moderate Unionism received a further setback in the early spring when Brian Faulkner, who had recently been elevated to the peerage, was killed in a horse riding accident. The number of capable Unionists who could provide an obstacle to Dr Paisley's hegemony over the Protestant electorate was diminishing.

Within the DUP such rapid changes in the political scene were interpreted as signifying the inevitable triumph of Dr Paisley's cause. By the spring of 1977 the inner circles of the DUP had developed a very high conceit of themselves, which helps to explain the way in which the events of the next few months were to shape themselves.

The officers of the DUP credited themselves with having created a political machine which had broken the 'Lundy' Unionist Party and destroyed the dangerous ploy of a Voluntary Coalition. These officers looked on Dr Paisley as a man of destiny providentially raised up by Almighty God to lead Ulster in its hour of travail. The Free Presbyterian Church was perceived to be the sole authentic voice of historic and reformed Protestantism.

Filled with pride at their achievements, and confident in the rightness of their policies,[16] the DUP prepared to commit themselves wholeheartedly to the tasks of defeating the IRA and enforcing the implementation of the Convention Report on the Government. In the event the enterprise would be exposed as a serious miscalculation, and the reason why the DUP misread the mood of ordinary Ulster people turns on their failure to comprehend that no single section of loyalism could, single-handed, confront the Government and hope to win.

As a first step, the DUP staged a two day party conference in mid-April. Three hundred delegates heard Dr Paisley deliver a ninety minute address during which the DUP leader launched a personal attack on the leader of the Vanguard rump, William Craig. Paisley alleged that the SDLP had weaned Craig away from the UUUC Convention manifesto by encouraging the Vanguard leader to imagine that with the co-operation of the SDLP he could be the Prime Minister of a devolved government. Paisley also explained to the delegates that he had only joined the UUUC Coalition because Harry West and William Craig had 'spoken out' when the Ulster Special Constabulary was disbanded.

In effect, Paisley was playing down the political significance of the Coalition and Paisley continued this indirect attack on the Coalition by advising the Party faithful that some of the Ulster Unionists in the

Convention could have drifted towards a power sharing policy if the DUP had not been in place to pressurise them.

However, it was Paisley's comments on the security situation which were most calculated to articulate the fears and apprehensions of his listeners: 'The refusal of the Government to introduce the death penalty is but another encouragement to the IRA. The Government prefers dead policemen, dead soldiers and dead civilians to dead terrorists.'

Turning to the decision of the police to prosecute five loyalists from Armagh for operating a vigilante road check, Paisley contended that 'Republicans can block roads and the IRA men can hold up cars, but the Government takes no action. The Ulster Service Corps, however, are to be made a public example – why? Simply because they are Protestants.'

With new local government elections due to be held in May, this DUP Conference was being stage managed for the purpose of maximising the commitment of the Party's workers to the forthcoming election, and Calvert acknowledged as much when he wrote that the Conference 'was used as a launching-ground for the local government elections'.

There is, however, a curious conjunction between this Conference and the two events which succeeded it, the scheduled local government elections held on 18 May and the 'constitutional stoppage' called by the Action Council for midnight on Monday 2 May. In Calvert's history of the DUP the sequence of these events is most revealing, because the 'constitutional stoppage' fulfils a subordinate role to that of the local government elections upon which Calvert placed much of his emphasis. As the 1977 strike proved to be an ignominious failure, Calvert has probably chosen an approach, not unknown in hagiography, where virtue is heavily underlined and folly is minimised.

A week after the DUP Conference ended the *News Letter* published a large half page advertisement on behalf of the Action Council. The advertisement carried echoes of Paisley's earlier 'Call to the Protestants of Ulster', because it was entitled 'A Solemn Call to the Loyalists of Ulster'. Like so much of Paisley's crusade, echoes of the Covenanters could also be discerned.

The advertisement was the manifesto of those who were planning another 'constitutional stoppage', and in it the Action Council declared that 'The British Government is actually using the Union to destroy the traditional Unionist concept of that Union. . . . The British Government has not only failed but has no intention of giving Ulster equality with the rest of the United Kingdom'.

The advertisement then delivered a calculated blow at the moderate and constitutional policies of the Unionist Party: 'It is a dangerous practice for any Unionist party to promote the notion that blind obedience to Westminster will keep Ulster free from a United Ireland'.

Not only did the advertisement conclude with verses from Rudyard Kipling's poem 'Ulster 1912', but *News Letter* readers were advised that 'the Action Council is now giving the leadership for which you have been waiting'. This final statement illustrates the conceit of those who had embarked on this policy of confrontation and disguises the fact that the leadership offered by the Action Council was being imposed on the Province from above by an alliance of duly elected political representatives and paramilitary enforcers. No attempt had been made to consult with grass-roots loyalist opinion, and the fact that neither the Unionist Party nor the Orange Order was willing to lend itself to the proposed action was to have a crucial bearing on subsequent events.

The constitutional stoppage was to be organised by sectional interests within the Ulster Protestant electorate and neither the changing political situation heralded by the arrival of Roy Mason nor the Action Council's failure to maintain a broadly based and united loyalist front, gave the strike leaders sufficient reason to stay their hand. On 26 April 1977, the Action Council issued an ultimatum to Roy Mason. The Secretary of State had just seven days in which to demonstrate a new determination by the Government to defeat the IRA, and to come to terms with the import of the Northern Ireland Convention Report, or a strike would be called.

On the same day, Rev. Martin Smyth, in his capacity as the Grand Master of the Orange Order, gave a detailed explanation as to why the loyal institution had been reluctant to affiliate to the Action Council. Smyth stated that there was alarm that the leadership of the Order might be taken out of the hands of Orangemen. This could be interpreted as a reference either to the role of the UDA within the Action Council or to the possibility that Paisley was manipulating the whole undertaking for his own party advantage.

The Orange leader also referred to another very widely held fear which seriously undermined the solidarity of the Protestant population as they faced up to the import of the 'solemn call' and impending strike action. This was the belief that extreme left-wing elements were 'prepared to take advantage of the frustrations of loyalists to take over the country'.

The Alliance Party subscribed, in part, to this alarm over the proposed constitutional stoppage, claiming that the real objective was independence for Northern Ireland. The Party also accused the politicians in the Action Council of using people for their own cynical ends.

Another factor which divided the loyalists was the fear that industrial disruption would adversely affect the unemployment situation in the Province. David Allen, a prominent member of Baird's group and a councillor in Ballymena, received death threats from extreme loyalists following his statement to the effect that the unemployment figures pointed strongly against any form of strike action.

The Protestant population was obviously deeply divided over the necessity for strike action, the ultimate intentions of the strikers themselves, and the consequences which would inevitably follow from any disruption for the future economic development of the Province.

For their part, the United Unionist Action Council imagined themselves to be in an identical situation to that which prevailed in May 1974. The Action Council believed that when Mason rejected their ultimatum, which they correctly presumed that he would, and the leaders shouted 'stop', the Province would grind to a halt.

Others were not so sure. A Roman Catholic workman in the Ormeau Bakery advised a colleague who was also a known activist in the DUP that Paisley's strike would fail. When the surprised DUP member asked his colleague how he had arrived at such a conclusion, the Roman Catholic replied that without the co-operation of the Orange Order Paisley could not possibly succeed. The Orange Order had been criticised by many of its own rank and file for a lack of militancy in the late 1960s and early 1970s, so the DUP man was not unnaturally intrigued by this analysis, but the Roman Catholic workman's supposition was well founded. Paisley had been unable to maximise Protestant support for direct action and as a result his scheme would misfire.

The constitutional stoppage began on 3 May and staggered on for ten days amidst an atmosphere heavy with menace, lawlessness and growing Action Council hysteria. Throughout the strike many factories stayed open and at a crucial juncture Paisley failed to win over the power station workers, whose participation could have given the faltering strike renewed impetus.

The façade of Unionist unity subsided under pressure from this further example of loyalist militancy, and the UUUC coalition fell apart when Molyneaux, the leader of the Official Unionists, warned Parliament on 5 May that the strike had endangered the link between Ulster and Great Britain.

That week also saw the nominations for the impending local government elections and as Calvert has coyly explained: 'in the midst of the stoppage the DUP nominated 109 candidates in twenty-three district council areas'. The Government's controlled handling of the media in the Province made an important contribution to the ultimate collapse of the strike, during which intimidation and murder took place. There were also violent clashes at the Republican village of Toomebridge. There an angry crowd of three hundred set fire to a loyalist convoy of fourteen tractors and later pushed four agricultural vehicles into the River Bann.

As the signs of the imminent collapse of the strike became all too apparent, the utterances of Paisley and Baird had become more vitriolic and intemperate. Dr Paisley went so far as to suggest that if the strike did not succeed he would resign from political life.[17]

On 18 May the Action Council came to terms with reality and called off the strike. Five days later the Province went to the polls in the local government elections. Calvert has stated that 'most of the DUP candidates were on the local stoppage committees and were so heavily engaged in organising pickets and protest meetings that little canvassing was done'. It is hard to escape the conclusion that in the minds of the DUP, at least, there was an inter-connection between the strike and the local government elections.

Calvert has admitted that it was the use of Government propaganda and the willingness of the Orange Order hierarchy and the Unionist Party to support Roy Mason which led to the defeat of the Action Council strike.

The strike may have had serious economic consequences for the Province, lives may have been lost and property destroyed but, remarkably, the reputations of Dr Paisley and his Party escaped unscathed. Why this should be the case turns on the results of the local government election. The Unionist Party suffered a severe reverse and lost thirty-four seats while the DUP gained seats at the expense of both the Unionists, whom the DUP publicly acknowledged to be their arch rivals, and the other loyalist candidates, including Baird's Party, which the DUP had cynically set out to destroy.

It would be wrong to assume that if these local government elections had been held after the dust of the industrial disruption had settled, then the results might have been different. Although time might have given the Protestant population the opportunity to reflect on the recklessness of Paisley and Baird's strike call, the reality is that the strike, even though it proved unsuccessful, was believed by many loyalists to have been a useful political gesture; to such folk the fact that Paisley is seen 'to be doin' somethin'' and 'to shout out' is enough. In addition there is the recurrent problem that the Unionist Party has never been able to exploit to the full the many vulnerable points in the DUP's style of politics, and this gives little grounds for supposing that the Unionists were denied an opportunity to mount a full-blooded attack on the DUP's policy of direct action.

W. D. Flackes does, however, suggest that one consequence of the bitter recriminations which passed between the Official Unionists and the DUP over the strike call and the lawlessness and violence which ensued was that it 'undoubtedly robbed the DUP of many OUP second preference votes'.[18] If Flackes is correct then it means that the DUP's electoral successes would have been even more spectacular in 1977 than they in fact were. Though the strike was an ignoble failure the DUP were able to wrest victory out of despair because their local government election gains indicated widespread approval amongst loyalists for their policy of demagoguery and confrontation.

Notes and References

[1] Derek McAuley, 'Ulster Vanguard: The study of a faction within the Ulster Unionist Party 1972–1973' (unpublished BSSc dissertation dated 1981, Political Science Department, Queen's University). McAuley presents a perceptive account of the development of Ulster Vanguard.

[2] R. J. Lawrence, S. Elliott, M. J. Laver, *The Northern Ireland General Elections of 1973*, HMSO Cmnd. 5851, 79.

[3] *Report of the Northern Ireland Assembly*, 31 July 1973, col. 6.

[4] Robin Evelegh, *Peace-Keeping in a Democratic Society: The Lessons of Northern Ireland*, London 1978, 113.

[5] Robert Fisk, *The Point of No Return*, London 1975, 43.

[6] The *Irish Times*, 7 December 1973.

[7] The Linenhall Library in Belfast has made strenuous efforts to catalogue and collate much of the ephemeral literature, pamphlets, broadsheets and the like which have been printed through the troubles. In this case the quotations are drawn from *Under the Stone*, Vanguard Unionist Party, Belfast, April 1975. It is anonymous.

[8] Eric Gallagher and Stanley Worrall, *Christians in Ulster 1968–1980*, Oxford 1982, 96–102.

[9] Ian R. K. Paisley, *Call to the Protestants of Ulster*, Belfast 1975. See also *News Letter*, Friday 31 January 1975.

[10] See Dervla Murphy, *A Place Apart*, Harmondsworth, Middlesex 1979.

[11] W. D. Flackes, *Northern Ireland: A Political Directory 1968–79*, Dublin 1980, 174.

[12] 'Points on a new United Unionist Party', prepared by the Democratic Unionist Convention Group for presentation and discussion at the United Ulster Unionist Council Steering Committee meeting on Thursday 7 August 1975.

[13] I was at that time Secretary to the UUUC Convention Parties and consequently had access to the relevant minutes of the Coalition meetings.

[14] *The Workers Weekly*, 20 September 1975.

[15] Interview with Marvyn Gowdy.

[16] See Chapter I for a detailed discussion of Protestant Unionism; also John Harbinson, *The Ulster Unionist Party*, Belfast 1973, 223–226.

[17] This word 'unique' must be used cautiously. The emphasis on 'Protestantism' by the DUP is 'unique' amongst Ulster Unionist parties, but the DUP is far from unique in a universal sense.

[18] The *Irish Times*, 13 December 1973.

CHAPTER IV

The Roots of
Ian Paisley's Ideology

I welcome an election. As soon as I can I will come before the electorate again because I believe that the only discipline in a democracy is the ballot box. I have been defeated in elections, I have won elections, but I have always accepted the ballot box. The Hon. Gentleman does not know the hard road by which I came to this House. I did not always have a majority. I saw candidates lose their deposits time and again, but I did not lose faith in the democratic method.

> Ian Paisley, speaking in the House of Commons
> *Official Reports (Hansard)* Vol.87 No.14 c.907, 27 Nov. 1985

This is moral majority Bible country, with Christian television channels and radio stations, where hotels display prominently detailed lists of every church service and preacher. Bob Jones, the president of the university, writes in the foreword to the university handbook: 'The area is progressive and vibrant but distinctly conservative, maintaining traditional American values'. Which would be recommendation enough for many Ulster Unionists, and in part explains why Dr Paisley has such close ties with the university, of which he is a trustee.

> *The Observer*
> 24 January 1982

Covenanting convictions in a contemporary setting

Ian Paisley is conscious of his roots. Unlike so many of his contemporaries Paisley has not lost faith in the religion of his forefathers. Though the DUP leader's Protestant beliefs set him apart from other politicians, those beliefs have made a crucial impact upon his political success. They have enabled the DUP leader to construct a unique and innovative ideology. This ideology has been shaped by Scottish seventeenth century Presbyterian political theory with its emphasis on a form of contractual allegiance, and by twentieth century American Fundamentalist revivalism with its strong populist appeal and love of country. Paisley's particular talent has been to graft on to the political principles of his covenanting forefathers all the energy, financial acumen and brashness of the Fundamentalist Protestant sects of the United States.

The skill of Paisley in fusing ancient and largely forgotten Presbyterian political precepts to a contemporary transatlantic phenomenon has helped to differentiate the DUP from other alternative forms of Unionism which fitfully emerged in the past to challenge the hegemony of the Ulster Unionist Party. Paisley's innovative role has been to proclaim a message which has a considerable appeal to the ordinary grass-roots Ulster Protestants, as election results indicate, but the message itself combines paradox- ically the political ideas of seventeenth century Calvinistic Covenan- ters with the momentum of arminian revivalism. It is ironic that in Ulster, sometimes called 'Scotland's invisible colony', political ideals which are now a matter of historical curiosity in the secularised political culture of modern Scotland should remain potent and palpable. In seeking to discover how this came about, it is necessary to understand something of the impact which Scottish political theory still makes upon the attitudes of loyalists and why it is that in defying the will of the sovereign Parliament at Westminster Ian Paisley and his followers reveal that they hold to a view of sovereignty which neither is shared nor understood by the political establishment in London.

Though Paisley has organised congregational bus tours of the covenanting memorials of Ayrshire and the *Protestant Telegraph* regularly carried historical features on similar themes and recounted the adventures of some of the many Covenanters who fled into North Antrim as refugees from 'the killing times', comparatively few in the Province have made the connection between the convictions of the Covenanters and the ideology that lies at the root of present-day political attitudes. Many ordinary Protestant people in the Province do appear, though, to have an intuitive or traditional view of politics which holds to a concept of political obligation and contractual allegiance which is alien to the political thought of the majority of the inhabitants of Ireland and which has long since been overtaken by more sophisticated concepts of social democracy and sovereignty in Britain. The widely noted position of the Orange Institution, that its allegiance is to the British Throne 'being Protestant' (sic), implies that in circumstances where the monarchy was no longer Protestant the

Orangemen could withhold their loyalty to the Crown. Part of Paisley's success derives from his ability to seize upon these instinctive attitudes of Protestants in Ulster and articulate their ideas on their behalf, but because such concepts are rooted in the past Paisley's support within the Province is more than balanced by the lack of comprehension and even derision expressed by outsiders.

Although, as the Dutch geographer, D. M. Heslinga, underlined in his study, *The Irish Border as a Cultural Divide*, there already was a significant Scottish presence in North-east Ireland before the Plantation of the Scottish King James I, it was the plantation policy of the Stuart king which rooted in the Ulster landscape ideas which continue to exert a powerful, if largely unrecognised, influence over the political imagination of the Protestants in Northern Ireland.

It is generally accepted that it was the tenacious Presbyterian convictions of the Scottish segment of the Ulster Plantation which helped to ensure the survival of that particular scheme of plantation where the earlier plantations of the Tudor monarchs in central Ireland had failed.

The new settlers brought into Ireland the reformed religion, but the settlers, whether Scottish or English, also brought to the Province their own ways of looking at things, including their politics. As A. D. Lindsay in his little classic *The Essentials of Democracy* explains, these settlers already had an inherently democratic outlook because:

> The inspiration of modern democracy came from men's experience of the entirely satisfactory character of democratic government in the Christian congregation – came therefore especially from the Independents, the Anabaptists, and the Quakers – from the men who had accepted more wholeheartedly than other Protestants the reformation doctrine of the spiritual priesthood of all believers.[1]

Lindsay further acknowledged the Presbyterian contribution to modern democracy because, noting that 'Presbyterian government is another example', he went on to remark that in Presbyterianism, 'the original unit of democratic church government – the congregation – is represented at the Presbyteries as Presbyteries are represented at Synod and General Assembly'.

The Ulster settlers, imbued with an inherently democratic spirit, encountered an ancient, sophisticated and paternalistic Gaelic society which was not only pre-Reformation but was also pre-democratic. Along with the religious divide introduced into North-east Ireland at the time of the Stuart Plantation there were also different views of society expressed in the Gaelic attitude to life and the early Protestant democratic idealism of the settlers.

When Irish nationalism emerged in the nineteenth century the sources of its democratic inspiration came from continental Europe, the Enlightenment, the United Irishmen, the French Revolution, Daniel O'Connell, and finally Thomas Meagher's association with the Paris Commune of 1848; all these threads helped to promote a concept of democracy with different roots from those of the Protestants in Ulster.

The early seventeenth century settlers in Ulster were of an independent turn of mind and as the century progressed there was a deepening awareness of Puritan democratic sentiment in England, augmented by the experiences of the Covenanters in their struggle with the Stuart kings. It has been said that the Covenanters were:

> . . . the pioneers of full civil and religious freedom. In all their covenants and contendings they stood for 'free assemblies' and 'free parliaments'. They stood for the rule of the people against the domination of arbitrary princes. They resisted the totalitarian claim of their day that the king was supreme in all causes, religious as well as civil.[2]

Foremost among those who made an intellectual contribution to the Covenanters' political theories was Samuel Rutherford; as his letters show, he took considerable interest in events in Ireland, but he is best remembered for his treatise written in 1644, entitled *Lex Rex*. In his argument Rutherford refuted the Stuart monarch's divine right doctrines. *Lex Rex* identified three 'species of government, such as government by one only, called monarchy, the government by some chief leading men, named aristocracy, the government by the people, going under the name democracy'.[3] Rutherford contended that 'all three forms (of government) are from God' and that God did not institute any particular form of government in the Bible. Rutherford then developed his argument in order to demonstrate with reference to the precedent in the Old Testament that 'the people made the King, though under God; and that he (Mizpeh) was yet a private man till the states of Israel chose him'.

The impact of these democratic ideals created a particular form of assertive and conditional political allegiance in the North-east of Ireland which has long been recognised: 'political opinions in Ulster were apt to be independent with a distinctive flavour of settler radicalism', and has also formed the basis of David Miller's more recent study *The Queen's Rebels*,[4] in which he discussed notions of contractual obligation, and conditional loyalty, and their relevance to the development of Protestant political thinking.

Protestant political thinking in Ulster continued to be influenced by undercurrents in central Scotland. One example of this is to be found in the career of the obscure Church of Scotland minister, Jacob Primmer, who lived at the turn of the century. Primmer's importance derived from the fact that he was a precursor of Ian Paisley himself. During his controversial career in which he organised massive anti-popery 'conventicles', Primmer acknowledged his indebtedness to the Covenanters by using their motto, 'Christ our King and Covenant' on his banners, and by his attempted revival of 'the spirit of the Covenanters'. A year before his death in 1914, Primmer advocated in his pamphlet *A New Political Party Wanted*[5] the setting up of an aggressively Protestant party which would 'fight the foreign Papal foe'. While Primmer's biography fails to examine the extent to which the Covenanting political theory of men like Rutherford influenced Jacob Primmer, Ian Paisley's writings provide firm evidence of the extent to which the Ulster leader is indebted to Covenanting theology.

In his book, *The Crown Rights of Jesus Christ*,[6] Paisley endorses such Covenanting sentiments and also acknowledges the influence which the later writings of Dr William Symington (1795–1861), one time Professor of Theology for the Synod of the Reformed Presbyterian Church of Scotland, had on his thinking.

More controversially, Dr Paisley has sought to argue in discussion that the Covenanters had made a distinctive additional contribution to the political thought of the earlier Protestant Reformers, Luther and Calvin. Paisley has contended that Calvin and those of his generation had not entirely freed themselves from some of the Church of Rome's influence in regard to the relationship of the subject to his prince and that the Covenanters had not merely a more democratic approach but a more Scriptural perception of the right relationship between the governing authority and the governed.

Ian Paisley emphatically rejects any form of pietistic acquiescence in the rule of a government authority whose state interests are in conflict with the law of God. In his book he quotes the following famous well thumbed passage in Paul's Epistle to the Romans: 'Let every soul be subject to the higher powers. For there is no power but God: the powers that be are ordained of God. Whosoever therefore resisteth the power, resisteth the ordinances of God; and they that resist shall receive to themselves damnation.'

And Paisley avers, quoting from the famous Scottish preacher and writer Robert Haldene, that there is no implied requirement to submit 'to laws contrary to the law of God'. 'No Scripture', writes the Ulster leader, 'has been more misunderstood and more wrested by unbelieving men to their own destruction'!

Like the Covenanters, Paisley possesses a robust and iconoclastic view of the powers and authority of established government. He writes:

In society the authorities are ordained of God in regard to their office or powers but not in regard to their characters. The chief magistrate is divinely ordained, the office is sacred, but a Hitler who usurps and abuses the office is not divinely ordained, neither are the laws of such a tyrant to be obeyed when they oppose the law of God.

It is the Ulster leader's understanding of Scripture and his identification with the Covenanters that supplies the foundation upon which Ian Paisley constructs his campaign of opposition to Westminster policies which he sees as inimical to Protestant interests in the Province.

Ulster loyalism consolidated: the Orange Tradition

Ian Paisley's identification with the Scottish Covenanters, like the Presbyterian beliefs of many of those who are adherents of the Presbyterian Church in Ireland, or the beliefs of many of the Church of Ireland's members in Ulster, are subsumed within a wider tradition: that of loyalism or Orangeism. The existence of the Orange tradition in Ulster has helped to differentiate the north-east corner of Ireland from the remainder of the island. While it may be an over-simplification to assert that the twin Orange enthusiasms for the Protestant religion and the British Crown motivated the Ulster Unionist movement in the late nineteenth and early twentieth centuries, the militancy which this populist and loyalist tradition injected into those political and social forces in north-east Ireland which sought to maintain the Union during the Home Rule crisis helped to determine the eventual outcome of a struggle which led to the partition of Ireland and the founding of Northern Ireland.

The Orange tradition unifies Ulster Protestants whether, as in Paisley's case, their roots lie in Scotland, or whether their origins can be traced back to the English Puritans, the Huguenots or those of the native Irish who were converted to the reformed faith during the religious revivals that moved Ulster in Plantation times.

The Orange tradition has successfully assimilated waves of Protestant immigration into north-east Ireland over the generations and Paisley uses the flags, symbols and music of the Orange tradition to amplify and project his political message. Louis Gardner was right, therefore, to place Paisley's relationship to this Ulster Protestant tradition in a context which omits any reference to the role of the United Irishmen and the rebellion of 1798. Gardner noted that:

> In politics, Ulster nonconformist ministers have followed two vastly disparate allegiances, the ultra-loyalist and the liberal-nationalist. Paisley represents a contemporary, non-violent version of the Protestant militia phenomenon which first emerged in 1641 and has reappeared in later generations through such media as the Peep O'Day boys, the original Orange Societies and the (Ulster) Volunteers of 1912. Its achievement has been to ensure that when Government has faltered in its obligation to defend the Loyalist garrison, private Ulster citizens always step into the breach to redress the deficiency and fight a soldier's battle, against whatever odds, until the position is stabilised.[7]

Gardner's statement not only serves to illuminate our understanding of the Orange tradition, but Paisley's role within it. The quotation compares closely with the assessment of the noted historian, A. T. Q. Stewart. Writing in *The Narrow Ground*, he identified important characteristics of this Protestant tradition in Ulster, including a radical strain which comes through in Paisley's social concern for underprivileged constituents:

> The Presbyterian is happiest when he is being radical. The austere doctrines of Calvinism, the simplicity of his worship, the democratic government of his church, the memory of the martyred Covenanters, and the Scottish refusal to yield or dissemble – all these incline him to that difficult and cantankerous disposition which is characteristic of a certain kind of political radicalism. His natural instinct is to distrust the outward forms of civil government unless they are consonant with his religious principles. On the other hand, his situation and his history in a predominantly Catholic Ireland have bred in him attitudes which seem opposite to these, making him defensive, intolerant and uncritically loyal to traditions and institutions.[8]

A. T. Q. Stewart's observations have an added importance: they not only give support to the general argument about the role of Ian Paisley and the impact of the Covenanters' ideals, but Stewart's comments do something else as well. Towards the end of this extract from *The Narrow Ground*, reference was made to the Ulster radical's 'natural instinct to distrust the outward forms of civil government', and in the concluding sentence of the quotation the Ulster radical's history was said to 'have bred in him' a defensive and intolerant spirit and an uncritical loyalty to 'traditions and institutions'. These three characteristics of what has been referred to as the Orange tradition, a distrust of government or authority, a defensive or narrow-minded intolerance, and an uncritical loyalty with its implied anti-intellectualism, or at least an unwillingness to contemplate change, are all traits which will resurface as the place of modern American fundamentalism in Paisley's thinking is explored.

The American fundamentalist momentum

Over the years, Ian Paisley's identification with American fundamentalism and his personal empathy with some of the movement's foremost preachers has become increasingly evident, but before discussing how Paisley's close affinity with American fundamentalism evolved, it is useful to define precisely what is meant by the term 'fundamentalist', because the term now has a wide application which includes other religions like Judaism and Islam, although originally fundamentalism was a strictly Protestant phenomenon.

The fundamentalist movement originated in the United States of America at the turn of the century. At that time a reaction set in among conservative Protestants who were responding to some of the more liberal constructions which a new wave of theologians was placing upon the Bible. Conservative theologians and scholars decided to defend the veracity of Scripture, and this led to the 'five fundamentals' being defined at the Presbyterian General Assembly in 1910. Within the next five years a list of doctrines known as 'the Fundamentals' was published.

Over the years a slight shift has taken place in the use of the term fundamentalist, so that the term, according to Wells and Woodbridge in their book *The Evangelicals*, has come to be associated with 'separated bodies (religious institutions, churches practising separation) having inferior educational systems and a polemical outlook'.[9] Wells and Woodbridge elaborated upon the shift in the meaning of the term fundamentalist as follows: 'The term has come in general parlance to represent not only the advocates of the traditional fundamentals but also those who are militant, schismatic, antischolarly, dispensational and premillenarian'. And it is in this limited historical sense that the term is employed.

Ian Paisley seems to have been attracted by the appeal of American fundamentalism at an early stage in his religious ministry. Paisley was in contact with a fundamentalist educational seminary as early as 1954 and the seminary conferred on the young Belfast preacher an honorary degree. By 1957, *The Revivalist*, the official organ of the Free Presbyterian Church as it was styled, was reprinting with approval the published sermons of Dr Bob Jones, founder of the Bob Jones University. Later another honorary degree was conferred on

Dr Paisley by Bob Jones in 1966 and in 1967 Ian Paisley undertook a six week tour of Canada and the United States during which Paisley's close association with his fundamentalist colleagues was consolidated. This transatlantic journey was only one of many undertaken by the Ulster Protestant leader who responded to invitations from his American fundamentalist friends by inviting them to preach in the Martyrs Memorial and at other Free Presbyterian Churches in Ulster.

One significant indication of Ian Paisley's close association with fundamentalists occurred during the World Congress of Fundamentalists held in Edinburgh in June 1976. The Congress published a statement of beliefs and Ian Paisley was one of the five religious leaders who sat on the 'Committee on the Definition of Fundamentalism', as it was called, which drew up the fifteen point statement released to the international press.

Apart from the fellowship which the Ulster Free Presbyterians and these American fundamentalist preachers shared with each other, Rev. Ian Paisley's church sells fundamentalist literature and displays a growing interest in developing the kind of educational institutions which fundamentalist churches had founded in America.

The doctrines of the Free Presbyterian Church have become strongly fundamentalist in character, and this is strikingly confirmed by the use of 'an appeal' at the close of revivalist services when the Free Presbyterian minister, following a well-established and familiar fundamentalist religious practice, calls on sinners to 'decide' for Christ. Calvinists insist that God is sovereign, and that a man lacks the ability to 'decide' for Christ because his will is not 'free' but damaged by sin, and this belief that salvation is from God is often associated with the doctrine of predestination. But the differences between fundamentalism and Calvinism extend beyond the theological issue of the way of salvation to other crucial areas of doctrine. For example, fundamentalists hold to the infallibility of the Bible while some who treasure their Calvinist heritage like the eminent theologian Karl Barth or Professor Torrance of the Church of Scotland, reject the infallibility of the Bible while still regarding the Scriptures as the principal source of authority; this is an illogical position, fundamentalists claim. More importantly, Calvinist theology is necessarily linked to John Calvin's *Institutes of the Christian Religion*,[10] which is a system of theology; fundamentalism lacks such a coherent body of doctrine and to some extent must be regarded as more pragmatic in its theological formulations. This departure of Paisley's Free Presbyterian Church from the Calvinist theology of Presbyterianism provoked former associates of Ian Paisley, like Rev. Jack Glass of Glasgow, and Rev. George Hutton of Larne, into criticism of Paisley's growing enthusiasm for a form of Protestant Christianity which was less rigorous in its theology, and which tended to measure spiritual blessing in the material terms of large congregations and an expanding church income.

Although the theological distinctions between Protestants who are Calvinists and Protestants who are fundamentalists may appear somewhat esoteric to those who have a secular outlook, the significance of this subtle theological debate took on a new importance in 1980 with the emergence of a highly politicised variant of fundamentalism in the United States in the form of fundamentalist pressure groups like the Moral Majority. These religious groups sought to influence the outcome of the Presidential election that year as part of a wider campaign to reverse the liberalising tendencies associated with the permissive society. It is apparent that Ian Paisley's close conformity to the pattern of American fundamentalism has given rise to some noteworthy similarities of style between the political activism of movements like the Moral Majority and the much smaller local fundamentalist influenced phenomenon in Northern Ireland, the Democratic Unionist Party.

For example, Jerry Falwell, the leading figure in the Moral Majority movement, has written a brief foreword to a conservative American political handbook, *The New Right: We Are Ready to Lead*,[11] in which he speaks out on behalf of those Americans who are 'God-fearing', suspicious of the Government in Washington, regard Communism as a serious menace, and who are manifestly patriotic in their enthusiasm for the 'American Way'. Falwell expressed such sentiments when he wrote:

> Too many of our top governmental officials, including judges in high places, legislators, bureaucrats, and politicians, have cared more about getting a vote than about courageously standing for what is right and good for America. Considering that the stability of any group whether it be a family or a nation, rises and falls upon leadership, it is no wonder that we find America depraved, decadent and demoralised today.

Although Jerry Falwell is more ecumenical than Dr Paisley in his willingness to co-operate with like-minded Jews and Roman Catholics associated with his moral crusade, it is worth reflecting that in a similar situation Ian Paisley welcomed Roman Catholic support for his petition against reform of the laws affecting homosexuality. A broad similarity of aims and emphasis exists between politicised fundamentalists in the United States and Ian Paisley's Party; and this is expressed in the commitment of both movements to a patriotic idealism, a distrust of Government, the perception that their liberties are threatened by outside forces, and a determination to resist those changes in society which reflect a liberalisation in moral attitudes.

These general observations are supported by a number of comparisons which may be drawn between specific aspects of the political style which American fundamentalists and Dr Paisley's Party have in common. The BBC's Everyman programme broadcast on 2 November 1980 gave a detailed appraisal of the politicised aspect of American fundamentalism. Dr Henry Kissinger remarked on the programme that the average academic in America had underestimated the strength of evangelical sentiment in the United States. The former American Secretary of State's perception of the movement took into consideration the historical context of the contribution which the 'Protestant tradition of achievement' had made to American society. This was the context in which Dr Kissinger made his assessment that in the Reagan Presidential campaign we were witnessing 'a reaction to the liberal democratic critique'. American senators interviewed on the BBC programme trenchantly criticised the fundamentalists for their political tactics which made use of the 'single issue' and ruthlessly attacked their opponents by attempting to discredit them and by denigrating their family life. These criticisms are identical to the criticisms which Harold McCusker MP voiced about the bitter inter-Unionist faction fight in the Armagh constituency between his Unionist Party supporters and activists in the DUP.

The use of the 'single issue' and of highly charged rhetoric targeted at individual politicians have both been significant facets of Ian Paisley's political style which suggests that there is a close comparison between politicised fundamentalism in the United States and the DUP. Two other features of the moralistic campaign of these fundamentalist pressure groups have been identified. *The Observer* noted that the movement was 'wide open and abjectly vulnerable to authoritarian thought', while *The Guardian*, writing of the Moral Majority's support for Reagan considered that 'facts were treated in a remarkably cavalier fashion'; the tone of these articles echoes sentiments which have previously been encountered in comments made about Ian Paisley's political style.

These observations which the media have passed on America's politicised fundamentalists are similar in content to statements about Protestant attitudes in Northern Ireland, particularly as they are reflected in the DUP, but what is even more striking is the similarity between the sentiments of journalists and earlier criticisms levelled at American fundamentalism in its religious aspect by evangelical theologians. Such criticisms are of special interest not only because there is the inherent suggestion that the fundamentalist characteristics which have been outlined are ingrained features of the movement but because these facets of fundamentalism have more than a passing similarity with A. T. Q. Stewart's description of Protestant radicalism in *The Narrow Ground.*

J. I. Packer in his book *Fundamentalism and the Word of God* has argued that over the years fundamentalism developed a momentum which carried the movement away from its intellectual origins, as a scholarly and theological reaction to the liberal interpretation of the Bible. Packer, noting this change of emphasis which overtook fundamentalism in the 1920s, has remarked that: 'partly in self-defence, the movement developed a pronounced anti-intellectual bias; it grew distrustful of scholarship, sceptical as to the value of reasoning in matters of religion and truculent in its attitude towards the arguments of its opponents'.[12]

Packer's criticism is comparable with a note on fundamentalism given in the *New International Christian Dictionary*, stating that: 'due to the tactics of certain leaders, the fundamentalist image eventually became stereotyped as closed-minded, belligerent and separatistic'.[13] It is not difficult to account for the strong similarity of approach on salient issues and similarity in political technique exhibited by the politicised revivalist preachers of the United States and Ulster, but what seems more remarkable is the comparison which suggests, however tenuously, that there is a similarity of outlook between the adherents of Protestant fundamentalism in the United States and Ulster Protestant radicals, because both groups are generally re-garded as being 'closed-minded', 'defensive', 'belligerent', and 'separatistic'. And although reservations need to be expressed about the differing emphasis which the more conservative American fundamentalists and the socially alert DUP would adopt to issues of state welfare and social betterment, it appears that both movements share many characteristics.

Part of the explanation may be that the American Presbyterian Church was largely the pioneering achievement of Scots-Irish settlers who migrated from Ulster in the mid-eighteenth century. Twentieth century American fundamentalism owes more to Baptist denomina-tions in North America than to Presbyterianism, but fundamental-ism was originally a transdenominational movement and it did not become a vigorous social and ecclesiastical sub-culture on the North American continent without benefitting from Presbyterian influences.

Many of the features which have been described so far are largely negative, but American fundamentalism also has a positive side. It is Ian Paisley's success in adapting these positive characteristics to the Northern Ireland situation which suggests that he has shown considerable skill in bringing about this synthesis between a contemporary American religious phenomenon and Ulster's Orange tradition.

The main features of American fundamentalism are not only exhibited in the Free Presbyterian Church of Ulster but they have also exerted considerable influence over the political style of the DUP. Dr Paisley's Party has shown itself to be a dynamic and energetic Party, strongly emphasising the need for success to its activist supporters, and regularly renewing its commitment to the political struggle by translating each election campaign into a zealots' crusade on the salient issue of the moment whether that be 'security', a Protestant voice in Europe, or achieving devolved powers for a Stormont Assembly.

Ian Paisley's religious beliefs have motivated his larger-than-life revivalist ministry. They have also provided the foundations and intellectual presuppositions upon which the DUP leader constructed his political ideology. It is an ideology which expresses Paisley's determination to defend the Protestant and Unionist cause in Northern Ireland in terms which identify closely with Ulster's Orange tradition and the folk symbols of loyalism. The manner and the verve with which Paisley communicates his beliefs and policies have been adapted from those American fundamentalist circles in which Ian Paisley has moved for more than half a lifetime. One further consequence of Paisley's success in grafting together covenanting roots and fundamentalist zeal has been to give the Ulster leader a theology which is pragmatic and flexible: could a politician ask for anything more?

Implication of Paisley's politics

There are few Westminster politicians and no European MEPs from the United Kingdom who have come in for more sustained criticism than Ian Paisley. The charges made against the DUP leader cover the gamut of political invective, but the most persistent criticism made of Paisley is that he is the leader of a nascent fascist movement in Ulster.

Golo Mann,[14] the eminent German historian, has described the important part that 'opportunism' played in the rise of the Nazi Party. Is it to be assumed that there is some parallel between the Democratic Unionist Party and the Nazis in the Wiemar Republic? There are strong comparisons and there are striking differences, but though opponents of the DUP criticise Dr Paisley in terms that equate the DUP with the Nazi Party, the results are inconclusive.

A detailed comparison of the DUP with the National Front in Britain and the Nazi Party in the 1930s suggests that any attempt to characterise the DUP as a crypto-fascist movement has to overcome problems both of history and philosophy. The DUP's economic policy, such as it is, has been derivative and apart from a parochial emphasis on Northern Ireland's economic needs, the economic programme of the DUP advocates limited state intervention and a mixed economy. There is no attempt to describe the Province's future economic performance in terms that would even remotely conform to the development of a corporate state.

The economic programme of the DUP is quite dissimilar from any economic policy advocated by fascist political parties or movements, while the intellectual roots of the DUP establish that its philosophical origins differ markedly from fascism.

In the matter of political technique, it is better to err on the side of caution. And it is in the techniques which Dr Paisley and his Party employ that opponents of the Ulster loyalist Party discern the silhouette of nascent fascism. The role of Rev. Ian Paisley as party leader and spiritual oversight of the Ulster Free Presbyterian Church has been interpreted as that of a 'Reichsleiter' or dictator. The internal political organisation of the DUP in which leadership from the top rather than democratic initiatives from the rank and file members provides the impetus for the Party, adds weight to the arguments of the Party's detractors.

The tactical use of loyalist bands, of banners, flags and street protest also carries with it an echo of the methods of Naziism in the Weimar Republic or the drum corps and serried ranks of Union Jack-carrying National Front supporters in Britain; there is substantial difficulty with this argument. Mass political demonstrations, the use of bands and political mobilisation at street level are traditional in Ireland; consequently there is a similarity, but too much must not be read into it.

Arguably, the other important similarity of political technique which the DUP shares with Naziism is the build up of the 'fear of encirclement'. Ulster is represented as being threatened from within by the terrorism of the Provisional IRA, the anti-constitutional postures of the SDLP and the treachery of moderate Unionists. The DUP claims that both the Dublin administration and the West-minster Government have malevolent intentions towards the loyal 'democratic majority' in Northern Ireland, and the Party presents a view of a Province under external pressure and internal threat. It has been suggested that by the calculated exploitation of 'the fear of encirclement', Rev. Ian Paisley and the DUP have tried to limit the rational and legitimate political options open not only to the British Government but to those parties in Northern Ireland which strive to channel debate away from the barricades and towards reconciliation.

Dr Paisley's pronouncements which warn of the dangers which confront Ulster loyalists are given added potency by the reality of the Troubles, while policy decisions carried out by the British Government have sometimes been so lacking in candour that they increase the climate of fear and suspicion. The extent to which Ian Paisley is said to exploit a 'fear of encirclement' which bears comparison with Hitler's political technique is also modified by the use which is made of the technique; Paisley's use of the technique is defensive, to consolidate the intransigent, whereas Hitler adopted the technique as an instrument of aggression.

It is also to be observed that denunciations of Rev. Ian Paisley as a fascist have invariably misfired, making little impact on either the Protestant leader or his supporters. When Captain Terence O'Neill made a blistering attack on Ian Paisley in the Chamber at Stormont on 15 June 1966, in which he drew attention to the rise of Paisleyism and the 'parallel in the rise of the Nazis to power' it served only to alienate many of O'Neill's supporters. John Harbinson, commenting upon this in *The Ulster Unionist Party*, has suggested that: 'many in the Unionist Party . . . did not see the parallel. What they saw was an attack on the traditional Unionism of Carson and Craig, who had shown contempt for established authority . . . organised monster processions – and appealed to patriotism.'[15] However, this explanation may not in itself be sufficient to explain why these persistent accusations may actually have added to Paisley's standing among Unionist voters. Equal consideration has to be given to the proposition that for years, Irish nationalists, with an unmistakable gift for hyperbole, had castigated the Unionist governments of Northern Ireland and their supporters as 'fascists'. A classic example is quoted in *Irish Action* where reference is made to a speech by De Valera in Liverpool on 10 October 1948. There De Valera stated that: '. . . The Ulster Unionists talk of their hatred of Nazi-ism and Fascist rule, but it was established there (in Northern Ireland) before it came on the continent'. By denouncing Paisley as a fascist, O'Neill was paying the Moderator of the Free Presbyterian Church a back-handed compliment, the import of which was to confirm Paisley's assertion that he was a 'traditional Unionist'. Furthermore, the attempts to categorise the DUP as a crypto-fascist movement oversimplify and smudge contrasting forms of political leadership, operation and organisation.

In fusing Fundamentalism to the loyalist or Orange tradition, Dr Paisley has created an ideology which is more flexible than that of the rival Unionist Party. Paisley's more pragmatic approach to highly salient issues in Northern Ireland politics is no more clearly demonstrated than on the continuance of the Union itself. Over a decade, spanning the years between the fall of the Stormont

Parliament in 1972 and the emergence of Jim Prior's 'Rolling Devolution' initiative in October 1982, the DUP produced a variety of responses to this crucial issue of how to maintain the Union.

It is possible to explain this flexibility, which the DUP has shown towards the issue of the Union, as an inevitable reaction to shifts in the policy of successive British Governments towards the Province, and as an attempt to outflank Westminster's commitment to the principle of power sharing. However, the more likely explanation is that the defence of the Protestant interest has a higher salience for the DUP than maintenance of the Union. From this perspective, the DUP's reactions and apparent inconsistencies on this issue are transformed into an entirely consistent and instinctive determination on the part of Ian Paisley and his Party first and foremost to defend Protestant Ulster, and thereafter to promote policies whether in the form of total integration, devolution or, ultimately, independence, which seem most likely to secure and safeguard Ulster's Protestant and separatist cause at any given point in time. In this respect, Paisley's approach to Unionism represents a departure from the position adopted by the Official Unionist Party and indicates the degree to which the fundamentalist, Orange synthesis has modified the DUP's perception of Northern Ireland's relationship with the rest of the United Kingdom.

It is only by examining in detail the variety of responses which the DUP has made to this issue and by contrasting the Party's policies with those of the rival Official Unionist Party over the period that the prior claims which Protestantism and loyalism exert over the Party become discernible.

Dr Paisley and Desmond Boal announced their support for a policy of total integration of Ulster with the rest of the United Kingdom in the aftermath of the Heath Government's action in abolishing the Stormont Parliament. By advocating a policy of 'total integration', the DUP took a calculated step which had a two-fold objective. Firstly, by campaigning for total integration the DUP hoped to outflank the Official Unionist Party and further discredit the Stormont Parliament which was suspected of having 'misruled' the Province for fifty years. This meant that the DUP stood aside from the controversy surrounding the demise of Stormont, not because of any thoroughgoing analysis of the failure of the Stormont Parliament as an institution but in order to achieve a tactical objective. The political gain was that the collapse of Stormont undermined the standing, power of patronage, leadership and recruiting powers of the Official Unionist Party. Secondly, the leaders of the DUP believed that 'total integration' would nullify the various diplomatic attempts by the government of the Irish Republic to involve itself in any future political settlement of what is termed the Northern Ireland question.

However, the concept of total integration provides a classic example of a policy which, though it is worthy of detailed consideration, fails to awaken popular interest because it has been defined in inaccurate terminology. The term 'total integration' seemed to suggest that Ulster would be absorbed or in some sense 'constitutionally digested' by the Westminster Parliament; and this at a time when many loyalists were highly critical of the Government's inept handling of the continuing civil disturbances in the Province. Whatever merit 'total integration' might possess as a strategy for resolving the constitutional uncertainty in Northern Ireland, many loyalists refused to give consideration to the proposal because it seemed to them that their first duty was to defend the good name of the recently prorogued Parliament at Stormont and to campaign tenaciously for its restoration.

Consequently the DUP was soon to discover that it had committed itself to an innovatory policy which was not widely understood by those loyalist voters whom the new Party hoped to attract. Nevertheless the DUP did attempt to press the merits of the case for 'total integration' upon the Unionist population. Oliver Gibson, who was the Chairman of the County Tyrone Democratic Unionist Association, wrote a pamphlet, *We Are Not Divided*, in which Paisley and Boal's joint call for integration was strongly supported. Gibson wrote:

Every Ulsterman would dearly wish to have the parliament and powers of pre-1969. However, we must be realistic. It was the Official Unionist regime which gave away these vital powers. How can the same people demand them back? A tenth rate Stormont is no safeguard to the majority who wish to remain within the Union.

To this prominent member of the DUP, the policy of integration pursued by Boal and Paisley was 'realistic'; it also faced up to the problem that the Official Unionist Party had failed to uphold the Stormont parliamentary system. In addition, Gibson surmised that, in the long term, the Unionist population would not be willing to settle for a 'Stormont of administrative status' and that, therefore, total integration was the solution which would best secure the interests of the majority.

The DUP's early enthusiasm for total integration was short-lived and the Party began to edge itself back towards a position on the Union which was compatible with the sentiments of the loyalist grass-roots. During this same period an intense struggle continued with the Official Unionist Party, the moderate leadership of which took encouragement from the belief that a restoration of the Stormont Parliament was possible provided the Unionist Party gave evidence of a willingness to share power with the SDLP.

The formation of the United Ulster Unionist Council in January 1974 provided a formal structure for a growing coalition of interests between the DUP, the Unionist Party right wing led by Harry West, and William Craig's Vanguard. The UUUC confirmed its commitment to a restored Stormont without power sharing at Executive level in the Northern Ireland Convention Report, to which the DUP lent its unequivocal support. Though the DUP abandoned total integration as party policy, the concept remained a matter of lively debate within the Official Unionist Party because Enoch Powell continued to insist that integration offered the best way forward for Ulster.

By the late 1970s, therefore, the DUP appeared to have settled on a policy which strongly supported a devolved government for the Province, but Dr Paisley soon provided evidence that his approach to the Union was pragmatic. This was illustrated by the repeated calls (on 26 March 1978 and again on 2 July 1979) which Dr Paisley made for a referendum on the Northern Ireland situation to be held throughout the United Kingdom. These calls for a referendum are in accordance with two of the characteristics of the DUP's ideology: the Party's distrust of government and its willingness to abide by the will of the people as expressed through the ballot box.

It may even be suggested that in calling for a referendum, Dr Paisley was able to merge two components of the Party's ideology. Firstly, the referendum demand underlined the DUP's commitment to the democratic ideal; what more noble and foolproof way of resolving the Ulster crisis could there be than to let the people of England, Scotland and Wales vote on the problem? The proposal of a referendum suggests that the DUP was confident that it could campaign successfully on the issue. What outcome, though, did the DUP want to achieve? This is where the second component has to be considered. A referendum could provide a bridge between the Union which has existed between Northern Ireland and the rest of the United Kingdom since 1922, and some new inchoate constitutional arrangement, perhaps taking the form of an autonomous or independent Ulster.

Rev. Ian Paisley's demand for a referendum as a constitutional device to break the political deadlock over the Province's future political development fused the DUP's public advocacy of the democratic principle with the independence of mind and mistrust of government associated with the Ulster Protestant radical tradition. Though the Alliance Party and the Official Unionist Party stigmatised Rev. Ian Paisley's referendum scheme as prejudicial to the

Union, the DUP had reason to believe that the outcome of such a constitutional device would not damage the political fortunes of the DUP. If the vote in Britain confirmed Northern Ireland's position within the United Kingdom, the DUP would emerge as the champions of the Union who had put the issue to the ultimate test, the people, but should the vote reflect a mood of withdrawal or rejection of the Province then in Rev. Ian Paisley's words: 'I could see the way ahead as an independent Ulster'.

The Dublin Summit in December 1980 between the British Prime Minister, Margaret Thatcher, and the Taoiseach of the Irish Republic, Charles Haughey, caused anxiety in Northern Ireland, and the issue of the Union once again came to the forefront of the political debate in Ulster. The run-up to the local government elections of May 1981 presented Dr Paisley with an opportunity to underline the message of the 'Carson Trail' and at a press conference to launch the DUP's local government manifesto, the Party proclaimed itself to be 'granite hard for the Union'. The phrase echoed an earlier sentiment expressed by Mrs Thatcher in an attempt to allay Unionist fears that she was 'rock hard for the Union'; the implication of Rev. Ian Paisley's comment was that while Mrs Thatcher's willingness to enter into secret talks about the future of Northern Ireland with the Haughey Government in Dublin called into question the value of her assurance, Paisley would prove to be the authentic voice of those determined to defend the Union. Once again an intuitive 'distrust of government' modified the responses of the DUP. At the same time, the fact that Dr Paisley was launching an electoral campaign in which he would seek to confirm the personal endorsement he received at the European elections of the previous June injected a 'democratic' dimension into the episode.

The DUP's local government manifesto pledged the Party to work for the restoration of the Stormont Parliament; the commitment was as unqualified as it was unequivocal. Although total integration had long ago ceased to form any part of the DUP's political programme, what was noticeable was that in the eight year interval the DUP had failed to formulate any critical reappraisal of the Stormont parliamentary system. The DUP manifesto held out the possibility that the restoration of the Stormont Parliament, with the DUP returned as the majority party, would bring stability and progress to the Province. The Party appeared to adopt the position that its acceptance of voting by Proportional Representation (which had worked to the DUP's advantage) and commitment to co-operate with the SDLP in the committee system of any future devolved institution represented a serious attempt to meet some of the demands of the minority. The DUP, however, remained opposed to the concept of 'partnership in government', which suggests that the kind of devolved institution favoured by the Party would lack the stability necessary to 'secure the Union'. It remained an open question whether an assembly would prove any more adequate a constitutional mechanism for resolving the intractable problems of Northern Ireland in the future than Stormont had between 1922 and 1972.

The parochialism of the political attitudes which the Stormont Parliament had fostered, and the limited political competence of many of the representatives who served that parliamentary institution suggested that however much a devolved administration appealed to a substantial section of the loyalist community, the negative forces which such an assembly encouraged would crystallise into a new rigidity of attitude.

Within eighteen months these observations were put to the test when the Northern Ireland Secretary of State, James Prior, formally opened the new Northern Ireland Assembly. The DUP welcomed the initiative, claiming that the Prior proposals offered the possibilities of 'getting power back into Ulster hands', and of eventual majority rule. However, the DUP had refused to address itself to the problem that the new institution lacked legitimacy as both the SDLP and Provisional Sinn Fein had boycotted the institution. The DUP's determination to achieve a full restoration of majority rule was not of assistance to the Government which had to face the dilemma posed by an Assembly which had been boycotted by the minority section of the community. Although there had been dramatic changes of stance in the DUP's policy towards the Union between 1972 and 1982, each pragmatic shift in Paisley's politics had sought to keep Protestant interests in Ulster uppermost.

Another issue which has been influenced by the innovative ideology of the DUP is that of Unionist unity. Although the Protestants of Northern Ireland have shown a marked tendency toward division and discord throughout history, the enthusiasm for Protestant or Unionist unity is well ingrained in the loyalists' political consciousness. Indeed, it could be argued that, paradoxically, one of the major themes of the Orange tradition is the concept of a united Protestant movement. This attachment to unity finds expression in the sentiments of loyalist politicians and more especially in the symbolism of the Orange Order, with its banners proclaiming 'unity is strength' and testifying to a Protestant brotherhood 'cemented with love'. But this loyalist grass-roots desire for Unionist unity has drawn only a limited response from Dr Paisley, whose rise to political prominence was achieved outside the established Ulster institutions of the Unionist Party, the Orange Order or the mainstream Protestant denominations. Ian Paisley's political experience as an

Ian Paisley reviews members of the 'Third Force', November 1981.

Paisley's 'Day of Action' in Belfast City Centre, 1981.

Protesting against 'It's a Knockout' on a Sunday, April 1981.

outsider who succeeded in gaining political power may provide an important insight into why the DUP leader appears to under-estimate the value to be derived from a coalition or union of loyalist political interests, while his wholehearted commitment to fundamentalism with its strong emphasis on separation suggests that Paisley's experiences have been reinforced by his religious principles. It seems probable that the separatist emphasis in Dr Paisley's spiritual ministry has been transmitted into the political arena and the sequel to this is that Rev. Ian Paisley's enthusiasm for separation and his achievement in gaining power outside the established channels have created obstacles to the achievement of a reconstructed Unionist Party. Dr Paisley's attitude is in contrast with that of Dr Henry Cooke, the early nineteenth century Ulster Presbyterian leader, who made the unity of Church of Ireland adherents and Ulster Presbyterians an integral part of his public, and often highly political, ministry.

How the DUP's ideology stifles internal dissent

The fundamentalist characteristics of 'closed-mindedness', 'defensiveness' and 'anti-intellectualism' have placed the leader of the Party in an exalted position of authority. Dr Paisley is regarded by his followers as the one who knows best, the leader raised up in the Providence of God to take his stand for Ulster in the crisis hour, and whose pronouncements on policy are not to be challenged, except in those circumstances where it is clearly indicated that the leader has not committed himself to a particular line of action and that consequently the issue is still open for discussion.

The Party's 'closed-mindedness' has given the DUP an internal cohesion which has tended to discourage dissent while producing a psychological response among the membership which is perhaps best described as the Lundy syndrome. Lundy was the archetypal traitor to the Ulster Protestant cause and, as a result of his dishonourable conduct during the siege of Derry in 1688, his name had entered the Ulster vocabulary as an epithet for the most reprehensible forms of treachery. In the early and belligerent stages of Rev. Ian Paisley's campaign against the Unionist governments at Stormont in the 1960s, eminent Unionist politicians and Prime Ministers such as Captain Terence O'Neill, Major James Chichester-Clark and Brian Faulkner were all subjected to virulent denunciations as 'Lundies', betrayers of the Ulster cause.

It was not long before Dr Paisley had re-invested the word 'Lundy' with declamatory resonance and the term of abuse has gained wide currency throughout Northern Ireland. This rebounded on the DUP, because before long inner-party meetings of the Party would sometimes generate an inhibited and claustrophobic attitude in which moderating responses to the issues under discussion were never offered for debate. Party activists who might have privately entertained less extreme views feared being denounced as 'Lundies' – traitors – not only to the Party but to Ulster. Some DUP adherents believed that the Party would prove to be the political saviour of the Province and to them any sign of political deviance raised suspicions about the 'loyalty' of their more open-minded party colleagues.

Willie Wilson, a North Antrim local government councillor, provides an interesting study of the manner in which DUP activists could find themselves isolated within the Party's ranks and effectively quarantined away from the internal decision making processes of the Party. Councillor Wilson failed to conform to the pattern of allegiant responses usually associated with DUP councillors: he was not a member of the Free Presbyterian Church, and while such church membership is not a specific requirement for those who aspire to represent the DUP in local politics, the problem became acute in this case because Councillor Wilson was not noticeably vigorous in his identification with any other evangelical sect or denomination; Councillor Wilson also credited himself with having an independent turn of mind, and he submitted a series of articles to the *Ballymena Observer* in March 1976. In the articles the DUP Councillor put on record his own personal political philosophy. In a letter to the writer, the North Antrim Councillor expressed his hope that the content of the articles would gain 'a degree of acceptance on the other side', that is, across the sectarian divide.

Articles such as those submitted to the *Ballymena Observer* indicated a willingness to engage in rational debate and an attempt to win a wide basis of support, and these attitudes conflicted with the DUP party members' adherence to separatistic and exclusivist doctrines. Willie Wilson's deviance from the norm resulted in his being perceived as an 'outsider' and this resulted in his influence over local party decisions being seriously diminished.

Another example of this Lundy syndrome occurred in the case of the DUP Mayor of Larne, Councillor Roy Beggs. In October 1980, the Mayor saw it as his civic duty to participate in a cross border courtesy visit to Dun Laoghaire, even though such cross border contacts had been specifically prohibited by the DUP's rules, and this led to Beggs being disciplined by the Party. Councillor Beggs was a highly articulate and respected member of Larne Council who would undoubtedly have presented a competent Unionist case to any social or political gathering to which he might have been invited in the Irish Republic. When account is taken of lack of detailed information which many citizens of the Irish Republic have about the political circumstances in the North such meetings could only prove beneficial. The DUP's Executive thought otherwise, and Roy Beggs was suspended by the inner caucus. Although the suspension held out the prospect that after a cooling-off period Beggs would be entitled to regain full membership, the suspension signalled that the Party could not reconcile its inward-looking ideology with Beggs' concept of Unionism.

Party members who might sympathise with a moderate stance on salient issues such as provocative street demonstrations, or the question of Sabbath Observance in a particular local government area, face the difficulty that they must argue their case within the Party under the inhibiting psychological discipline of the Lundy syndrome. A heated exchange or an argument pressed too closely could create a situation in which a DUP councillor or party member might suddenly find himself crossing an invisible line which his local fellow party members see as separating them from those whose policies would weaken the 'Protestant' cause and endanger Ulster.

The psychological implications of the DUP's closed-mindedness have been described in terms of a 'Lundy syndrome' but this defensive outlook is complemented by an anti-intellectualism which may have cramped the DUP's range of options and which has undoubtedly intensified the parochial attitude which pervades the Party. This attitude has isolated the Party from those who might otherwise be sympathetic to the DUP in Great Britain and, as a result, the intense alienation experienced by the loyalist population has inevitably increased.

Paisley's alienation from mainstream evangelicalism

In the September 1981 issue of the evangelical journal *Themelios* David Kibble wrote an article entitled 'The Kingdom of God and Christian Politics'; the article called for a commitment by Christians to political activism in Great Britain and the author stated his grounds for believing that a Christian's participation in the political life of the nation has Scriptural authority. One of the matters arising from Kibble's article is relevant to this book. Kibble referred to Northern Ireland in passing but he omitted any reference to the DUP, the inference to be drawn from this being that the writer did not perceive the DUP to be a Christian party which had anything to offer or to teach other Christians in the United Kingdom. And in this Kibble was simply following a general line adopted by many evangelical writers in Scotland, England and Wales who have detached themselves from their evangelical brethren in Ulster in general and from the political activism of Dr Paisley in particular. A further example of this disassociation from the political style of Ian Paisley also appeared in print in 1981. Dr MacLeod, writing in the magazine of the Free Church of Scotland, attempted to draw a distinction between Paisley's politics and the sentiments of other evangelicals in Ulster, to whom he offered the following advice: 'Many – perhaps the vast majority – of these (Ulster) evangelicals are already completely out of sympathy with Paisley's methods and objectives. But they must stand up and say so. The time has come to isolate him, and to denounce him as a man who has shown a callous intransigence beyond that of any Roman Catholic politician.'

The writers of both these articles would hold to theological propositions which approximate to those of Ian Paisley, and all three could be described in general terms as evangelical Protestants; despite this apparent common ground, Paisley's style of politics had alienated Dr MacLeod and had no relevance for David Kibble despite his interest in Christian activism. This reaction to or disassociation from the politics of the DUP has much more to do with Paisley's conduct than with an anti-intellectualism which is characteristic of the Party. Such articles demonstrate that the politicised Protestantism of Ian Paisley has failed to attract the sympathies of those who ought to have been most receptive to an appeal from Ulster's evangelical Christians.

In fact there is nothing surprising about this, because an earlier critic of Ian Paisley's political style was the Ulster-born industrialist, Sir Frederick Catherwood (presently a member of the European Parliament). Catherwood considered the political crisis in Northern Ireland in a pamphlet entitled *Christian Duty in Ulster Today*, in which he wrote: 'There has been a vacuum in the teaching about the Christian's place in society and into that vacuum stepped men with a fixed and narrow purpose and . . . their wrong but dogmatic view has forced its way to the front'. There is no doubt that this is intended as a criticism of Rev. Ian Paisley's boisterous political crusade, and to remove any doubt from the reader's mind as to the target of his criticism, Catherwood alluded a little later in the same passage to 'wild voices' (sic). Evangelicals of the Catherwood school differentiate their political commitment from the reactionary and dynamic activism of Dr Paisley and the DUP.

Turning to the United States of America, the discussion becomes more complex. There, Protestant philosophies have been influenced by the traditional attitude to participation adopted by evangelicals accustomed to working with a British-style parliamentary system, but Americans have also been open to the political perceptions of Reformed theologians on the continent of Europe. The consequence of this is an interesting dichotomy between fundamentalists who act as moralistic pressure groups or react to the 'communist threat' and those who theorise about what the Christian's role in the political life of contemporary society ought to be. If we concentrate upon contemporary political trends within evangelical circles in North America and Great Britain significant similarities of attitude emerge.

This has occurred because in both the political systems middle-class evangelical intellectuals have theorised about the Christian's role in politics, while the more populist fundamentalists have shown a greater willingness to participate in the system. But the inadequacy, the lack of rationality, in the theoretical position of such fundamentalists has left them open to the charge that they use the tactics of the demagogue.

The problem is that in making the transition from the role of a revivalist preacher expounding an authoritative message to that of a politician, fundamentalists like Ian Paisley or Jerry Falwell carry into the political arena some of the trappings and techniques of their preaching ministry: the use of emotion, colourful language and the ability to dominate an audience through the use of oratory. It is this blurring of his preaching style with political techniques which has provided Paisley's critics with the opportunity to castigate him as a demagogue.

Despite the accusation of demagoguery, his oratorical skills give the politically motivated fundamentalist greater power and one dismal consequence of this is that other evangelical Christians in Northern Ireland who hold differing political views and who might endorse imaginative approaches to the divisions in the Province stifle their own views for fear of being denounced from either the pulpit of the Martyrs Memorial Church or from the hustings.

Another alternative evangelical voice to that of Paisley is Jacques Ellul, who has been described as having been 'of tremendous influence among many of the more radical young evangelicals'. Ellul is a prolific writer whose range of interests includes sociology and theology. Ellul argues that it is no part of the Christian's task to propound a Christian political theory, and he rejects the concepts both of a Christian culture or a normative Christian social ethic.

Ellul's writings on the inter-related themes of Christian apologetics and contemporary society are speculative and non-exegetical in their application of texts drawn from the Bible; and consequently Ellul is not to be easily identified with a specific Protestant theological system. He is reformed and Protestant in his convictions and methodology but he propounds a form of radical Christian individualism which has been described as 'Christian anarchism'.

For these reasons it is to be noted that the application of some of Ellul's practical views on the Christian's role in society would not simply break with the established political pattern in Northern Ireland, but it would be rejected by the DUP as a heretical form of Protestant thinking.

The radical nature of Ellul's thought is well exemplified in his work *The Ethics of Freedom*; there he states: 'If Christians are to be in political life to bear witness, if this is in truth their only motive, then Christians are needed in all parties and movements. Only in this way can the scandal of the political divisions of Christians be avoided.'[16] However, as this analysis of the DUP's ideology indicates, members of the Party are motivated not only to 'bear witness' but to sustain other political objectives as well. Like activists in other Unionist parties, who also testify to their Protestant principles, the members of the DUP have been mobilised in response to a range of ideological commitments, and it is other political attitudes which mask their Christianity. In addition, in considering Ellul's argument, mention should also be made of the fact that in conservative theological circles in Ulster the 'scandal of the political divisions of Christians' is not an issue which weighs heavily on the conscience. This presents serious obstacles to an application of Ellul's practical Christian ethics in Ulster.

Ellul then extends his argument as follows:

> If Christians take up differing positions knowing that these are only human, and having it as their primary goal to bear witness to Jesus Christ wherever they are, their splitting up into various movements, far from manifesting the incompetence of Christian thought or the inconsistency of faith, will be a striking expression of Christian freedom. For in effect the result is that Christians join different parties with the same motive, namely, that of proclaiming Jesus Christ explicitly to their neighbours. Hence they are more united among themselves by their faith than they are with their political associates. This is what really counts.

There is a second difficulty here which becomes apparent: both Roman Catholic Irish nationalists and Ulster loyalists invest their particularistic and exclusive aspirations with divine approval; consequently there is no sense in which Unionist and Irish nationalist ideologues comprehend that their 'differing positions . . . are only human'. Nevertheless it is transparently obvious that Jacques Ellul's 'Christian anarchism' brings to the problems of political violence in Northern Ireland a radical call to bear witness to Jesus Christ in disassociation from the cultural imperatives of both Unionism and Irish nationalism.

The Dutch philosopher, Herman Dooyeweerd, establishes a more concrete theory for Christian political action than the atomistic Christian idealism of Jacques Ellul. Dooyeweerd explains the rise of Christian parties as a consequence of 'the insight that in the last instance the struggle between the political standpoints is ruled by an unbridgeable contrast between the religious basic motives'.[17] He specifically excludes the development of what he refers to as 'the old English dual party system' of liberalism and conservatism from this acknowledgement of 'the deeper fundamentals of the party principle'. For Dooyeweerd, the political struggle is between the totalitarian political ideologies and the anti-totalitarian political standpoints; in other words, the political cleavage is between a Christian worldview and the ideologies of atheistic socialism and Marxism; there is no attempt to place the political contest in the arena of Reformation and counter-Reformation theology.

Dooyeweerd identifies a spiritual crisis within the Western culture and views secularisation as contributing to the advancement of anti-Christian political trends. To reverse this drift and to educate the electors into an awareness of the need to restate a basic Christian apologia, Dooyeweerd calls for a 'Christian party-formation on a non-ecclesiastical basis'.

He elaborates upon the nature of Christian political parties and regards the 'Anti-Revolutionary Party' in the Netherlands as a model for those Christian parties which achieve genuine independence from ecclesiastical authority. As this is not always the case, contrasting examples are enumerated. Dooyeweerd believes that the formation of factions within a church for the purpose of political association cannot be justified. He contends that misunderstanding about the inner nature of the Church as compared with political parties is occasionally expressed by 'political parties which have bound themselves to a particular ecclesiastical confession, or to the guidance of a church authority, or strive after a privileged position of a particular church'. Finally, Dooyeweerd states that the term ecclesiastical parties can also be used of those parties 'which have expressly bound themselves to a Christian political belief in the formerly defined sense, without accepting any ecclesiastical binding'.

The DUP does not associate itself with a corpus of Christian political theory in any clearly defined sense. The Christianity, or the Christian causes, which the DUP seeks to uphold in the political life of Ulster are Christian causes identified as worthy of support by the Free Presbyterian Church and Rev. Ian Paisley in his role as Moderator of the denomination. Secondly, there is confusion in the minds of both the DUP spokesmen and members as to where the line between the Christian witness of the Free Presbyterian Church ends and the political action of the DUP begins. This dualism is in no way negated by the fact that membership of the DUP is not restricted to Free Presbyterians. When, therefore, Dooyeweerd acknowledges the possibility of 'a serious confusion' arising between 'the inner nature of a Church and that of a political party', we have to examine whether this aspect of this study can have any relevance to the DUP. In so far as the DUP is inherently bound 'to the particular confession of the Free Presbyterian Church of Ulster', no DUP member could publicly advocate a liberalisation of the 'Ulster Sabbath' or homosexual reform, and as the leadership of the Party is vested in the person of Rev. Ian Paisley, that is, the DUP looks 'to the guidance of a Church authority', then it becomes apparent that Dooyeweerd's analysis is relevant to the DUP.

Dooyeweerd's general observations also suggest that there are aspects of the philosophy of the DUP which the Professor might criticise as being inappropriate to the inner nature of a Christian party. He foresees, for example, that essential political convictions of party members may be endangered by 'a dictatorial power-formation of an elite or a leader, in consequence of an overstrained party discipline'. Dooyeweerd also counsels against 'the competition for the favour of the voters by deceitful slogans and promises'. This last point must mean that there are ethical considerations which must guide a party in the formulation of policy if it is not to abandon party principle in favour of opportunism. Dooyeweerd regards opportunistic parties as lacking 'a firm basis of political principles', and doubts whether such parties will not suffer from a weakened structure due to the absence of any stable convictions amongst their members. As the activists of the DUP exhibit a very high degree of moralistic fervour and conviction, it is difficult to conclude that Dooyeweerd's strictures on 'opportunism' could be applied, in this instance, to the DUP.

There are two further problems which arise from this discussion. Firstly, Calvin taught in the following quotation that ultimate political authority derives from God, and therefore the demagogue, by courting popular support, subverts the relationship established by the Providence of God, between those in government and the governed:

For (Paul) states both that power is an ordinance of God (Rom. 13:2) and that there are no powers except those ordained by God (Rom. 13:1). Further, that princes are ministers of God, for those doing good unto praise; for those doing evil, avengers unto wrath (Rom. 13:3–4). To this may be added the examples of holy men, of whom some possessed kingdoms, as David, Josiah, and Hezekiah; others, lordships, as Joseph and Daniel; others, civil rule among a free people, as Moses, Joshua, and the judges. The Lord has declared his approval of their offices. Accordingly, no one ought to doubt that civil authority is a calling, not only holy and lawful before God, but also the most sacred and by far the most honourable of all callings in the whole life of mortal men.[18]

And it is in accordance with such an argument that an article published in the *Journal of Christian Reconstruction* warned against 'the generally accepted way to stay alive, politically speaking, to seek to please either the power brokers or the greatest number of constituents'. Catherwood also emphasises that the Christian's belief in democracy is to be constrained by a higher principle: that government of men rests on the authority of God.

And this approach has also been endorsed by Norman De Jong in his book *The Christian and Democracy* in which he concluded: 'God has instituted government in which He places some persons in authority over others. The authority which comes to expression, then, is not derived from the consent of the governed, but is delegated by the God who is omnipotent. From Him comes all power and authority.'[19]

Rev. Ian Paisley, by appeasing some of the least desirable qualities in the Ulster Protestant electorate, has invited criticism from other Protestants who urge that the politics of the demagogue ought to be shunned by the Christian political activist.

Another criticism inherent in the DUP's endorsement of what has every appearance of being a demagogic campaign is an ethical one. The Christian is exhorted in the Bible to measure his words with care, and to refrain from 'bearing false witness against his neighbour' (Exod. 20:16). Rev. Ian Paisley and the DUP behave in a way which suggests that there are few restraints on the kind of abuse with which the DUP chooses to lambast its political opponents.

Now these demagogic tactics, and the massed street rallies which accompany them, are a well documented feature of the will to power in politics; the criticism is not that the DUP uses such tactics, but more precisely, that members of the DUP, having made moralistic claims about themselves and their policies, then contradict their well publicised Christian convictions by the unscrupulous use of rhetoric. And this criticism is levelled not just at the person of the DUP leader, but also at many of his Party who demonstrate a similar recourse to bellicose political action on the street and at the shop-floor level.

This facet of the DUP's political operations can only be understood and rationalised by recognising a certain antinomian ambivalence within the Christian thinking of the Free Presbyterian Church and the DUP which permits such activists to use vehement and denunciatory language, that the greater good, the maintenance of 'Protestant Ulster' might be secured.

There is, though, another of the DUP's characteristics which Dooyeweerd disapproves of, and that is the deference and loyalty which many DUP members show to their leader. Dooyeweerd asserts that the 'politico-ethical solidarity' of party members 'can never imply a blind obedience and self-surrender to the Party's interests and insights'. He concludes that such self-surrender is evidence of a 'totalitarian party-discipline' which in turn has its origins 'in a pseudo-religious commitment to the party's totalitarian political ideology, which includes the belief in its infallibility'.

It is the conviction of many DUP militants that their Party has, single-handedly, sustained the fight to preserve Ulster's identity. This has now promoted a form of super-loyalty among some of the Party's adherents, and led them to abstain in crucial elections such as the Fermanagh and South Tyrone by-election in April 1981, when Harry West, the Official Unionist candidate, was narrowly defeated by Bobby Sands, the H Blocks protester. By abstaining these DUP zealots proved that their 'loyalty' was untainted by any hint of compromise with Official Unionism. Jean Coulter, a former member of the Northern Ireland Assembly, has stated that this Paisleyite reluctance to vote for Official Unionist candidates in first past the post elections is well established and that supporters of Rev. Ian Paisley would abstain rather than vote for another Unionist who did not measure up to their estimation of loyalism.

Such a belief in the infallibility of the DUP is upheld by party activists and public figures alike, as the following comments made by David Calvert in his history of the DUP illustrates: 'The Democratic Unionists have pioneered the loyalist cause and have been foremost in galvanising the Unionist electorate for Ulster's deliverance'. This uncritical support for the Party recalls Dooyeweerd's reference to 'blind obedience', and helps to distinguish the Ulster Protestant party from the ideal kind of Christian party which Dooyeweerd advocates as having both justification and relevance in the face of what he terms the 'present spiritual crisis of Western culture'.

The 'antinomian ambivalence' within the thinking of the Free Presbyterian Church and the DUP, which allows the Party to exploit vehement rhetoric in pursuit of its political goals, may well be another consequence of Dr Paisley's pragmatic theology. These ethical problems seldom trouble the ranks of the DUP leader's supporters. Ian Paisley 'speaks out for the loyalists'; it is the man with the message that the loyalists crowd in to hear.

Dr Paisley's role, therefore, as both spiritual leader of the Free Presbyterian Church and leader of the DUP is of great importance, because at critical moments in the evolution of the DUP the Party's development has been modified because Paisley was able to call upon the resources of the Protestant sect which he leads to provide what could be termed logistic support for the Party. This being the case, an insight into the personality of the party leader himself becomes essential.

Ian Paisley's charisma: from gospel appeal to populist support

The personality of Ian Paisley overarches the Party which he leads. What kind of man is Ian Paisley and what are his political aspirations? Ian Paisley's character is full of so many paradoxes and contradictions that an answer to these two direct questions is far from easy. Ken Heskin has noted that Paisley's personality 'defies simplistic analysis',[20] and Heskin was unable to arrive at a firm conclusion as to the motivating forces in Paisley's life.

Paisley's career is open to the interpretation that he has imposed his self-proclaimed leadership on Ulster's loyalists, and that his electoral successes have retrospectively validated an assertion of this right to lead. Paisley seems at times both to misunderstand the relationship between the Free Church and the DUP and to play down his role as leader.

A striking illustration of Dr Paisley's attitude to the relationship between the Church and Party is derived from personal experience. When it became obvious that my days within the DUP were numbered, I asked Dr Paisley, on the doorstep of his manse, whether my departure from the Party would affect my membership of the Free Presbyterian Church. Paisley seemed taken aback by this question and he replied by insisting that the Free Presbyterian Church and the DUP were distinct entities; and in theoretical terms this is the situation because adherence to the Free Presbyterian Church does not confer rights of membership in the DUP. In the event, the sequel to this political row with Dr Paisley was a break in fellowship with the Free Presbyterian Church and this personal experience conforms to a more generally observed pattern in which activists who were members of both the Church and the Party found that they were unable to continue in fellowship with the Church once they had split with the Party.

In the course of the House of Commons debate following the Hillsborough Agreement signed on 15 November 1985, Ian Paisley provided an insight into his own understanding of the relationship between himself and the people: 'The best thing for a man in this place (House of Commons) is to know that his people are for him. The important thing is that the grass roots that I represent know that I represent them the way they should be represented.' Is this an important clue to Paisley's political role in Northern Ireland? Is

Paisley's career that of a spokesman, a representative voice, rather than that of a leader of vision who will strike out for new territory knowing that where he leads others will follow?

Those who oppose Paisley's politics or reject his theological presuppositions find little difficulty in summing up the Ulster loyalist leader: to Paisley's critics he is nothing more than a charlatan and the apparent inconsistencies in his behaviour are held up as evidence of an underlying hypocrisy in the Free Presbyterian Moderator's behaviour.

This hostile view of Paisley cannot explain Paisley's hold over the affections and imagination of so many ordinary Ulster voters who respond to Paisley in a way that accords him the status of a folk hero. Paisley's photograph beams down from the wall of the living room, his portrait is lovingly painted on Lambeg drums, stories about his latest comings and goings are recounted enthusiastically and he is looked upon by many humble loyalists as a man who not only responds to circumstances as they would respond if they could, but whose brash and aggressive approach to authority has placed him in a unique position to affect and improve the circumstances of ordinary people.

An insight into this facet of Paisley's populist appeal has been provided by Wallace Thompson. In this case, however, Thompson stands as the representative of all those who have spent any length of time in Ian Paisley's company. Thompson and Paisley had spent a long day together in rural Ulster on a fund raising trip on behalf of the DUP. Late into the evening and before setting out on the long journey back to Belfast, Paisley and Thompson called at the home of a DUP supporter and his family for a bite of supper. It was very late and Wallace Thompson admits to having been exhausted by the day's activities. The head of the house got into conversation with 'the big man' and informed him that a neighbour further down the lane had run into serious difficulties as a result of some problem which she had with the authorities.

Paisley immediately insisted that he speak to the person concerned, and despite the lateness of the hour – it was nearly midnight – Paisley met with the family who were in distress, heard their story in great detail and undertook to do something about it.

Even later, as the car sped back to Belfast, Paisley was able to tell his companions sharing the journey with him all the ins and outs of this constituency problem. Thompson was impressed by Paisley's willingness to hear this complaint despite the fact that Paisley had had a very taxing day and also by Paisley's facility for remembering in great detail all the aspects of the problem. Asked whether Paisley had actually dealt with the problem, Thompson said that as far as he could remember Paisley had, adding that one other striking feature was Paisley's ability to recall people's names and needs years after he had first encountered them. Paisley, it seems, would meet people in their homes and be able to recall that a daughter had got married some months previously, or to enquire after a brother-in-law who had had a serious operation. Wallace Thompson was greatly impressed by Ian Paisley's talent for remembering ordinary folk and his ability to talk to them about the things that really mattered in their lives.

The picture painted in this conversation is shared by many of those who have been close to Ian Paisley for a time. There is a mutual affection shared between Paisley and his supporters, especially in rural Ulster which is less afflicted by the cynical attitude towards politics and politicians which seems to prevail in loyalist circles in Belfast. This affection is expressed in a very free and easy manner which enables Paisley to knock on the doors of the people whom he is close to, literally at any hour of the day or night, knowing that whatever their condition, whether the folk are in carpet slippers and dressing-gowns or dressed to go out to Sabbath evening service, he will be warmly received and offered a cup of tea while conversing over the reason for his visit.

This view of Paisley as a man without affectations who is genuinely at one with the people helps to explain why he enjoys such affection among his many supporters and assists in an understanding of why his supporters are willing to tolerate or turn a blind eye to some of the darker areas of his personality.

It is those who work most closely with Ian Paisley, his office staff and some of his relatives, like Rev. James Beggs, his election agent, who know only too well that Paisley has an unruly temper which can apparently be provoked by something as trivial as an unwanted phone call from some newspaper. Allied to displays of bad temper, those who work with Ian Paisley also have to cope with his readiness to make totally impracticable demands upon his staff. When the Puritan Printing Press was operative, Paisley was liable to set down a schedule for the production of election literature and posters which was aimed at getting his literature before the electorate first and which took no account of the operating constraints under which his printers had to work. Paisley's brusque insistence that others meet deadlines or fulfil commissions takes no account of the practicalities of the situation and is another of the dark facets of the man's character – dark and demanding because the underlying motivation seems to be that if he, Paisley, puts so much energy into the cause and overcomes all kinds of obstacles, then his supporters may be expected to do the same.

Paisley appears to conform to Max Weber's concept of a charismatic leader, as being one who 'is set apart from ordinary men and treated as endowed with supernatural, superhuman or at least specifically exceptional powers or qualities'.[21] Weber went on to stress the relevance of 'how the individual is actually regarded by those subject to charismatic authority, by his "followers" or "disciples"'.

Some sociologists would argue that it is misleading to suggest that Paisley's style of authority conforms to Weber's definition of charisma. From their standpoint Paisley is a traditional and ideological leader. The evidence is different: Paisley's ideology is innovative and the loyalist leader flamboyantly expresses elements of both the 'heroic' and the 'sacred' in his personality. Ian Paisley's dominance of the political scene, and the manner in which he upstages rival Unionist politicians, give weight to the view that he is a charismatic figure.

Paisley emerges in this book as being both paternalistic and authoritarian in his dealings with others. Probably the paternalistic and authoritarian traits in the DUP leader's personality shade into one another to some degree, so that while outsiders might perceive the DUP leader to be an authoritarian character, the perception of those who are loyal is not so harsh and Dr Paisley comes across to them as a guide and mentor, a kind of father figure, knowing better than others what is the best course for everyone to take. In this way features of his behaviour, which outsiders who lack the zeal for Protestantism which inspires Paisley and his followers would find appalling or at least off-putting, are accepted by party activists and church members alike as 'a wee flaw' in the leader's make-up which ought not to be allowed to detract from his undoubted standing with his supporters as a 'folk hero'. This helps to explain why party activists perceive the DUP to be a truly democratic Party while those outside the Party would regard the influence of Free Presbyterianism and the greater influence wielded by the party leader himself as in some respects a negation of democracy.

Ian Paisley in his private dealings with colleagues and his supporters in rural Ulster displays a generosity of spirit and deeply-felt concern for the misfortunes and needs of others, but against this must be set an unruly temper and a tendency to demand more from his staff than is warranted, but these are traits in Ian Paisley's personality with which the public at large is generally unfamiliar.

Dr Paisley usually comes to the attention of most people through his oratorical skills or his competent handling of a discussion in a televised interview; therefore Ian Paisley's oratorical skills deserve to be considered. It is through the highly refined use of oratory that

Paisley has been able to dominate loyalist politics. One of the recognised indices of the influence of television over modern political communication and the interaction between leaders and the led has been the decline in the importance of oratory as a projection not merely of the politician's personality, but as the vocal instrument through which he gains mastery over the audience. The relationship between the orator and his mass audience, and the subtle interweave of basic human emotions, of egotistical fulfilment on the part of the speaker and communal awe experienced by the crowd, are subjects which have lost currency in recent studies of political leadership. The advent of wireless between the wars and the possibilities inherent in television after the Second World War modified leadership styles, while the banality of modern English as rendered in the speeches of political figures in the United States and Great Britain has meant that eloquent speakers are noted more for their uniqueness than for their superior development of what was formerly regarded as an essential prerequisite of the politician's craft.

Consequently we have to turn to a study like Robert Michels' *Political Parties* in order to find an adequate commentary on the role of oratory in the advancement of a political career. Michels stresses two important factors which are relevant here: 'The prestige acquired by the orator in the minds of the crowd is almost unlimited. What masses appreciate above all are oratorical gifts as such, beauty and strength of voice, suppleness of mind, badinage; whilst the content of the speech is of quite secondary importance.'[22]

The first point that Michels makes centres on the 'prestige' which the gift of oratory confers on the speaker.

In Northern Ireland where a large proportion of its population attends church regularly, a high preaching standard is expected of those who enter the pulpit and the congregations in their turn regard themselves as competent judges of those who are or are not 'good speakers'. Consequently, Rev. Ian Paisley's mastery of the vocal arts advanced his reputation in a Province which has a surfeit of competent preachers.

Another factor which Michels stresses is that of the content of the speeches made. Michels advises that the actual content is of secondary importance; and it is in the realisation of this fact that Rev. Ian Paisley has been able to achieve an affinity with the crowds, whether they be fifty supporters and onlookers in the main street of Rasharkin, County Antrim, during an election campaign, or thousands of factory workers in the Victoria Park, Belfast, an affinity which few other contemporary politicians have been able to equal. Rev. Ian Paisley presents not a lucid, articulate argument, but a series of word pictures, of verbal cartoons, some of which are witty, others full of pathos, but the overall effect is to stir the emotions of his hearers so that they are left in no doubt as to the cause which Rev. Ian Paisley is promoting at that time.

Nevertheless, it would be a mistake to analyse Dr Paisley's oratorical gifts solely in terms of his skills as an open air speaker. Dr Paisley has a number of speaking styles which are all variations of a basic technique and these styles are employed to suit the circumstances of the gathering he is addressing, and ironically Dr Paisley has come across as least effective when speaking in Parliament. This may be because his speeches from the back of the famous grey landrover which he uses when campaigning have a studied anti-intellectual tone to them; the thought presented to the crowd is invariably underlined by a 'them and us' theme and the division may either be between the betrayed Unionist people and the party bosses of Glengall Street or the Protestants of Ulster and their Irish Republican foes. And while the mental shift that is needed to cope with an audience seated in a hall is great, it is not so great as the change in style, structure and intonation needed for a speech delivered before other Members of Parliament in the House of Commons at Westminster whose social and educational background renders them ill suited to the establishment of a populist appeal amongst the electorate.

Dr Paisley's control over gatherings of supporters has encouraged other party activists to think of Rev. Ian Paisley as indispensable to the progress of the Party, while aspiring politicians within the DUP make a studied attempt to affect a similar speaking style to that of their party leader. Both of these characteristics tend to bolster the leader's egotism and they also reinforce the monolithic appearance of the Party to outsiders who note the similarity in speaking style and read into this phenomenon the conclusion that the subliminal suppression of individualism by DUP party activists is a manifestation of their own hero-worship of the leader. One critic described this facet of the Party in the following terms: '. . . (T)he Democratic Unionist Party . . . whatever the topic of discussion all behave as if they have been cloned off Ian Paisley'. Ian Paisley's technical skills in the use of language have also been directed to negative ends. There are two aspects to this: firstly, it was Paisley's use of bellicose and vehement language which attracted the attention of the media early in his career and secondly, through the DUP leader's declamatory attacks – the way in which he singles out individuals for abrasive comments – it is possible to identify a will to power, a quest for dominance which has provided an underlying motivation in Dr Paisley's political career. In this respect Paisley's oratorical gifts have served him well as an instrument of power.

23 November 1985: Paisley and Molyneaux on the platform as 300,000 converge on Belfast City Hall to demonstrate against the signing of the Anglo-Irish Agreement.

Paisley refutes the claim that he had not read the Anglo-Irish Agreement before rejecting it.

The Voice of Protestant Ulster.

Ian Paisley's oratorical skills, his ability to 'get the message across', reflect the public aspect of Paisley's charismatic style of leadership. The DUP leader's charisma is also sustained through his ability to subsume the struggles of Ulster within his own personality; and the passion, emotion and drama with which Paisley can enliven the message which he proclaims has an electrifying effect on his supporters. To people who yearn for meaning in the midst of confusion, and to those who experience an extreme sense of alienation because their archaic moral values and old-fashioned patriotism has cut them adrift from contemporary British society, Paisley acts as an interpreter. The present is to be understood in terms of the past. Dr Paisley's talent for absorbing and reinterpreting the Ulster Protestant cause has given him the added ability to respond emotionally and instinctively at moments of danger and crisis.

The pragmatism inherent in Paisley's success in grafting Covenanting conviction and Fundamentalist emotionalism together also suggests that there is an undisciplined streak in the Protestant leader's character. There is evidence to sustain the argument that Ian Paisley lacks, or has never been subject to, many of the usual disciplines and constraints that help to mould an individual's personality, and that therefore Dr Paisley's instinctive reactions may be more dynamic than might otherwise be the case.

Without becoming involved in an intimate discussion of Ian Paisley's home life, the following facts are known. Ian Paisley did not have a particularly noteworthy scholastic career, yet Ken Heskin believes that the DUP leader is 'a very intelligent man'; it may well be that Ian Paisley harboured a marked reluctance to submit to the general discipline of school or the personal discipline of private study. Thereafter, Paisley studied at the Theological Hall of the Reformed Presbyterian Church and at the Barry School of Evangelism in South Wales. However, Paisley was an unaffiliated student; he did not submit to the oversight or guidance of a denominational group – in effect he asserted his independence. Paisley's later career as a revivalist preacher and emergence as a major political figure in Ulster underline the argument, because the DUP leader has remained very much an independent and an outsider struggling to achieve prominence on his own terms and not according to the established channels.

If this analysis of Ian Paisley as someone who is self-willed, who has consciously rejected, or alternatively never been brought under, those institutional forms of discipline which influence the development of most personalities, then many of the apparent paradoxes in Ian Paisley's public career and gospel ministry become more intelligible.

The outbursts of temper which Paisley sometimes exhibits in his private dealings with his staff may occur because he is conscious that he is not under the restraint of public scrutiny. The element of indiscipline or self-will in the DUP leader's character may also help to explain why he is a man of extremes who tends to see people and circumstances in black and white terms. Perhaps the most significant point to be stressed concerns the relationship between this self-willed trait in Ian Paisley's personality and the difficulty in arriving at a satisfactory explanation of the deepest motivations in the DUP leader's life, his wants and goals, because Paisley's instinctive reactions have made it even more difficult to arrive at an accurate assessment of his political aims. It seems highly probable that more than high office, Ian Paisley desires the adulation of the crowd, of his supporters, and to some degree the authoritarian aspect of Paisley's personality may be transformed in response to a process which Weber has termed 'legitimisation by plebiscite'. This suggests that having initially asserted his right to lead, Dr Paisley may have moderated his style of leadership once it became apparent that his claims were endorsed by a substantial percentage of the Unionist electorate.

The importance which Ian Paisley attaches to the enthusiasm which his supporters manifest towards him is not based entirely on a postulated relationship between voter support for the DUP leader and Weber's theory of the 'routinisation of charisma'; it is also a matter of observation. Anyone who has had experience either of one of Ian Paisley's church services, the use he makes of political rallies, or his passionate enthusiasm for electioneering must be impressed not only by the manner in which Ian Paisley is able to stamp his 'presence' on a particular meeting but equally by his personal reaction and response to the affection and adulation of his supporters. Ian Paisley needs the people whom he leads. And therein lies the great dilemma, not only for Ian Paisley, but for the Party over which he has had such a formative influence. While the high excitement displayed by serried ranks of loyalists may give satisfaction, may fulfil a major goal in Ian Paisley's life, his ability to strike out for other goals, to aspire perhaps to government office and responsibility, is inhibited by a deep-rooted fear that compromise of those loyalist principles he has espoused could result, not in an executive role in the affairs of the Province, but in a loss of esteem among the very people who have made Ian Paisley their own. Is it possible that Ian Paisley is just as much a prisoner of the Lundy syndrome as so many of the members of the Party which he leads?

Notes and References

[1] A. D. Lindsay, *The Essentials of Democracy*, Oxford, 2nd edn., 1967, 19; also pp. 35–36.

[2] J. Barr, *The Scottish Covenanters*, Glasgow 1946, 230.

[3] S. Rutherford, *Lex Rex* or *The Law and the Prince*, Harrisonburg, Virginia 1980, 1. Rutherford took a keen interest in the welfare of the Presbyterians of Ulster.

[4] D. Miller, *Queen's Rebels: Ulster Loyalism in Historical Perspective*, Dublin 1978.

[5] J. Boyd Primmer, *Life of Jacob Primmer: Minister of the Church of Scotland*, Edinburgh 1916, 311–312. Primmer noted that 'nothing will equal agitation, and that on a grand scale. That is what the Reformers did. There must be great meetings which will arrest public attention. Small meetings will not do.'

[6] Ian R. K. Paisley, *The Crown Rights of Jesus Christ*, Belfast 1985.

[7] Louis Gardner, *Resurgence of the Majority*, Belfast 1970, 31.

[8] A. T. Q. Stewart, *The Narrow Ground: Aspects of Ulster 1609–1969*, London 1977, 83.

[9] D. F. Wells and J. D. Woodbridge, *The Evangelicals: What They Believe, Who They Are, Where They Are Changing*, Grand Rapids Michigan 1977, Revised Edition, 29, 30.

[10] J. Calvin, *Institutes of the Christian Religion*, Philadelphia 1960.

[11] R. A. Viguerie, *The New Right: We're Ready to Lead*, Falls Church, Virginia 1980.

[12] J. I. Parker, *Fundamentalism and the Word of God*, London, 1st edn., 1958, 32.

[13] J. D. Douglas (Ed.), *The New International Dictionary of the Christian Church*, Exeter 1974, 397.

[14] G. Mann, *History of Germany Since 1789*, London 1968, 396–400.

[15] J. F. Harbinson, *The Ulster Unionist Party 1882–1973, Its Development and Organisation*, Belfast 1973, 149.

[16] Jacques Ellul, *The Ethics of Freedom*, Oxford 1976, 379.

[17] H. Dooyeweerd, *A New Critique of Theoretical Thought*, Vols. III and IV, USA 1969, 623.

[18] Calvin, *Institutes*, Book IV xx 4, 1490. See also J. T. McNeill, *Calvin: On God and Political Duty*, Indianapolis, USA, 2nd edn. 1977.

[19] N. De Jong, *Christianity and Democracy*, USA 1978, 163.

[20] Ken Heskin, *Northern Ireland: A Psychological Analysis*, Dublin 1980, 119.

[21] Max Weber, *On Charisma and Institution Building*, Chicago 1968, 48.

[22] Robert Michels, *Political Parties: A Sociological Study of the Oligarchical Tendencies of Modern Democracy*, New York 1959, 71.

CHAPTER V

Triumph and Betrayal

Confounding the assumptions and doctrines of Enlightenment secularism (in both its original liberal-bourgeois and later Marxist guises), religion has continued to play an important role in the politics of the 'Old World'. Both Northern Ireland and Poland stand as contemporary reminders that, despite rumours to the contrary, God is not dead so far as European politics are concerned.

John Madeley
Politics and the Pulpit: The Case of Protestant Europe

A consistent motivational conflict is apparent in Paisley's career. He is very aware of his own abilities . . . At the same time, while wishing to see these appropriately recognised, he has often lacked the confidence to put them to a proper test.

Ken Heskin
Northern Ireland: A Psychological Analysis

The DUP, the guardians of public morality

With the failure of the 1977 Paisley strike and the local government elections over, the political initiative passed back to the Northern Ireland Secretary of State. On 8 June Roy Mason announced that the SAS would be used in covert operations against the terrorists. More troops would be used in the Province and the force levels of both the RUC and the part time UDR were to be increased. The Unionists and the Action Council interpreted these security decisions by the Secretary of State as a vindication of their divergent approaches to the continuing crisis. Probably Roy Mason's major concern was to ensure that the Queen's Jubilee visit to Northern Ireland would take place without serious incident. The Queen's visit took place on 9 and 10 August and apart from a minor incident during a visit to

Coleraine, the brief Royal tour was a tremendous personal triumph
for the Queen.

During the month the DUP appointed Wallace Thompson as Party
Finance Officer. Calvert has described this addition to the small
professional staff which administered the Party as 'the next step in a
planned expansion of the Party organisation'.[1]

By the late autumn, the DUP's role as the main loyalist alternative
to Official Unionism received a further boost when in a succession of
events, William Craig was first appointed to a research post by the
Council of Europe and then on 20 November, Craig announced that
Vanguard would cease to function as a political party. Both leader
and Party disappeared from the political arena and, in theory, Ernest
Baird and the United Ulster Unionist Party which he led ought to
have been in a position to consolidate the Vanguard Party's share of
the loyalist vote. However, Baird was unable to capture Vanguard's
potential electoral support. Consequently there was a cumulative
effect to Craig's decision to wind down Vanguard's political interest
which emphasised the fact that the loyalist alternatives to the DUP
had become progressively depleted as the decade wore on.

Like some great leviathan, the troubles were devouring the lives of
thousands of people, and corroding the political fortunes of leaders in
both the nationalist and unionist sections of the community. The
pressure on the Unionist population to change their political
allegiance and orientation continued to be the underlying feature of
political life in Ulster in 1978. The year began with the Eire Premier,
Jack Lynch, emphasising his belief that a united Ireland was the only
solution which offered peace. This political leverage on the Unionist
population led to both the DUP and the OUP breaking off desultory
talks with the Northern Ireland Office. A few weeks later, the
Provisional IRA launched a horrendous fire bomb attack on the La
Mon Hotel in which twelve people died and twenty-three were
injured.

As the spring began Ernest Baird and Paisley invited Harry West
and the Unionist Party to begin talks. The stated aim was to avoid a
situation where rival Unionist candidates contested the same Westminster seats. West rebuffed the two loyalist leaders and released the
text of a confidential letter to the press. Two factors influenced the
decision of the Ulster Unionists. The collapse of Craig's Vanguard
Party and the death of the moderate Unionists' most articulate
politician, Brian Faulkner, had opened up new horizons for the
Party. There was every prospect that West's Party would regain some
of the activists who had left the Unionists in the early seventies.
Whether such prodigals came from Vanguard or the Unionist Party
of Northern Ireland, they would share a common detestation of

Paisley-style politics. This factor may have given West sufficient cause to reject the overture from Paisley and Baird, but there was another aspect to West's refusal. The inner circles of the Glengall Street Party had noted the fact that Paisley had climbed to prominence on a coalition ladder and some of the Unionist Party's officers argued cogently that to enter into talks with Baird and the DUP or to attempt to revive the UUUC coalition would only redound to Paisley's advantage.

Paisley reacted to the breakdown in these negotiations at a Special Delegates meeting of DUP activists in Portadown. At the meeting Paisley castigated the Unionist Party and catalogued in trenchant manner the numerous failures of his rival loyalists. The DUP would recruit more members and expand across the Province with the declared objective of taking upon itself 'the leadership of the loyalist people'.

The emphasis of DUP activity now shifted away from the person of Dr Paisley and the locally elected councillors began to assert themselves, sometimes in an aggressive manner which was calculated to attract the interest of the local press. The impression was assiduously created that DUP councillors had a detailed knowledge of the needs of their local area constituents and were determined to press the needs of their people at every opportunity. And there is little doubt that the Party expected its councillors to work unstintedly on their constituents' behalf. With seventy-four Council seats and this determination to serve the loyalist population, Calvert has claimed that in the spring of 1978 'the DUP was growing in stature. It had become a party with an impeccable credibility . . .' (sic).

The distinctive feature of the DUP's entry into community politics was the well publicised emphasis which the DUP councillors placed on moral issues. In the autumn of 1977 the Party had launched a 'Save Ulster from Sodomy' campaign which aimed to mobilise support against any proposed changes in the law affecting homosexuals in Northern Ireland. By the time it had concluded in February 1978 the campaign had attracted 70,000 signatures, and it has been suggested that some Roman Catholics supported this campaign to frustrate any relaxation in the law as it related to homosexual behaviour. However, the bulk of the signatures came from the large body of evangelical Christians in the Province. Opposition to the liberalisation of legislation as it affected homo-sexuals was but one of a number of moralistic issues raised by the DUP: other matters which came under discussion ranged from the contents of English literature textbooks containing blasphemous language which were used in schools, to the recurring problem of Sunday observance.

The Protestant Unionist Party had campaigned vigorously on behalf of Sabbath Day observance in the past, and now that the DUP had gained control of Ballymena Council and held the balance of power in thirteen other councils, the Party mounted a protracted campaign to impose a stricter form of Sabbatarianism upon those council districts in which the DUP had the numerical strength and influence to bring about changes in the local district bye-laws.

In crucial votes the DUP representatives were able to rely on the support of other loyalist councillors or Unionist Party councillors who felt that it would be injudicious to be seen to be voting against their Protestant colleagues on the local council and with the Roman Catholics, in favour of bye-laws which encouraged the local citizenry to desecrate the Lord's Day. The effects of this moralist endeavour created all kinds of anomalies where, for example, the district council might vote to close a leisure centre on a Sunday but had no power to enforce strict Sabbatarianism on a private golf club in the same district.

The debate on the issue of Sabbath observance became very intense, and some Unionist councillors argued that when the electors voted for the DUP councillors they did not give such councillors a mandate to pursue their own pietistic convictions or impose what was in effect the moral and ethical standards of a fundamentalist sect on the community at large. For their part, the DUP adopted the position that as their councillors had been democratically elected they had a mandate to impose stricter forms of Sabbatarianism on the local community. In effect, the DUP was claiming that a general endorsement of their election manifesto enabled them to claim specific authority on issues which did not weigh as heavily with DUP voters, many of whom did not share the doctrinal views of the DUP with the same intensity and commitment as the Party's members and representatives.

The DUP had not worked out a theoretical justification for these pietistic impositions on the community; instead the Party turned to the Word of God for its authority on how the Sabbath was to be observed, and relied on the ballot box to give its representatives the mandate to vote through controversial bye-laws to give effect to their interpretation of the Bible.

Inevitably this moralistic posture provoked a reaction from the libertarians in the Province. A cartoon wall poster appeared in Belfast consisting of a collage composed of the facial features of Dr Paisley and the Ayatollah Khomeini.

There is, of course, a parallel which is much closer to home than Iran! It is possible to contrast the authoritarian and moralistic impositions of the Roman Catholic Church in the Republic of Ireland as they have affected censorship and private morality, and the censorious spirit exhibited by those DUP councillors who have taken upon themselves this role of the guardians of public morals. The Party's crusade was endorsed by the evangelical section of the Province's population, and conservative Protestant sects which may not even encourage their adherents to vote or participate in politics have applauded the moralistic fervour of the DUP in its defence of Biblically inspired principles of conduct.

Critics of the DUP, whether from the Unionist or Nationalist side of the political fence, or for that matter high minded religious folk, noted serious inconsistencies in the DUP's concern about raising the Province's moral standards.

The DUP's belligerence, its uncharitable spirit towards the Party's political opponents, the ruthless pursuit of political office even to the extent of the use of personation at election time, and the technique of character assassination as a means of ostracising former supporters, all these traits led the many critics of the Party to conclude that the DUP's councillors ought first to consider the beam that was in their own eye before attempting to cast out the mote that was in their brother's.

This programme of religious defence which had been embarked upon by the DUP's newly elected councillors would continue to be an aspect of the Party's policy in the future, but the more immediate task was to consolidate and prepare for the next opportunity which might present itself. In keeping with these objectives, the DUP staged a party conference in early June 1978. Before the conference delegates met, *The Irish Times* caustically noted that 'almost all the motions (to be proposed at the conference) are directed against other parties or against other ideas'.

The highlight of the conference was the speech by the party leader, but the address was largely taken up with a restatement of the religious motivations behind the Party's political programme and, apart from a fierce attack on the 'fascist' Roy Mason and a claim that the link with the United Kingdom was becoming weaker and increasingly meaningless, it is impossible to detect any strand of idealism or amplification of policy which was anything other than a re-echoing of the rhetoric which had become the stock-in-trade of Dr Paisley. Indeed many of the phrases employed were resurrected from speeches and statements that had been made in former years and this feeling of déjà vu underlined the impression that the DUP had suffered a form of regression and manifested characteristics which were suggestive of neo-Protestant Unionism.

Dr Paisley's leadership over the Party had become so well established that there was no genuine public discussion or internal party debate at the 1978 party conference, the first occasion upon which the whole Party could have considered the strike debacle of the previous year. What Dr Paisley offered at the conference was a histrionic restatement of the Party's ideology, and when the opportunity was later presented, through the publication of the year book, for reflection upon where the DUP was going, the opportunity was set to one side. Instead refuge was sought in the well tried expedient of invoking the glories of Ulster's Protestant past.

In July the DUP took over a suite of offices at 296 Albertbridge Road which had previously been occupied for a time by the Ulster Workers Council, and in the autumn as part of the Party's strategy for further advance a recruitment leaflet was prepared.

5 October marked the tenth anniversary of the Civil Rights march in Londonderry, and by 1978 those who wished to commemorate the event consisted in the main of extreme Irish Republicans, as the more moderate factions within the Northern Ireland Civil Rights Association had long since severed their connections with that body. Tension increased in Londonderry when it became evident that the Irish Republicans intended to hold their commemoration parade along the route of the original march, because this meant that the parade would begin in the largely Protestant district of the Waterside. The RUC did allow the parade to take place on 8 October and, as a direct result, serious disturbances ensued. The DUP had organised a counter-demonstration and it was the counter-demonstrators who came into conflict with the police.

The following weekend the DUP organised a second demonstration to protest at the failure of the police to prevent the Republican commemoration from taking place in a Protestant area. The large number of loyalists who participated in this demonstration succeeded in marching to the Guildhall Square and, although there were further disorders, the loyalists interpreted the episode as a vindication of their determination to oppose what they saw as further police concessions to Irish Republican agitation.

These incidents in Londonderry in October 1978 brought to an end what had been a quiescent phase in the DUP's development. The confrontation with Irish Republicans showed clearly that though the United Unionist Action Council had collapsed the DUP had not abandoned its willingness to resort to street agitation and was prepared to confront the authorities in circumstances which could be construed as being in defence of the loyalists' interests. Further, the ability of the DUP to mobilise such a large loyalist crowd on the parade to the Guildhall Square reflected favourably on the Party's claim that it gave leadership and political direction to grass-roots loyalist opinion. These demonstrations also marked a turning point in the fortunes of the DUP in Londonderry City. After the Party had given a show of determination to confront the authorities in Londonderry, there was a significant increase in political support and the Ulster Unionist Party was forced on to the defensive in the Londonderry area.

1978 closed with a small but significant increase in the DUP's membership and a delegates' conference in November was used to consolidate this growing party support.

A Protestant voice in Europe

The following year, 1979, stands out as one of the most important years in the DUP's history, because it was in 1979 that Dr Paisley established his claim to speak for the Protestants of Ulster. Paisley's claim was based upon the democratic will of a majority of those who chose to vote in the EEC election. As the *News Letter* commented when Dr Paisley's first preference vote was known: 'The Euro-election has given him the greatest triumph so far in his eventful life'.

This triumph, however, had only been achieved after a 'fierce battle' at a secret meeting of the Presbytery of the Free Presbyterian Church of Ulster. The controversy erupted over Dr Paisley's decision to put himself forward for the European election and the argument extended to the not insignificant question of whether Rev. William Beattie should stand as a second DUP candidate in the EEC election. The background to this opposition to Dr Paisley's desire to stand for Europe turns on the religious attitudes which the Free Presbyterian Church had adopted to the EEC.

Two leading Free Presbyterian ministers, Rev. John Douglas and Rev. S. B. Cooke, had made a detailed study of the EEC, and these ministers saw in the Common Market a fulfilment of Old Testament prophecy. Dr Paisley, who has always been very cautious about eschatological preaching and who did not regard sermons interpreting Biblical prophecy as a major part of his church ministry, was of a similar mind to his Free Presbyterian colleagues. The European Economic Community was a political manifestation of mystery Babylon; the Common Market, based as it was upon the Treaty of Rome, was an expression of the Papacy's political influence in Western Europe.

It was the contention of Rev. John Wylie that the decision of Dr Paisley to stand for election to the European Parliament was at variance with these spiritual insights. The issue which Rev. John Wylie had raised touched a raw nerve within Free Presbyterianism, and for the following reason.

One of the crucial doctrines propounded by the Free Presbyterians was that of Biblical separation; this doctrine lay at the heart of Dr Paisley's criticism of the Presbyterian Church in Ireland and the other major Protestant denominations which were linked to the World Council of Churches. It was Dr Paisley's contention that evangelical Christians could not be unequally yoked together with those who were theological modernists or sacramentalists looking to eventual union with the Church of Rome. This doctrine of separatism had been applied rigorously in all kinds of circumstances; now Dr Paisley was actually arguing that he should stand for election to, should seek a place within, this supra-national institution, this creation of the Great Apostacy.

Although there is some indication that a number of senior activists within the DUP also harboured reservations about the party leader's decision to contest the EEC election, the real debate, the heated controversy, occurred at a secret Presbytery meeting[2] from which the vast majority of DUP party members were not only excluded but of which they were, in all probability, kept in total ignorance.

Rev. John Wylie had been a personal friend and colleague of Dr Paisley in the formative days of both the Free Presbyterian Church and of Protestant Unionism. John Wylie had shared a jail term with Rev. Ian Paisley in 1966. Therefore the criticism which Wylie levelled at the Moderator of his church cannot simply be set to one side. Though Wylie had been out of sympathy with the absorption of the Protestant Unionist Party by the DUP, his religious convictions also bore the stamp of an older generation. Wylie was much less influenced by American Fundamentalism, and he had never regarded success either in financial terms or church attendance as a measure of true spirituality.

It was for these reasons that Rev. John Wylie could not only claim the right to be heard in the Presbytery meeting, but expect that his opinions would carry some authority. Inevitably, though, his opposition to the proposed candidacy was ineffectual. The Presbytery endorsed their Moderator's desire to stand for the European Parliament. Nevertheless, Wylie had given expression and leadership to an inchoate body of Paisleyite opinion which had concluded that Dr Paisley's intended candidature was inconsistent with the Free Presbyterian Church's identification of the Common Market as the political expression of Mystery Babylon. The irony was that although Wylie was not alone, others within the DUP who shared Wylie's Protestant principles and correctly interpreted Paisley's decision as being an entirely pragmatic one did not even know that such a controversial meeting had taken place; the critics within the DUP had either to bite their tongues or withdraw from the Party.

There is little doubt that Paisley more than anyone else in that Presbytery meeting would have recognised the force and principle which lay behind John Wylie's opposition to the endorsement of the Moderator as an EEC candidate. However, the political pressures to run were extremely strong, though another factor has to be taken into account.

The other factor was that of Paisley's own personality. Paisley's egotism was so marked that it is difficult to believe that the DUP leader could have resisted the temptation and challenge presented by a Province-wide election in which he could vindicate his own assertion that he was the 'Voice of Protestant Ulster'. There is a little anecdote about Dr Paisley that well illustrates this aspect of the DUP leader's personality. The story goes that in the late 1950s, when Ian Paisley and Norman Porter were conducting tent campaigns on behalf of the Evangelical Protestant Society, both preachers would repair home together for supper. At the supper table the *Belfast Telegraph* for the previous evening would be produced and Paisley, armed with a twelve inch ruler, would scan the pages of the paper for reports of their latest exploits. Apparently Paisley was alternately elated or depressed depending on whether it was Ian Paisley or Norman Porter who succeeded in gaining the longest number of newspaper column inches in the previous evening's editions.

Paisley's egotistical designs on Ulster's European election vote may well help to explain why the Presbytery refused to endorse Rev. William Beattie as a second candidate in the forthcoming European election. As the minutes of these Presbytery meetings are not available for public scrutiny any assessment as to why Rev. William Beattie did not receive the approbation of the Presbytery must be treated with caution. Had the DUP put forward two candidates in the 1979 European election then Rev. Ian Paisley would have been denied the opportunity to maximise his personal vote across the whole Province, and a smaller vote for Paisley would have robbed the DUP leader of his remarkable triumph over the two rival Official Unionist candidates, Taylor and West, whose combined first preference votes were 54,519 short of the total number of votes cast for the DUP leader.

The decision of the Presbytery of the Free Presbyterian Church to endorse Dr Paisley, thereby enabling him to go forward as the sole candidate for the DUP, proved to be of great importance, because the ultimate consequence of this decision was to inflict more damage on the diminishing prestige of the Ulster Unionist Party and permit Dr Paisley to exult in his remarkable electoral achievement: 'a twentieth century miracle', he said.

There were also sound political reasons why the DUP ought to put forward a candidate in the forthcoming European election.

A call for an abstentionist vote on a matter of principle would not be widely understood amongst the Unionist electorate which, unlike the nationalist population, had no tradition of abstentionist politics. Furthermore, from a partisan standpoint the election would be as much about keeping out candidates that the voters did not approve of, as positively voting favoured candidates into office. Had Paisley chosen not to contest the election the Unionist Party would have taken advantage of the situation and used the election campaign to regain some of the ground which it had conceded to the DUP.

In seeking to maximise the Protestant vote Paisley would also ensure that the SDLP would not receive a disproportionately high percentage of the votes cast and, apart from the political argument, the publicity which would be generated by the European election would inevitably enhance the prestige, or it could be said the notoriety, of the candidate who emerged as the political leader endorsed by the largest number of the Province's voters.

As Paisley paused before launching himself pell-mell into electioneering, it is worth reflecting on the very considerable advantages displayed by the political machine which Paisley had helped to engineer and which he now controlled.

There had been an intense, though one-sided, ideological debate on the proposed candidacies of Dr Paisley and Rev. William Beattie, yet literally only a whisper of what had been said had leaked out. Even then, the leaks never reached the press or television. The contrast with the misery of the Unionist Party could not have been more marked. The Unionist Party, like the British Labour Party, seemed to attract more media attention and comment about the Party's internal splits, factions and feuds than about its policy and commitments. Paisley would go to the hustings asserting that a vote for the DUP would give Ulster a Protestant voice in Europe, secure in the knowledge that any voices of dissent within the Free Presbyterian-DUP nexus were for all practical political purposes inaudible. Considering the widely held notion that Ulstermen are not afraid to speak their own minds, this was no mean political achievement.

On 3 March 1979, the DUP met in Portadown town hall and formally nominated Dr Paisley as the Party's European election candidate. Later that evening, Paisley gave an address entitled 'How Ulster loyalists can destroy the Common Market conspiracy and use the European election to secure devolved government for Northern Ireland'. This title encapsulated the two main themes that were to dominate this DUP campaign. Paisley was representing himself not only as a vociferous anti-Marketeer, but as the candidate who alone had the political clout to retrieve a devolved administration for the Province.

Rev. James Beggs, Paisley's taciturn and highly competent brother-in-law, who had acted as Paisley's election agent in North Antrim, now took on the task of election agent for the European election campaign. Organising committees were set up in each of the twelve Westminster constituencies and twelve sub-agents were appointed.

This first European election in Northern Ireland had hardly been launched when events at Westminster, where the Labour Government of Jim Callaghan had been struggling to hold on to office, suddenly interrupted the proceedings.

The bitter infighting between the DUP and the Ulster Unionists had spilled over into the corridors of the Palace of Westminster. Both parties used the floor of the House of Commons as a megaphone through which the follies of their rivals could be bellowed at the listening electorate in Ulster.

When on 28 March Jim Callaghan's Government faced a vote of no confidence, the Labour Government had the solace of knowing that two Official Unionist MPs, John Carson and Harold McCusker, would support the beleaguered Government in the division lobbies. Callaghan's Government fell, but in Northern Ireland it was this well publicised demonstration of the splits within Ulster Unionism which caught the public eye. It was not a good augury with which to open an election contest which would entail a struggle for supremacy with the DUP.

The DUP's European campaign was held in abeyance while the Party contested five Westminster seats. The DUP also benefited indirectly from the defection of the Ulster Unionist MP for North Down, Jim Kilfedder, who decided to establish his own Party and then proceeded to conduct a successful fight to retain his parliamentary seat[3] against the writer, who had been selected as the Official Unionist candidate.

When the results were declared on 4 May, it was learned that Dr Paisley had retained his seat in North Antrim, but the DUP created a sensation by taking two seats in North and East Belfast from the Unionist Party.

There were two highly significant aspects to this breakthrough by the DUP in East Belfast. Firstly, the DUP had broken the old alliance between the Unionist Party and the Orange Order and replaced it with a radical loyalist alternative. In addition, in both North and East Belfast the DUP had been able to call upon the covert assistance of paramilitary groups in mounting its election challenge.

In East Belfast, for example, DUP Party activists, some of whom were members of Sandown Road Free Presbyterian Church, worked throughout polling day to 'get the voters out', while simultaneously a group of UDA men were engaged in taking voters to the polls in support of the DUP candidate. Each group acted as if it were unaware of the existence of the other.

In North Belfast, the DUP candidate, Johnnie McQuade, was a local folk hero and Second World War veteran, and his personal following was well established. Nevertheless in that constituency also, the paramilitary involvement made a contribution to the DUP's electoral triumph. These two results indicated that the DUP was succeeding in winning over working-class loyalist support in Belfast.

The DUP also contested Armagh, where the Official Unionist, Harold McCusker, comfortably beat off the DUP threat posed by David Calvert, while in West Belfast the DUP candidate, William Dickson, trailed behind the Official Unionist, Tommy Passmore, in a seat which Gerry Fitt held for the SDLP with a comfortable majority of 8,235 votes.[4]

With the Westminster results behind it, the DUP turned to face its discomfited Unionist rival and Dr Paisley resumed his European election campaign. The question at issue now was whether the three DUP seats would give an added impetus to Dr Paisley's campaign.

Dr Sydney Elliott, having examined the slight increase in the DUP's percentage share of the vote in the Westminster election, argued that the political consequences were far reaching: 'The Democratic Unionist share of the poll rose to 10·2 per cent from 8·5 per cent in October 1974; this was small considering that three additional candidates were in the field. However, the three victories provided an enormous boost to the party confidence'.[5]

Polling day in the European election was 7 June and in the interval between the Westminster election and polling day, Dr Paisley had toured almost all the Province's constituencies twice and conducted numerous meetings, which were invariably preceded by a band parade. Dr Paisley is said to have covered 122 miles on foot and travelled over 4,000 miles by car.

The count began on Monday, 11 June and by the early evening Dr Paisley had been elected on the first count with a total of 170,688 votes which was 27,628 votes above the required quota. This vote was all the more remarkable because it is probable that Dr Paisley received between 40 and 50 per cent of the total number of Protestant votes cast in the EEC election. This was the first occasion on which electors right across the Province had had the opportunity to vote for the DUP and the vote was taken as a conclusive vindication of Dr Paisley's assertion that he was the authentic leader of Protestant opinion in Ulster.

Dr Paisley had no doubt in his own mind that his very considerable achievement of June 1979 would lead to a reassessment of the role of the DUP in government circles. While the DUP leader reflected on the new political situation which he believed was heralded by his triumph in the European election, the Unionist Party was forced to come to terms with its declining fortunes. Harry West, the former Stormont Cabinet Minister, resigned as party leader and the Party turned to Jim Molyneaux, the MP for South Antrim at Westminster, to guide the Party and restore its tattered pride.

Molyneaux had always been on the right of the Party and his emergence as leader marked the final stage of that 'long march' through the Party which had been embarked upon by the right wing when they decided to challenge the progressive policies of the reforming Stormont Prime Minister, Terence O'Neill, in the late sixties.

It would now be more difficult to distinguish between the policies espoused by the Unionists and those put forward by the DUP. Both parties were opposed to a devolved power sharing Executive, both parties were positively committed to the Northern Ireland Convention Report, and both parties placed a vigorous anti-terrorist campaign high on their respective lists of priorities. It was this close alignment between the two warring Unionist parties which led Dr Paisley to misjudge seriously the political stance which the Unionist Party would shortly adopt and it was the similarity of aims, separated by a storm of invective, which led an increasingly high proportion of loyalist activists to despair of Unionist politics altogether and 'opt out' from the seemingly interminable and increasingly futile skirmishing between the two major divisions in the Unionist bloc.

The General Election in June had brought about a change of government at Westminster and a new Secretary of State for Northern Ireland had been appointed by the Conservative Prime Minister, Margaret Thatcher. Airey Neave, who had been the Conservative Party's spokesman on Northern Ireland while the Party had been in opposition, had been assassinated by the INLA and the new appointee, Humphrey Atkins, came to his office without the kind of experience or detailed knowledge of the Province which had been acquired by Neave. It would be part of Humphrey Atkins' task to negotiate with the DUP and its leader, Dr Paisley; it was evident that the Party had reached a significant turning point in its brief history.

It was an important turning point because Dr Paisley had proved, to his own satisfaction and to that of the media, that he was the leader of Protestant Ulster, and his personal hegemony over the Unionist electorate had been underlined by the DUP's two dramatic Westminster parliamentary gains. It was the cumulative effect of both the Westminster and European elections that made the impact.

Other successes enjoyed by the DUP in the spring of 1979 also had long term effects on the development of the Party. After his success in East Belfast, Peter Robinson, the new DUP MP, unobtrusively began to consolidate his position as the heir apparent, the inevitable successor to Paisley, the party boss. Robinson continued to build up his personal fief in Castlereagh where DUP candidates whose first loyalty would be to Robinson rather than to Dr Paisley found advancement. Now that an increased and onerous political role was falling on Paisley's broad shoulders, the DUP leader's capacity for involving himself in the day-to-day administration of the Party was noticeably diminished.

Paisley's decision to appoint Jim Allister to a professional post as EEC adviser effectively created a micro-managerial class centring on Robinson and Allister. Robinson and Allister together with an inner circle of young DUP members, some of whom were graduates, soon began to influence the selection of future candidates and give coherence to the Party's pragmatic policies. For the first time since the departure of Desmond Boal the Party had ceased to be a hostage to the human frailty of its leader – after the spring of 1979 the possibility opened up that the DUP could have a future in the event of Dr Paisley's departure from the political arena.

Nevertheless it was Dr Paisley's leadership through which the changing image of the Party was reflected. In a noisy and sensational outburst at the opening of the new European Parliament in Strasbourg on 17 July, Paisley, the first of the newly elected MEPs to speak, excoriated the European Assembly over the fact that the flag of the United Kingdom was being flown upside down – this being a distress signal! By this incident, which Paisley conducted in characteristically belligerent style, the DUP leader demonstrated that protest and confrontation remained an acceptable tactical option for the Party. Paisley continued his protests on the following day, when he attempted to interrupt Jack Lynch, the Irish Republic's Taoiseach, who was making a speech in his capacity as President in Office of the European Council.

Paisley for P.M.

From the end of July 1979 until May of the following year, the DUP adopted a low profile; demonstrations and confrontation gave way to modest political manoeuvres aimed at achieving a political agreement through participation in the constitutional talks initiated by Humphrey Atkins.

Though the Atkins conference was abortive, it did create an unusual political situation because the new right-wing leader of the Official Unionists, James Molyneaux, created a major political upset by refusing to attend the Atkins conference at all. Molyneaux's decision had the knock-on effect of pushing the DUP closer to the centre of Ulster politics. This unexpected development gave rise to widespread confusion among the loyalist rank and file. In particular, the DUP's supporters were discomfited to discover that their leaders had placed the Party in an exposed position which gave the Unionist Party the opportunity to go on the offensive by claiming that the DUP was weakening on the Union. Whatever advantage the Official Unionist Party might have gained by outflanking the DUP over the Atkins conference was largely dissipated by the Party's inability to curtail public wrangling between its spokesmen over party policy.[6] One faction of the Official Unionists privately agreed with the integrationist line of Enoch Powell, but another vociferous faction pressed the case for devolution. As the Unionist Party had been orientated towards a provincial government at Stormont throughout most of the years of its existence, parochialism was deeply entrenched within the Party's structure and whatever Molyneaux's private convictions may have been he found himself leading a Party which was unable to reconcile the Ulster localism with Powell's adherence to the Union.

The seemingly endemic faction fighting within the Official Unionists put the leadership under intense strain, forcing Molyneaux to sacrifice clarity on policy in order to keep the Party intact. This gave the DUP a considerable advantage because Paisley's Party was able to represent itself to the Ulster electorate as a political movement which spoke with one voice. The end result was that Molyneaux's strategy of out-manoeuvring the DUP was nullified by the widely publicised personality wrangles and policy disagreements within his own Party. Molyneaux's decision not to participate in the Atkins talks left the DUP sitting at the conference table.

In late July Paisley attacked the widely canvassed suggestion that Pope John Paul's intended visit to Ireland in two months' time should include a Papal visit to the City of Armagh, but horrendous events on 27 August caused the Pope to reconsider and subsequently cancel this controversial aspect of his itinerary. A shocked nation learned that the Provisional IRA had assassinated Earl Mountbatten of Burma and a number of his holiday friends at Mullaghmore in the Irish Republic. A few hours later, the IRA inflicted the biggest death toll in a single incident in the course of a decade of violence when they carried out a bomb attack which killed eighteen soldiers at Warrenpoint in County Down.

With the Pope's visit to Ireland curtailed to the Republic, Paisley adopted the position that the visit was an event in a foreign country and therefore no concern of his. Paisley was, in effect, asserting that the border was not only a political frontier but a spiritual frontier as well. This debatable stratagem could not hide the fact that Paisley could have responded to the Papal visit with much more religious fervour had he so desired, for there had been a time when he would have toured every Free Presbyterian Church to preach anti-Popery and win over those of wider Protestant sympathies to adherence to the Free Presbyterian Church. But there would be no monster Protestant rallies in Ulster on this occasion, and Paisley observed a low profile throughout the visit. His approach is in marked contrast to that which the Free Presbyterian Moderator adopted when John Paul visited Britain in May 1982. On that occasion Paisley, according to the statements of some Orangemen in Scotland, thrust himself to the head of various Protestant groupings which set out to oppose the Pope's British tour. By the end of the Pope's visit the impression had been created by the media that all opposition to the Papal visit was master-minded and engineered by Dr Paisley and a handful of Free Presbyterian clerics imported to England for the specific purpose of demonstrating against the Papal visit.

Dr Paisley's conciliatory mood during the autumn of 1979 was complemented by a reassessment being made of Paisley and his Party by the civil servants and Conservative politicians who administered the Northern Ireland Office. It was probably a combination of Paisley's sensational election to the European Assembly and the 1979 phase of Paisley, the moderate leader, that led these policymakers to contemplate the possibility that the DUP leader could head a new devolved Executive in Northern Ireland.

This attempt to reach an understanding with Dr Paisley was reflected in the attitude of the press. An example of this appeared in *The Irish Times*, which had previously treated Paisley with unremitting hostility. One article, written by John Healy, arrived at the erroneous conclusion that 'Mrs Thatcher and Lord Carrington got rid of Rhodesia in record time when they put their mind to it. All that's left now is Northern Ireland and Mrs Thatcher's ability to recognise that if she facilitates the Big Man (Paisley), by first breaking the link, he and Hume have the political talent to find a political solution in a matter of months'.

This 'Paisley for P.M.'[7] campaign remained a talking point until early 1981 and was based on the premise that Paisley had turned over a new leaf after his substantial triumph in the European election and that it could safely be assumed that the DUP leader would maintain his conciliatory political stance in the future. This reasoning was based on two serious misunderstandings. The first mistake arose from the notion that the politics of the DUP were conducted in accordance with a coherent philosophy which was open to progressive adjustment and modification, and the second error was prompted by a misreading of Paisley's dominant position within Ulster loyalism.

In reality the DUP's approach to politics was erratic, because the contradictions within the DUP's paradoxical ideology had never been resolved. Secondly Paisley was a leader in the sense that he was chiefly an articulation of loyalist grass-roots opinion and not because he had either the vision or moral fortitude to persuade his supporters to make radical choices. Whenever Paisley found himself in an unfamiliar situation and with his support slipping away, his instinctive reaction was to fall back upon the trusted and tried political tactics of the past – belligerency and protestation.

For months the DUP had found itself in an unfamiliar role, participating in negotiations with the Secretary of State which the Unionist Party had unexpectedly decided to boycott. The DUP's supporters were puzzled and alarmed. The DUP was on the defensive. Then without warning everything was changed and the DUP was back in the role which the Party knows best, right-wing loyalist street politics.

In comparison with the repercussions which followed, this next event which took place in the city of Armagh was a small scale affair; only the three Westminster DUP MPs, Peter Robinson, Ian Paisley and, making one of his rare public appearances, Johnnie McQuade, participated. They were supported by about fifty other loyalist demonstrators, a very small turnout by comparison with other loyalist demonstrations. The protest itself took place on 8 May, on the occasion of the enthronement of the new Church of Ireland Archbishop, the Right Rev. Dr John Armstrong. It became known that the Taoiseach of the Irish Republic, Charles Haughey, intended to be present at the enthronement, so Paisley and his followers attempted to confront Haughey with their placards and bombard him with verbal abuse.

This was an archetypal Paisleyite demonstration and it conformed to the established ritual of these episodes,[8] because it was the RUC which restrained Paisley and his followers while the enthronement in the Cathedral continued uninterrupted.

Anne McHardy, writing in *The Guardian* the following day, in an article appositely entitled 'Paisley Pattern', observed that 'this was the first experience for the Northern Ireland Secretary, Mr Humphrey Atkins, of Paisley the rabble rouser, and it was neatly timed. Mr Atkins is putting the finishing touches to his plans for the future government of the Province, and all the signs are that he envisages a devolved administration which Paisley could head.'[9]

The realisation that Paisley's style of politics was reactionary, and that public demonstrations, which carry in their wake the inherent possibility of street disorders, were as characteristic of the DUP as the ability to achieve significant electoral successes, began to permeate the corridors of power and the columns of those quality newspapers which had briefly toyed with the notion that 'Paisley the P.M.' would prove to be a more restrained and mature politician than the well known 'street demagogue'.

Some weeks after McHardy's article, *The Irish Times* turned its attention to the phenomenon of Paisleyism. The writer, Conor O'Clery, came to the conclusion that 'those who have put their trust in the mantle of "respectability" which Paisley appeared to don at times during the last few years have constantly been disappointed'. Although the DUP protest at Armagh did not completely smother all talk of 'Paisley for PM' the demonstration on 8 May raised doubts about Paisley's capacity to provide restrained and constitutionally oriented leadership in a future devolved assembly, and the protest reflected on Paisley's personal political judgement.

The DUP leader had, through his EEC electoral success, gained political leverage over the British Government. In order to turn that leverage to his advantage, Paisley had to be flexible enough to talk to the Government in language which it could understand, while at the same time presenting a public profile which would give credibility to the Government's decision to negotiate with the leader of Ulster Protestant opinion. At the moment when this opportunity was beckoning, Paisley went off at a tangent and staged one of his stereotyped street demonstrations. The event in Armagh was predictable: it fitted into a pattern of DUP responses throughout a decade of 'constitutional uncertainty';[10] but the demonstration was also a soft option for Paisley.

Anne McHardy well understood the immediate advantage this protest gained for the DUP leader: 'In local political terms, the demonstration could do Mr Paisley considerable good. All the other Unionist parties joined him in criticising the invitation of Mr Haughey to the enthronement but their views were reported, if at all, in final paragraphs to the stories of Mr Paisley's doings.'

Dr Paisley had spurned the challenge to agree terms with the SDLP and the British Government; he preferred, instead, to remind his loyalist followers that the DUP had not 'weakened' and to reinforce his personal standing with the hardliners in Protestant Ulster.

Having missed an opportunity to engage in a realistic political dialogue with the British Government and the SDLP, the DUP turned in on itself and proceeded to consolidate its political base.

Calvert later remarked that 'throughout 1980 several more DUP branches were formed and the organisation spread into every corner of Ulster'. Financial problems had continually plagued the Party's organisers, but in June £12,000 was raised through a sponsored walk.

In the early summer, the Government produced yet another discussion document on the future of Northern Ireland, and the DUP replied by unambiguously ruling out the power sharing option, though the DUP remained of the opinion that the Government would offer firm proposals on devolution in the Queen's speech when Parliament reopened in November. Meanwhile, the Thatcher Government's concern about Irish events had been redirected by pressing problems on the Irish Republican side of the sectarian interface.

A further twist in the spiral of violence

On 27 October 1980, Republican prisoners in the 'H Blocks' at the Maze prison, near Belfast, began a hunger strike. Death fasts had a long tradition which stretched back through the annals of Irish nationalism, and it was evident that the issue of political status for IRA terrorist prisoners in the H Blocks had great potency for mobilising the nationalist population in both Northern Ireland and the Irish Republic.

This mobilisation of Irish Republican sentiment together with the concurrent violence in Northern Ireland greatly increased the pressure on the British Government to take some form of political initiative which would defuse the situation. Irish-American politicians in the United States of America went to great lengths to identify themselves with the widespread voicing of concern over the increased tension in the Province.

The British Government was resolute, and unwilling to make concessions to the Provisional IRA and INLA prisoners who were 'on the blanket' and engaged in 'the dirty protest', as the refusal to wear prison garb and the practice of smearing the cells with excrement were termed. The Thatcher Government sought the support of the Government of the Irish Republic in its determined stand and on 8 December 1980 a powerful delegation of Cabinet Ministers led by Mrs Thatcher met Charles Haughey, the Taoiseach, and two other colleagues in the Irish Government at a conference, which became known as the Dublin Summit.

At the conclusion of the Summit, a joint communique was issued which had the effect of raising the expectations of the Irish nationalists in the Province, as represented by the SDLP, and adding further to the mistrust and suspicion harboured by the Unionist electorate towards the Westminster administration.

The brief communique recognised, in a form that was open to the widest possible interpretation, what was termed 'the totality of relationships within these islands' and stated that both Governments would enter into joint studies on a 'range of issues . . . including possible new institutional structures'.

Ten days later the IRA prisoners in the H Blocks called off their protest and while there was controversy over the extent to which the British Government had finally capitulated to the demands of the 'men on the blanket', subsequent events were soon to establish that the prisoners themselves regarded the decision of 18 December to end the fast to the death as a surrender to the British Government.

The reaction to the Dublin Summit amongst the Unionists followed what was by now a well established pattern. The Official Unionists and the DUP both denounced the package but, while the Unionist Party was intent on offering a reasoned resistance to any measures which might endanger the Union, the DUP identified the Dublin Summit as an historic betrayal of Ulster Protestant interests:

> . . . it was only fitting that in 1981 when Ulster again was called to face a serious effort by a British Government to edge us out of the United Kingdom that Ulstermen should revert to the ways of their fathers, as today's generation with equal determination set about defeating the nefarious conspiracy hatched at the Dublin Summit was more subtle than the introduction in the 1912 Parliament of a Bill to establish a thirty-two county Irish Parliament it was just as dangerous for its end was the same[11] (sic).

The seriousness with which the DUP regarded the import of the Anglo-Irish agreement was soon demonstrated in a spectacular manner which briefly left the Unionist Party bereft of any appearance of offering opposition to the London-Dublin 'process'.

At midnight on Thursday, 5 February the DUP leaders, Robinson and Beattie, led a selected group of press men to witness Dr Paisley addressing a clandestine meeting of 500 loyalists drawn up in military formation who, in indication of their resolve, waved what were claimed to be firearm certificates against the cold night air. Of this band of vigilantes, Paisley said: 'This is a small token of men who are placed to absolutely devastate any attempt by Margaret Thatcher and Charles Haughey to destroy the Union and take from us our heritage'. This meeting, on a hillside near Ballymena, was the prologue to an extended political campaign which the DUP was about to mount, and the men who had been mobilised soon came to be known as 'The Third Force'. Was this to be the apogee of Dr

Paisley's numerous attempts to recruit a Protestant militia owing personal loyalty to him? Only time would tell.

Though this paramilitary formation drew widespread criticism from Protestant church leaders in the Province, Westminster politicians and the press leader writers, Paisley and the DUP pressed ahead with their policy of renewed confrontation. The DUP knew that many of the Unionist electorate rarely chose to look beyond the signs and symbols of reaction or bothered to question whether such stunts might in the long run be self-defeating.

Two days later, the party machine set up a specially summoned delegates' meeting which was held in Ballymena town hall. The purpose of the meeting was to consolidate the party activists in support of a policy of protestation and to apprise them of the form that this campaign on the streets of Ulster would take. The delegates learned that considerable sums of money were to be committed to an 'education campaign' and it was planned to distribute over 100,000 pieces of literature Province-wide.

Next the Party called a press conference on 9 February 1981 when it was revealed that an 'Ulster Declaration' closely modelled on the Ulster Covenant of 1912[12] had been published and that loyalists would be encouraged to sign the document.

The language in this declaration reflected a curious blend of style, drawing directly in places from the text of the original Ulster Covenant and then proceeding to incorporate contemporary usage as well. The twenty-line statement contained references which expressed 'sure confidence' that God 'will defend the right', and the threat which a united Ireland was presumed to pose to 'civil and religious freedom' was also given prominence. The declaration concluded that the Province was about to be subjected to 'an ongoing process of all-Ireland integration'.[13]

At this press conference the Party stated its intention to embark on another barnstorming campaign to be known as the 'Carson Trail'. The campaign began at Omagh on 13 February and concluded after eleven consecutive rallies with a massive demonstration of loyalist solidarity at the Carson Monument in the Parliament grounds at Stormont on Saturday, 28 March.

Though the DUP asserted that these histrionic protests at which Dr Paisley was able to display both his oratorical skills, and his sense of theatre, were targeted at the London-Dublin accord, other motives can be detected. The street protests were aimed at mobilising political support in time for the local government election which had been scheduled for May. There was an additional motive: the Carson Trial rallies were a propaganda stunt. This intention to counter the IRA hunger strike campaign of the previous winter was suddenly outflanked when on 1 March a Provisional IRA prisoner in the Maze, Bobby Sands, renewed the campaign for political status by going on a death fast.

Some days later Mrs Thatcher visited Northern Ireland and in the course of an address delivered during the visit, the Prime Minister went out of her way to allay Unionist fears that the Government intended to bring about the procured acquiescence of Northern Ireland in some form of future all-Ireland settlement. Mrs Thatcher directly challenged the DUP's understanding of the significance of the London-Dublin accord in the following words: 'Let me say with all the emphasis at my command that there is no plot. There is no sell out. Those who argue otherwise have simply got it wrong and are choosing not to understand the purpose of my discussions with Mr Charles Haughey.'

Despite Mrs Thatcher's intervention, Paisley continued to march along the 'Carson Trail' and a week after Mrs Thatcher's attempt to dampen down loyalist resentment, 15,000 people attended that Carson Trail Rally in Ballymena. Four more rallies took place before the Trail wound its way up the hill at Stormont buildings, to the accompaniment of numerous bands. *The Irish Times* estimated that the attendance at Stormont did not exceed 10,000 and that the DUP leader's disappointment with the poor showing communicated itself in his voice.

On the nationalist side of the divide, Sands' hunger strike had still not reached a critical stage when Frank Maguire, the independent Irish Republican MP for Fermanagh and South Tyrone, died, and this gave Sands the opportunity to intervene as the anti-H Blocks candidate in the subsequent by-election. This by-election, which Sands won, took place on 9 April, and the result is generally regarded as having provided evidence of an intensification of the polarisation within the Province.

While the Unionist Party and the DUP wrangled over whether a sufficient number of DUP voters had spoilt their ballot papers indirectly to have contributed to the electoral triumph of a convicted Provisional IRA terrorist, a rising crescendo of violence erupted across Northern Ireland. This dangerous situation prompted security chiefs to warn that the Provisional IRA intended to provoke the Unionist population into retaliation and civil war.

The by-election victory by Bobby Sands which inaugurated this emergency came only weeks before the long awaited local government elections. On 20 May 1981 the electors of Northern Ireland went to the polls for the ninth time since the DUP had been founded in 1971. The results represented a significant endorsement of the DUP's political style by 26·7 per cent of the electorate. An even more striking fact was that for the first time in ten years the DUP had councillors elected to every one of the twenty-six local district councils in Northern Ireland. This is how Calvert in his history of the DUP interpreted the DUP's electoral success:

> The results demonstrated that the DUP was the dominant force in Northern Ireland politics and the voice of Ulster Unionism. The DUP was now the largest party in 9 District Councils. In 5 Councils the DUP obtained more than 40% of the total votes cast. Of the 142 Councillors elected, 51 were elected on the first count having surpassed the necessary quota. Out of these 51 Councillors, 38 also topped the poll in their respective areas.

Calvert, surprisingly, does not overstate the significance of this result. Dr Paisley's ability to monopolise the articulation of the Unionist case and the strongly disciplined character of the DUP had the effect of increasing the DUP's political strength, to a degree which enabled the Party to take seats from the Official Unionist Party and to strengthen its hold on seats which in previous elections would have fallen to either the Vanguard Party or Baird's UUUP.

The local government results of May 1981 mark the peak of the DUP's electoral successes during the Party's first ten years. The votes cast for the DUP show an increase of nearly 7,000 votes over the previous personal vote obtained by Dr Paisley in June 1979, and as such these local government votes can be regarded as the sequel to Dr Paisley's triumph in the EEC election.

In June, the Carson Trail finally 'petered out', adding further weight to the suspicion that the Trail had been one prolonged electioneering campaign, and that it had been abandoned once its purpose had been served. The Republican protests and violence over the 'H Blocks' issue continued to dominate the headlines and Dr Paisley reacted by leading a 'military style' parade through the Tyrone village of Sixmilecross on 2 July. After the march Dr Paisley warned the crowd that: 'We have a choice to make. Shall we allow ourselves to be murdered by the IRA or shall we kill the killers?'

This parade in Sixmilecross was another stage in the evolution of the Paisleyite 'Third Force'. However, the overall effect of Dr Paisley's intention to mobilise paramilitary formations similar to those which had been drawn up in the Antrim hills during the previous winter sustains the belief that Dr Paisley and the DUP had committed themselves to a prolonged period of street politics, while the local election results indicated that the DUP's militancy had the backing of a significant percentage of Unionist voters.

By mid-summer, with the deaths of the other hunger strikers and murder stalking the streets, the political implications of Paisley's militancy were over-shadowed by the intensity of emotion, resentment and hatred engendered by the H Blocks crisis. Despite the intervention of humanitarian agencies like the Irish Commission for Peace and Justice, and the International Red Cross, it became evident that the British Government and the H Block hunger strikers were locked into a deadly struggle of wills. By early September there were signs that the resolve of the relatives of the Provisional IRA and INLA hunger strikers was starting to wilt, and it was at this critical moment in the crisis that Mrs Thatcher chose to replace Humphrey Atkins with a new Secretary of State, Mr James Prior. Mr Prior took up office on 14 September. Murders of members of the security forces continued throughout the rest of the month, but on 3 October it was formally announced that the hunger strike was at an end.

Since Bobby Sands had entered into a hunger strike on 1 March, sixty-four people had been killed, and this figure did not include the ten H Block protesters who had starved themselves to death; but any hopes that some semblance of normality might return to the Province were dashed when it became brutally clear that the catalogue of killing was not at an end.

The Provisional IRA and INLA continued to attack members of the security forces and at the end of October there was a series of murders of Roman Catholics committed by loyalist paramilitaries. Then on 14 November, Rev. Robert Bradford, Official Unionist MP for the Westminster Constituency of South Belfast and a colleague of Dr Paisley, was murdered at a constituency advice centre. According to the *News Letter*, Rev. Robert Bradford's assassination 'shocked the Unionist community perhaps more deeply than any other single act of the troubles'.

Two days later, a stunned House of Commons met to hear tributes paid to the murdered MP, but Dr Paisley, John McQuade and Peter Robinson made heated interventions which led to their suspension from the Chamber. The Speaker stated that the three DUP Members of Parliament were 'guilty of grossly disorderly conduct and of ignoring the authority of the Chair'. Outside the Houses of Parliament, Dr Paisley told the press that 'we have no other option but to call on the people of Northern Ireland to make it impossible for Mrs Thatcher and her ministers to govern the Province'.

One ironic repercussion of the DUP outburst in the House of Commons was that the 'grossly disorderly conduct' of the three MPs was the main item on television that evening while Mrs Thatcher's tribute to the fallen Ulster Unionist MP had to take second place.

Mr James Prior was among those who attended the funeral service for Rev. Robert Bradford in Dundonald Presbyterian Church. The Northern Ireland Secretary of State was subjected to abuse from elements in the large crowd gathered outside the church during both his arrival and departure. The next day the *Daily Telegraph* reported that 'ministerial colleagues were shocked when they watched the television pictures of Mr Prior being mobbed at the funeral and (they) saw the extent of outrage among the majority Protestant Unionist community'.

The incidents at the funeral service reflected the deepening divisions within the Protestant population. Though mourners apologised later to Mr Prior for the intemperate behaviour of their fellow loyalists, Dr Paisley, whose disorderly conduct in Parliament had provided an example for the mob at Dundonald to emulate, took a totally different view. Paisley claimed that Mr Prior should not have attended the service and that 'he was not wanted'. Later that evening Paisley announced that a Day of Action would be held on 23 November. That same night yet another member of the Ulster Defence Regiment, Albert Beacom, was murdered at Maguiresbridge in County Fermanagh.

The sermon which the local Church of Ireland minister preached at his funeral differed little from thousands of other sermons which had been preached at the gravesides of the victims of the violence down through the years. However, the address did raise important issues by questioning the attitude of the Roman Catholic bishops in Ireland and their people in Fermanagh towards Irish Republican terrorism:

> Roman Catholics of County Fermanagh, we don't expect you to be Protestant. We don't expect you to vote unionist. We do expect you to honour the law of god and to turn your face against all who defy it. How can we accept or understand your sympathy with our sorrow when you cast your vote for the representatives of those who have inflicted it upon us? . . . I wish to speak too, to the Roman Catholic Bishops of Ireland. You can do much to help the Protestants of this Province, and by so doing help your own people. Do not just condemn these murders, excommunicate those who boast of committing them. It is acknowledged that the action of your predecessors in the 1950s played a major part in bringing that terror campaign to an end. . . .[14]

The sentiments expressed demonstrate that Paisley was not alone in his denunciations of the Roman Catholic Church. There was a difference, however, between Paisley's belligerent anti-Catholicism and the questionings of the Church of Ireland rector in Aghavea. There is a hesitancy and a humility in the Church of Ireland rector's sermon; it is something which comes from the heart, born of the anguish of the moment, and it is in stark contrast to the undercurrent, 'the will to power', which courses through much of Dr Paisley's criticism.

Four days later, the Day of Action took place; the *News Letter* recorded that it was a 'massive victory for the Paisley approach'.

The same evening between 5,000 and 10,000 members of the Third Force marched through the town of Newtownards where they were reviewed by Dr Paisley. The Newtownards demonstration turned out to be the concluding chapter in the tale of the Third Force. As Christmas and the New Year approached, there was a sharp fall off in terrorist incidents, and it became apparent that, faced with increased security measures by the British Government and having created the terrible probability of some form of massive loyalist retaliation, the Irish Republican terrorists had decided to make a tactical withdrawal. Like the 'Carson Trail' the Third Force phenomenon began to fade away but, before it did so, a dramatic episode occurred which suggested that Paisley's 'stunts' had, to some extent at least, been counter-productive.

One of the last political acts of Rev. Robert Bradford before he was assassinated was to propose that a visit to the United States of America should be undertaken by Unionist politicians and laymen to 'tell the truth about Ulster'. To this end, a series of advertisements appeared in the *News Letter* in October asking the general public to subscribe to a fund in support of 'Operation USA'.

After the murder of the MP for South Belfast, it was announced that Mrs Norah Bradford would take up the place on the panel of unionist politicians left vacant by the death of her husband. Other members of the party included Mr John Taylor, an Official Unionist Member of the European Parliament, Peter Robinson and Dr Paisley. Inevitably, the presence of Dr Paisley on the 'Operation USA' panel gave a certain complexion to the proposed visit. A powerful lobby of Irish American Congressmen announced that they intended to frustrate Dr Paisley's entry into the United States and, after studying transcripts of Dr Paisley's bellicose speeches, the State Department refused Paisley an entry visa.

Operation USA went ahead as planned; the only alterations made to the publicity drive were to accommodate Mrs Eileen Paisley who took her husband's place, and to rearrange the itinerary so that Paisley flew to Canada instead of the United States. However, the refusal of entry to the United States inflicted some damage on Paisley because it showed that his fundamentalist backers carried much less clout in Washington than did the Irish American lobby, and there was another implication as well: Paisley's extremism might win him plaudits in Ulster, but it provoked international hostility to the Province.

As in the past, Paisley reacted sharply to this rebuff and the DUP began to moderate its activities, but not to such an extent that there was any diminution in the Paisleyite Party's ruthless determination to get the better of the Official Unionist Party at the hustings.

The Loyalists' tendency toward self-destruction

Early in the new year, the attention of both the DUP and the Official Unionist Party was taken up by the question of the vacant South Belfast seat. Rev. Robert Bradford had originally been elected as a Vanguard Unionist under the Coalition banner of the UUUC in 1974, but he had joined the Official Unionists in the aftermath of the Voluntary Coalition fiasco. This gave the DUP grounds for claiming that the seat should be fought by an agreed Unionist, and for some weeks there were rumours to the effect that Mrs Norah Bradford could be persuaded to stand. Mrs Bradford refused to stand, and the failure of the DUP to secure an 'agreed Unionist' marked an important turning point in the Party's fortunes. An 'agreed Unionist' would have neutralised the Official Unionists in the constituency and, in all probability, once elected, the new MP would have tended to support the Paisley faction to whose behind-the-scenes pressure he or she would have owed the seat.

The two Unionist parties selected rival candidates. The Official Unionists chose one of their best known political figures, Rev. Martin Smyth, the Grand Master of the Loyal Orange Institution, while the DUP selected the hardline fundamentalist minister and popular gospel recording artist, Rev. William McCrea. The contest would be fought out between two evangelical clerics who were conservative or right-wing in their politics. The by-election also provided an example of the DUP's function as an agent of politicisation because Rev. William McCrea was, like Ian Paisley before him, an outsider, who would in all probability never have been endorsed at any selection meeting organised by the Ulster Unionist Party. The contest turned out to be a bitter one and a classic illustration of self-destructive forces at work within the faction-ridden Protestant majority in the Province.

At the same time as the internal wrangling over prospective loyalist candidates to fight the Westminster by-election was taking place, the media were devoting considerable coverage to what has become known as the Kincora scandal. The police had undertaken to investigate newspaper reports of abuses at a Welfare Home in Belfast. In December 1981, three members of the staff at the Kincora home, one of whom was a member of the Orange Order, were gaoled on charges of committing sexual offences against the boys in their care. Dr Paisley attended a press conference on 26 January when he denied any involvement in the Kincora case, specifically denying that he had known that the convicted member of the staff who was also an Orangeman, was a homosexual. Dr Paisley conceded later that he knew the member of staff and that he had been informed in 1974 that the person in question was a homosexual but he did not know that he worked at a children's home.

This affair impinged on the election prospects of both the Unionist parties, because Rev. Martin Smyth was also involved on the periphery of the issue, but some activists to whom the writer has spoken claimed that the episode hurt the DUP at the time. There is no way of quantifying this, so all that is necessary is to note the political aspects of the affair.

The by-election was held on 4 March and Rev. Martin Smyth successfully warded off the challenge with a majority of 5,397 votes over the DUP, which trailed behind the Alliance Party candidate, a former Lord Mayor of Belfast, David Cook.

Though the DUP fought a vigorous campaign their percentage share of the vote (22·55 per cent) was down on their 1981 local government results (26·7 per cent); against this it must be borne in mind that the constituency areas were not completely identical. The Unionist Party had put up its strongest candidate, Martin Smyth, who had been able to call upon the support of a large number of party workers and activists from the Orange Order in Belfast throughout the by-election campaign, and these facts were of fundamental importance to the Unionist success.

However, other factors influenced the result and indicated that there had been some slippage in the overall support for the DUP. One of these was the phenomenon of the Third Force or 'Third Farce' as some of Paisley's critics had termed the venture. Protestants had become increasingly disenchanted with loyalist paramilitarism and were more inclined to trust their defence to the Government security forces.

With the invasion of the Falkland Islands by Argentina, attention shifted to the deterioration in Anglo-Irish relations. The decision of the Government of the Irish Republic on 24 May not to continue economic sanctions against Argentina was only one of a number of factors which led to a cooling in the relations between the United Kingdom and the Irish Republic. Other factors had included the failure of Jim Prior and the British Government to consult with the Republic's Government over a new British initiative for Ulster. This initiative, known as 'Rolling Devolution', committed the Thatcher

Government to the establishment of a new Northern Ireland Assembly which would proceed towards fully devolved powers by stages and had as its ultimate objective the creation of a power sharing administration.

The Dublin Government condemned the proposals and raised the further objection that the initiative did not take into account the Irish dimension.

The Falklands factor was a reminder that events external to Northern Ireland could have a highly significant impact on the interior political development of the Province. Unionists noted the hostility of the Government of the Irish Republic, took satisfaction from the discord created in Anglo-Irish relations as a result of the war in the South Atlantic, and were wont to contrast the resolve of the Thatcher Government in rescuing the Falkland Islanders from the hands of their aggressive foreign neighbour with what they conceived to be a lamentable failure of will in the face of Irish Republican terrorism in Ulster.

Prior's Devolution Bill did not become law without a struggle. There was a minor right-wing Tory revolt against the proposals by a faction which favoured integration. This right-wing Tory harassment of the Prior proposals only underlined the inability of the Unionists in Northern Ireland to consolidate the measure of pro-Ulster support which they enjoyed in Parliament. The more the Ulster Unionists fell under the influence of the inward-looking embattled mentality of Dr Paisley and the devolutionists the more they cut themselves adrift from those right-wing Tories and other allies in England whose political inclination was to support the Province.

Concurrent with these developments a bitter struggle began to take shape between Dr Paisley and Enoch Powell. This clash between the man who claimed to speak for Protestant Ulster and the Member for South Down, widely acknowledged to be the greatest parliamentarian of the last thirty years, was symbolic of the internecine feud within Unionism.

Powell's advocacy of the Union was based on his commitment to the concept of sovereignty; consequently Powell eschewed any hint of sectarianism in his approach to the Ulster question. Furthermore he had long argued that integration was the best safeguard, not only for the Unionists, but for the minority as well. Powell drew a distinction when he used the word 'Unionist' which other loyalist politicians often omitted. Powell accepted that numbers of Roman Catholics in Ulster also voted for the Union.

Early in 1982, Powell denounced the Prior proposals as one facet of a conspiracy organised in the main by high ranking civil servants in London and Dublin, the intent of which was to detach Ulster from the United Kingdom and create the political circumstances in which the unification of Ireland would become inevitable. As Molyneaux, the leader of the Ulster Unionists, agreed with Powell's arcane analysis, the Unionist Party's stance on devolution was pushed to the right of the DUP's. Paisley's Party supported the Prior proposals as a means of making direct rule accountable to the electorate.

This was the background to the confrontation between the two Unionist politicians in which Paisley denounced Powell as 'an Englishman' and later as a 'foreigner and Anglo-Catholic'. Paisley's rejection of Powell brought to the surface undercurrents of resentment, anti-intellectualism, and a tendency to isolationism. The paradoxes in Paisley's position were nearly as complex as the man himself. Here was the advocate of Democratic Unionism treating the leading parliamentarian of his generation to a vial of the DUP leader's vitriol, and the defender of traditional Unionism heaping ingratitude on an English politician who had chosen, not only to bear the same personal risks and dangers as Ulster politicians, but to advocate the cause of the Union with all the passion and integrity at his command.

The controversy between Paisley and Powell was only one aspect of the continuing struggle between the rival Unionist parties, and as the elections to the new Northern Ireland Assembly drew closer the contest quickened. However, to all but the most dedicated of loyalist activists this feud between the rival claimants to the mantle of 'traditional Unionism' was incomprehensible. The Official Unionist Party and the DUP were, after all, right-wing parties, both opposed power sharing, and both apparently wanted devolution within the United Kingdom framework. Political logic indicated that a faction-ridden Unionism would be able to exert even less leverage over the Government at Westminster than a united loyalist movement but, as with Paisley's antipathy towards Powell, political logic was no match for Protestant passion.

The elections were held to a seventy-eight member Assembly on 20 October 1982; and the attention of the media was directed to the 'notable success' of Provisional Sinn Fein, which gained five seats. There had been a total of 184 candidates representing some seventeen parties, and a few independents. The twelve Northern Ireland constituencies were used, although Molyneaux had fought a rear-guard action in Parliament to have this PR election fought on the basis of the boundary changes incorporating five extra seats at Westminster.

The results of the election confirmed the impression that the Official Unionists had gained ground despite the challenge from the DUP, whose share of the vote at 22·99 per cent was only marginally up on the percentage share recorded in March at the time of the South Belfast by-election (22·55 per cent).

In view of the difficulty which the ordinary loyalist must have experienced in aligning himself with one or other of the loyalist factions, it is hardly surprising that one of the most crucial factors which affected the Unionist Party's improved showing was the tactical decision taken by the Party to encourage its Westminster MPs to fight the October 1982 Northern Ireland Assembly election. Not all the Official Unionists did so, but in a PR election where Unionist first preference votes had a tendency to flow towards the better known loyalist on the ballot paper, the decision had the effect of maximising the Official Unionist vote in a number of key constituencies, while in other constituencies like Fermanagh and South Tyrone and South Down, where DUP support was weak, the fact that the name of an Official Unionist MP did not figure on the ballot paper did not materially affect the outcome.

Against the success registered by the Official Unionists, the DUP had to measure the solidarity and fervour of the representatives who had been returned as followers of Dr Paisley. Changes were apparent; Paisley was becoming increasingly a father figure in a Party of younger men, sometimes described as 'radical' because of their increased awareness of social needs and their reservations about pressing religious issues such as Sabbath observance too far. The impression that the DUP had gained added momentum as a result of an influx of radical young Paisleyites, some of whom had been elected to the Assembly, was offset by the stubborn reality that of the twenty-one DUP members elected, eighteen were adherents of the Free Presbyterian Church, and that of the five prominent young radicals, three were also adherents of the Free Presbyterian Church.

The Assembly by-passed

The first meeting of the Assembly took place in the main chamber at Stormont on 11 November, and it soon became apparent that an intriguing pattern of political alignments was in prospect. The DUP, led by Dr Paisley, swung into another extended phase of conciliation which had as its aim the winning of a measure of devolved power from the British Government, as a reward for moderation. One aspect of this moderate mood involved a covert coalition with the Alliance Party. This informal pact secured the election of James Kilfedder, the UPUP member of the Assembly, as the first presiding officer, and John Cushnahan, a Roman Catholic Alliance member, as the Chairman of the Assembly Education Committee.

The Assembly proved to be a shadow-play; nothing of substance emerged. The existence of this devolved institution encouraged the Alliance Party, the DUP and Unionists to act out roles implying that local politics in the Province had relevance. To this end, the DUP made much of the Assembly's scrutiny committees. The Official Unionists, preoccupied with maintaining party unity after a decade of defections, adopted an ambivalent attitude to the Stormont institution. Molyneaux's determination to suppress the internal Unionist Party debate between those who believed that if the clock could only be turned back there would be a Parliament once more at Stormont, and the integrationists, played into the hands of the DUP.

The rival Unionist parties circled each other, like Apache warriors in a knife fight, while decisions about their citizenship and territorial rights were being taken elsewhere. Over the years there had grown up a community of interest between the British and Irish Governments in finding a 'solution' to the Northern Ireland problem. This process of harmonisation was encouraged by John Hume, the leader of the SDLP, who articulated a sophisticated Irish nationalist approach to the crisis. In March 1983, Hume proposed the setting up of a Forum to bring forward an agenda for a 'New Ireland'. By this time there was a coalition government in the Republic led by the affable Taoiseach, Dr Garrett Fitzgerald of Fine Gael. Fitzgerald responded warmly to Hume's political initiative and another stage in the SDLP leader's gradualist approach to Irish unification had been reached.

Jim Molyneaux and Enoch Powell had achieved increased parliamentary representation for the Province at Westminster, so that when the United Kingdom went to the polls in a general election in June a total of seventeen seats were contested in the Province. Interest centred on the growing political strength of Sinn Fein as well as on the latest round of the struggle for supremacy in the loyalist camp. The Official Unionists did comparatively well taking eleven seats. The DUP retained their hold on three seats exchanging a loss in North Belfast for a gain in Mid-Ulster, where Rev. William McCrea warded off the Sinn Fein challenge from Danny Morrison. Gerry Adams, a leading advocate of the Provisionals' 'armalite and ballot box' strategy, took West Belfast, though not his seat at Westminster.

There was much ill-considered speculation that the onward march of the DUP had been halted. The DUP, somewhat untypically, had blundered. Ian Paisley could have won in another constituency, knowing that North Antrim would remain under DUP control. And the Party's short-sighted decision to discipline the popular Roy Beggs rebounded when Beggs won East Antrim for the Official Unionists. Other difficulties clouded the Party's fortunes, because the hapless Rev. William Beattie became embroiled in a highly publicised feud with the Paisleyite stalwart, William Belshaw of Lisburn. Belshaw, like Beggs, withdrew from the DUP and joined the Molyneaux camp.

By the autumn attention had switched back to the boycotted Assembly where the competition between the Ulster Unionists and the DUP took on a new aspect following the horrendous murders of three men and the injury of seven others worshipping in Mountain Lodge Pentecostal Gospel Hall at Darkley in County Armagh. The Ulster Unionist Party demanded a reappraisal of security from Jim Prior, the Secretary of State, and underlined their resolve by withdrawing from the Assembly the day after the outrage, 21 November. There were now more Assembly members boycotting Prior's devolution experiment than attending it.

In April of the following year, Chris Patten, the Under-Secretary of State, announced that a statutory rule had been made changing the name of Londonderry City Council to Derry City Council. The name change demonstrated the British Government's willingness 'to make Irish Nationalists feel more at home in the Province', but the Government's decision outraged loyalists who perceived the name change to be another feature of the cultural attrition to which they believed the majority were being subjected. This highly emotive episode brought to the fore another DUP politician, Gregory Campbell, and precipitated further division among the anguished loyalists who comprised the minority population in a predominantly nationalist city.

On 2 May, 1984, the long awaited Report of the Forum on a New Ireland was published in Dublin. The immediate aims of the Forum Report were to describe the prevailing political realities in Ireland and to urge on both governments the creation of political structures which would end 'the deep and growing alienation of Nationalists in the North from the system of political authority'.

Initially the British Government's response to the Report of the New Ireland Forum was cool and evasive. Both Unionist parties rejected the Report of the Forum and published brief critiques of the Irish Nationalist analysis, but both parties entirely underestimated the importance of the Report and the impact which it was to make on future British policy. The Forum Report was seriously flawed; it largely misconstrued the influence of religious beliefs in Ulster, minimised the Scottish dimension in the history and economic development of the Province and vacuously asserted that once Partition was resolved the violence would fade away.

Perhaps it was the impending European elections which had distracted the loyalists so that they failed to offer a serious challenge to the Forum document; whatever the reason, both parties rapidly shifted their attention to the European scene.

The 1984 European election turned out to be a considerable personal triumph for Dr Paisley, though the media tended to underplay his outstanding achievement in increasing the size of his first preference votes from 170,688 in 1979 to an extremely creditable 230,351. Though there had been an increase in the percentage turnout, this ought not to detract from Paisley's success. The result, however, might well have been different.

The Official Unionist Party could not agree on whether John Taylor, the politician and successful businessman who already held a seat in Europe, should be automatically endorsed or whether Harold McCusker, the passionate and articulate MP for County Armagh, should be thrown into the lists against Ian Paisley. A hard fought selection battle ensued in which John Taylor, who had been a Minister in the old Stormont Parliament, was supported by the Unionist Party's old guard and elements of Bill Craig's defunct Vanguard Party who had made their peace with Glengall Street; Harold McCusker attracted the support of the younger section of the Party and its right wing. Taylor, who had needed second preferences from Paisley to take a seat in 1979, was selected and Ulster was denied a contest between the Unionist Party's most popular spokesman and the leader of the DUP.

John Hume stood aside from the Unionist divisions and campaigned to thwart the growing political strength of Sinn Fein whose candidate was Danny Morrison. Hume was re-elected to Europe with 151,399 first preference votes, while Taylor was also successful, gaining a total of 147,169 votes, and being elected on the second count.

There had been a general decline in terrorist violence throughout the early years of the decade. The informer system of 'supergrass' trials, though controversial, produced a large number of convictions. However, the Provisional IRA's strategy of aligning the armalite rifle with an orchestrated political campaign indicated a determination to exploit their weaponry increasingly to psychological effect.

In the early hours of 12 October 1984, 20lb. of commercial explosive exploded above the suite of hotel rooms occupied by the Prime Minister and her entourage attending the Annual Conservative Party Conference at Brighton. Those who had survived the outrage in which five guests were killed, including Sir Anthony Berry MP, and thirty others were admitted to hospital, some, like Mrs Norman Tebbitt, with crippling injuries, assembled on the sea front in their night attire in stunned disbelief. It was the most severe shock which the Provisional IRA had managed to deliver to the British body politic. It remained to be seen, however, whether this shock treatment would bring about the required change of behaviour.

Just over a month later, on 19 November 1984, Mrs Thatcher met Dr Fitzgerald at another of the Anglo-Irish summits. The Report of the Forum, with its three recommended options, including a unitary Irish state, a federal Ireland or joint sovereignty, was on the agenda. Mrs Thatcher took everyone by surprise with the vehemence of her rejection of the Irish Government's proposals. Later Dr Fitzgerald told a private meeting of his supporters in Dublin that he found Mrs Thatcher's press conference response of 'out, out, out!' to the three options 'gratuitously offensive'.

As the winter wore on loyalists grew alarmed at the Provisionals' strategy of 'physical force and political action'. In the shadow of this threat from IRA bombers in politicians' suits, the rival parties moved closer together. On 28 February 1985 the Provisionals launched a mortar attack on Newry RUC station in which nine police officers died. The IRA, in a statement after the attack, stated: 'This was a major and well-planned operation, indicating our ability to strike where and when we decide'. Paisley and Molyneaux, reacting to the Newry attack, began to draw up the framework for a joint approach to the crisis.

The first test of this improvement in relations between the DUP and the Ulster Unionists came in the spring of 1985 when the Province went to the polls in local government elections. Following the 15 May poll in which a total of 566 council seats were contested the DUP gained 24 per cent of the vote, taking 142 seats, while the Unionist Party gained 190 seats with 30 per cent of the vote. Though the competition between the DUP and the Unionists had been limited the results confirmed the underlying trends: the rival loyalist parties were stalemated. Ian Paisley commanded most popular support among voters, but the Official Unionists were the stronger on the ground.

Much concern was also expressed at the strength of Provisional Sinn Fein, which chalked up 12 per cent of the vote and took 59 seats. Immediately after the results, the DUP and the Unionists announced that there would be no 'fraternising' with the Sinn Fein councillors and that the loyalists had been given a mandate by the electorate to 'smash' Sinn Fein. The council chambers became a battle ground as the loyalists mounted an inept and at times farcical campaign to exclude Sinn Fein from the Council Chambers. The Unionists' predicament was all the more acute because the Northern Ireland Office operated a double standard. The Secretary of State, Douglas Hurd, and his parliamentary colleagues in the NIO refused to meet Sinn Fein representatives, but expected the loyalists to work with the Provisionals in local government. Having previously rejected a Unionist appeal that all prospective candidates in the elections sign an undertaking repudiating violence, the Northern Ireland Office stance served to increase the pressure on the loyalists.

On 21 June, Bill Craig, who had suffered a protracted illness, wrote a private letter[15] to Molyneaux and Paisley, in which he warned of the direction the London-Dublin talks were taking. In the text of the letter Craig offered a chilling analysis of the military potential of the IRA. Although Molyneaux acknowledged the letter, Paisley, not wishing to be seen to resurrect the career of the fallen Vanguard leader, ignored it. Craig's premonition of danger ahead went largely unheeded. A few weeks later, responding to various straws in the wind, the loyalists did establish an *ad hoc* committee which was given the task of setting out a joint strategy towards any agreement between Thatcher and Fitzgerald. Once again, the loyalists had seriously underestimated the influence which the Irish Republic was able to exert over the British Government[16] and the *ad hoc* committee went complacently about its business.

Throughout the late summer and early autumn there were persistent stories in the press that the British and Irish Governments had reached an accord on Northern Ireland. The Northern Ireland Office played down reports in the Irish press that Dublin would be given a say in the North; then Sir John Hermon, the Chief Constable, caused the NIO further embarrassment when he reportedly told an American police audience in Texas that the Irish Republic's security forces had failed either to infiltrate the Provisional IRA or to commit sufficient resources to the defeat of terrorism. By November, informed sources were stating that an agreement had been reached; yet early in the week beginning 10 November, Jim Molyneaux assured a close aide that Mrs Thatcher would not give the Republic a say in the affairs of a region of the United Kingdom. Molyneaux was not alone in an assessment which was shared by others in the higher echelons of Official Unionism. When on 15 November Mrs Thatcher flew to Hillsborough Castle, formerly the official residence of the Governor of Northern Ireland, to sign the Anglo-Irish Agreement with the Taoiseach of the Irish Republic, the Unionist politicians were devastated. The sense of betrayal was so intense as to be tangible.

The Agreement, which comprised thirteen articles, established an Intergovernmental Conference. Ministers from London and Dublin would jointly agree policy on a wide range of issues. Premises at Maryfield, on the southern shores of Belfast Lough, were occupied by the secretariat which included civil servants from the Irish Republic. The Accord bore comparison with the 1972 proposals of the SDLP which envisaged an Ulster condominium. John Hume's long term strategy had brought dividends.

'Ulster Says No'

On Saturday, 23 November Ulster gave its answer. Thousands of loyalists carrying slogans reading 'Maggie's Munich Agreement' and 'Ulster Says No' converged on Belfast City Hall. The platform party, consisting of Unionist MPs and some Assembly members, huddled round the microphones against the bitter winds. Molyneaux, speaking first, had to cope with an inefficient public address system. His remarks made little impression: this was of small consequence, because the assembled thousands realised that their physical presence at the rally signalled a massive rejection of the Accord. Ian Paisley, in a sonorous voice, spoke next and fared better. Addressing the cheering crowds Paisley warned of a long battle demanding 'staying power' and he accused Mrs Thatcher of 'signing away to Dublin our inalienable right to equality of citizenship within the United Kingdom'.[17]

As the rally concluded, fourteen loyalist MPs signed an undertaking to resign their Westminster parliamentary seats and fight by-elections unless the Accord was scrapped. The British Government, meanwhile, had drawn up contingency plans to defeat any loyalist street violence. Initially, attempts were made to minimise the numbers rejecting the Thatcher initiative but when aerial photographs were published it became evident that this Edward Carson-like protest had attracted 300,000 supporters.

The 23 November demonstration marked the re-emergence of Ian Paisley as the dominant voice in loyalist politics. Paisley's demeanour on the platform suggested that he was pre-eminent among the loyalists. Many of those in his shadow that day had only gained a voice in Ulster politics because Paisley had succeeded in breaking the hegemony of the Ulster Unionist Party. Seen by many as a father figure who had mellowed with the years, Paisley advocated 'constitutional' opposition to the Agreement, though both he and Molyneaux stated that if democratic means failed, paramilitary violence could ensue.

The scene next shifted to Westminster where the Accord received the approbation of an overwhelming majority of MPs. In the course of the two-day debate Enoch Powell, drawing on the analogy of Scotland, contended that support for the agreement would 'undermine the authority of parliament as the law-making institution of the whole of this kingdom'. Scotland could only be treated 'differentially' in respect of its legal system because the people of Scotland gave their consent. The burden of Powell's speech was that the Government's actions had been immoral.

By 1 January 1986 all the Unionist MPs had resigned their Westminster seats. Before the by-elections took place the Government moved speedily to implement its policy. There was violence at Maryfield on the day that Peter Barry, the Republic's Foreign Minister and joint chairman of the Intergovernmental Conference, met Tom King, four miles to the south-west at Stormont Castle. Over the new year period, Young Unionists, led by Robert Lyle, joined Young Democrats on a five-day march from Londonderry to Maryfield. Carrying 'equal citizenship' banners and 'Ulster Says No' posters, the march attracted growing support, as once more the focus of dissent was the Secretariat, shielded by barbed wire and the RUC.

The DUP and Unionists formalised a coalition pact before the by-elections. Both leaders campaigned together, though not all their Unionist colleagues ran constituency campaigns with a like vigour, and the parties published an agreed manifesto. It appeared that loyalist politics had turned full circle, but the Agreement had brought a new clarity to the Ulster situation. It was now widely recognised that the failure over time of the British national parties to contest elections in the Province had condemned the electorate to years of sectarian politics. Remarkably, it was Ian Paisley, the fundamentalist firebrand, who articulated this issue in an eve of poll interview in the *Ballymena Guardian*. Asked about the need for a 'dummy candidate' in his constituency, Paisley replied:

> If this was any other part of the United Kingdom the Governing Party would have a candidate to test the issue. Where is the Governing Party? Where is King or his colleagues? Where is the Labour Party? Where is the SDP who are always lecturing us? Where is David Owen?

The by-elections were an anti-climax. Some 418,930 electors voted against the Agreement, representing 71·9 per cent of the total votes cast. There was a sustained campaign to minimise the significance of the poll. Dublin and London drew comfort from the fact that Seamus Mallon, the deputy leader of the SDLP, making aggressive use of postal voting, had taken Newry and South Armagh from the Official Unionists. This, it was suggested, proved that the Accord's aim of taking support from the Provisionals was enjoying success.

Throughout this period the Provisional IRA campaign continued, though Protestant clergymen no longer used the cliché 'mindless violence' to describe IRA rural outrages. Constable David Hanson had been murdered on the day of the Agreement, the 144th RUC man to be assassinated. Ian Paisley, having visited the grieving relatives, returned to take the evening service in the Martyrs Memorial. It took some weeks before word of what the Free Presbyterian Moderator had said[18] percolated through.

In the course of his opening prayer, Ian Paisley laid Ulster's plight before Almighty God:

> Thou dost know the tragedy and betrayal that has overtaken our Province; thou dost know how this people that have passed through such a severe ordeal in the past fifteen years; that have followed the coffins that bore the murdered bodies of their loved ones; that have shed their bitter tears over the tragedy after tragedy that has overtaken us; how, our God and Father, they have patiently endured the ordeal of fire, the ordeal of pain, the ordeal of assassination, the ordeal of bombing and maiming . . . and have now been basely betrayed . . .

Paisley worshipped the God of his fathers, the God of the Covenanters, and like the lowland Scots in 'the killing times' who did not baulk at 'denuding' the Stuart monarch of his kingly authority, the Ulster preacher turned to Margaret Thatcher. In a manner to which outsiders would have responded incredulously, Ian Paisley's prayer of the 17 November continued:

> We pray this night that Thou wouldst deal with the Prime Minister of our country. We remember that the Apostle Paul handed over the enemies of truth to the Devil that they might learn not to blaspheme. In the name of Thy blessed Self, Father, Son and Holy Ghost, we hand this woman Margaret Thatcher over to the Devil, that she might learn not to blaspheme. We pray that thou'dst make her a monument of Thy divine vengeance; we pray that the world will learn a lesson through her fall, and will learn a lesson through the ignominy to which she shall be brought . . . For wilt Thou not hear the cries of Thy people, and if Thou wilt not hear their cry, we are confident that Thou wilt hear the cry of innocent blood that comes from the soil of Ulster today; and, O God, in wrath take vengeance upon this wicked treacherous lying woman, take vengeance upon her O Lord and grant that we shall see a demonstration of Thy power . . .

Sitting in the taut silence of a packed Martyrs Memorial many must have wondered what had brought Ulster to such a pass, or provoked Paisley to such a torrent of indignation. Characterised by their detractors as having a 'siege mentality', the Ulster loyalists, unlike the SDLP, had been excluded from the Thatcher-Fitzgerald talks; not a single representative of the Governing Party, or any other national party, would contest the by-elections; and Government spokesmen affirmed that the result would be ignored.

Others had added bricks to the ramparts behind which Ian Paisley gave expression and a political voice to those within Unionism who most closely identified with the Orange tradition, and for whom the Siege of Derry remains a potent symbol of Ulster Protestant defiance, Irish aggression and the British Government's tardiness in sending relief.

Notes and References

1 David Calvert, *A Decade of the DUP*, Belfast 1981, 12.
2 See the criticism levelled at Ulster Free Presbyterianism in *The Constitution and Government of the Bible Presbyterian Church*, Larne 1980, Preface item vi, subsection 7: 'The despotic rule of a hierarchy, displayed in unprincipled inquisitorial power and clandestine meetings'.
3 See also an article by the author on the 1979 general election, 'Alarm Bells Ring for the Official Unionist Party', *Irish Times*, 19 May 1979.
4 W. D. Flackes, *Northern Ireland: A Political Directory 1968–1979*, Dublin 1980, 179–180.
5 Sydney Elliott, *Northern Ireland: The First Election to the European Parliament*, Belfast 1980, 20.
6 Jacques Ellul, *Propaganda: The Formation of Men's Attitudes*, New York 1965, 216. See especially: 'The system of committees, which express themselves weakly, leads only to sporadic and fragmentary action. Speed of action or reaction is essential to propaganda'.
7 This headline, 'Paisley for P.M.', was printed on the front page of a *Workers Weekly* broadsheet, vol. ii, no. 363 (28 November 1981), Belfast.
8 A. T. Q. Stewart, *The Narrow Ground: Aspects of Ulster 1609–1969*, London 1977, 148. Stewart here discusses the internal logic of rioting in Ulster at some length.
9 *The Guardian*, 9 May 1980.
10 This phrase was first used in a Bow Group pamphlet, *Do You Sincerely Want to Win?*, London 1973.
11 Sam Wilson, *The Carson Trail*, Belfast 1981, 9.
12 See A. T. Q. Stewart, *The Ulster Crisis*, London 1967, which gives a definitive account of the events of 1912.
13 Wilson, *Carson Trail*, 30, where 'Ulster's Declaration' is given in full.
14 The sermon is another example of ephemeral literature in Northern Ireland; there is no printer or author shown. The title is: *A Sermon Preached in Aghavea Parish Church on Thursday 19 November 1981 at the Funeral of Albert Beacom who was Murdered on his Farm by Republican Terrorists*.
15 I was given access to Bill Craig's letter in the autumn of 1985.
16 Simon Murphy, 'Irish and British Government Policy in Northern Ireland, 1968–1982', U.C.W. Aberystwyth.
17 *Belfast Telegraph*, 25 November 1985.
18 A tape of this prayer and sermon for the evening of 17 November 1985 is available from Martyrs Memorial Recordings, 356 Ravenhill Road, Belfast.

Selected Bibliography

ANONYMOUS, *Orangeism in Ireland and Throughout the Empire*, Vols. I and II, Thynne and Co. Ltd., London (no date given).

ARTHUR, PAUL, *The Government and Politics of Northern Ireland*, Longman's Publishing Group, Essex 1980.

BARR, J., *The Scottish Covenanters*, John Smith and Son, Glasgow 1946.

BELL, J. BOWYER, *The Secret Army: A History of the IRA 1916–1970*, Anthony Blond Ltd., London 1970.

BOULTON, DAVID, *The UVF 1966–1973: An Anatomy of Loyalist Rebellion*, Torc Books, Gill and MacMillan, Dublin 1973.

CALVERT, DAVID, *A Decade of the DUP*, Crown Publications, Belfast 1981.

CALVIN, JOHN, *Institutes of the Christian Religion*, Vols. I and II, J. T. McNeill (Ed.), The Westminster Press, Philadelphia 1960.

CARLTON, D. AND SCHAERF, *Contemporary Terror: Studies in Sub-State Terror*, MacMillan, London 1981.

CATHERWOOD, SIR H. F. R., *Christian Duty in Ulster Today*, Evangelical Press, London 1969.

COOGAN, TIM PAT, *The Irish: A Personal View*, Phaidon Press, London 1975.

DEUTSCH, RICHARD, AND MAGOWAN, VIVIEN, *Northern Ireland 1968–1973: A Chronology of Events*, Vols. I and II, Blackstaff Press, Belfast 1973.

DOLLAR, G. W., *A History of Fundamentalism in America*, Bob Jones University Press, Greenville South Carolina 1973.

DOOYEWEERD, HERMAN, *A New Critique of Theoretical Thought*, Vol. III–IV, The Presbyterian and Reformed Publishing Co., United States of America 1969; also *The Christian Idea of the State*, Craig Press, United States of America 1975.

DOUGLAS, J. D. (Ed.), *The New International Dictionary of the Christian Church*, Paternoster Press, Exeter 1974.

ELLIOTT, SYDNEY, *Northern Ireland: The First Election to the European Parliament*, The Queen's University of Belfast 1980.

ELLUL, JACQUES, *Propaganda: The Formation of Men's Attitudes*, Alfred A. Knopf, New York 1965; also *The Ethics of Freedom*, A. R. Mowbrays and Co. Ltd., Oxford 1976; *The New Demons*, A. R. Mowbrays and Co. Ltd., Oxford 1975.

EVELEGH, ROBIN, *Peace-Keeping in a Democratic Society: The Lessons of Northern Ireland*, C. Hurst and Co., London 1978.

FISK, ROBERT, *The Point of No Return: The Strike which Broke the British in Ulster*, Times Books, Andre Deutsch, London 1975.

FLACKES, W. D., *Northern Ireland: A Political Directory 1968–79*, Gill and MacMillan, Dublin 1980.

GARDNER, LOUIS, *Resurgence of the Majority*, No publisher given, Belfast 1971.

GIBBON, PETER, *The Origins of Ulster Unionism: The Formation of Popular Protestant Politics and Ideology in Nineteenth Century Ireland*, Manchester University Press 1975.

GROENNINGS, S., KELLEY, E. W. AND LEIZERSON, M., *The Study of Coalition Behaviour: Theoretical Perspectives and Cases from Four Continents*, Holt Rinehart and Winston inc., New York 1970.

HARBINSON, J. F., *The Ulster Unionist Party 1882–1973, Its Development and Organisation*, Blackstaff Press, Belfast 1973.

HESKIN, KEN, *Northern Ireland: A Psychological Analysis*, Gill and MacMillan, Dublin 1980.

HESLINGA, M. W., *The Irish Border as a Cultural Divide*, Van Gorcum and Co., Assen 1971.

HEZLET, SIR ARTHUR, *The 'B' Specials: A History of the Ulster Special Constabulary*, Pan Books Ltd., London 1972.

HOLMES, R. FINLAY, *Henry Cooke*, Christian Publications, Belfast 1981.

KELLY, HENRY, *How Stormont Fell*, Gill and MacMillan, Dublin 1972.

KITSON, FRANK, *Low Intensity Operations: Subversion, Insurgency and Peacekeeping*, Faber and Faber, London 1971.

LIJPHART, AREND, *The Politics of Accommodation: Pluralism and Democracy in the Netherlands*, University of California Press 1968.

LINDSAY, A. D., *The Essentials of Democracy*, 2nd edn, Clarendon Press, Oxford 1967.

MANN, GOLO, *The History of Germany Since 1789*, Chatto and Windus, London 1968.

MARRINAN, PATRICK, *Paisley: Man of Wrath*, Anvil Books Ltd., Tralee, County Kerry 1973.

MARTIN, DAVID, *A General Theory of Secularization*, Basil Blackwell, Oxford 1978.

MCALLISTER, IAN, *The Northern Ireland Social Democratic and Labour Party: Political Opposition in a Divided Society*, MacMillan, London 1977.

MCCANN, EAMONN, *War and an Irish Town*, Penguin Books, Harmondsworth, Middlesex 1974.

MCCREA, WILLIAM, *In His Pathway: The Story of the Rev. William McCrea*, Lutterworth Press, Marshall Morgan and Scott, London 1980.

MCNEILL, JOHN T., *Calvin: On God and Political Duty*, 2nd edn, Bobbs-Merrill Educational Publishing, Indianapolis 1977.

MICHELS, ROBERT, *Political Parties: A Sociological Study of the Oligarchical Tendencies of Modern Democracy*, Dover Publications inc., New York 1959.

MILLER, DAVID W., *Queen's Rebels: Ulster Loyalism in Historical Perspective*, Gill and MacMillan, Dublin 1978.

MOXON-BROWNE, EDWARD, *Nation, Class and Creed in Northern Ireland*, Gower, Aldershot 1983.

NELSON, SARAH, 'Ulster's Uncertain Defenders: A Study of Loyalists in Political, Paramilitary and Community Organisations in Belfast 1969–1975' (PhD thesis, University of Strathclyde), now published by Appletree Press, Belfast 1984.

O'NEILL, TERENCE, *The Autobiography of Terence O'Neill, Prime Minister of Northern Ireland 1963–1969*, Rupert Hart-Davis, London 1972.

PACKER, J. I., *'Fundamentalism' and the Word of God: Some Evangelical Principles*, Inter-Varsity Fellowship, London 1958.

PAISLEY, IAN R. K., *An Exposition of the Epistle to the Romans Prepared in the Prison Cell*, Marshall Morgan and Scott, London 1968; also *Nicholson Centenary 1876–1976: From Civil War to Revival Victory*, Martyrs Memorial Publications, Belfast 1976; *My Father and My Mother: Loving Tributes by their Younger Son*, Martyrs Memorial Publications, Belfast 1973; *The '59 Revival: An Authentic History of the Great Ulster Awakening of 1859*, 4th edn, Published by the Martyrs Memorial Free Presbyterian Church, Belfast 1970; *The Crown Rights of Jesus Christ*, Martyrs Memorial Productions, Belfast 1985; *The Ulster Problem: A Discussion of the True Situation in Northern Ireland*, Bob Jones University Press, Greenville, South Carolina 1972.

PRIMMER, J. BOYD, *Life of Jacob Primmer, Minister of the Church of Scotland*, William Bishop, Edinburgh 1916.

ROSE, RICHARD, *Governing Without Consensus: An Irish Perspective*, Faber and Faber, London 1971; also *The Problem of Party Government*, Penguin Books, Harmondsworth, Middlesex 1974.

RUTHERFORD, SAMUEL, *Lex Rex* or *The Law and The Prince*, Sprinkle Publications, Harrisonburg, Virginia 1980.

STEVENSON, DAVID, *Scottish Covenanters and Irish Confederates: Scottish-Irish Relations in the Mid-Seventeenth Century*, Ulster Historical Foundation, Belfast 1981.

STEWART, A. T. Q., *The Narrow Ground: Aspects of Ulster 1609–1969*, Faber and Faber, London 1977; also *The Ulster Crisis*, Faber and Faber, London 1967.

THIELICKE, HELMUT, *Theological Ethics Vol. II Politics*, William B. Eerdmans Publishing Co., Grand Rapids, Michigan 1979.

VIGUERIE, RICHARD A., *The New Right: We're Ready to Lead*, The Viguerie Company, Falls Church, Virginia 1980.

WALLER, P. J., *Democracy and Sectarianism: A Political and Social History of Liverpool 1868–1939*, Liverpool University Press 1981.

WEBER, MAX, *On Charisma and Institution Building*, The University of Chicago Press, Chicago 1968.

WELLS, DAVID F. AND WOODBRIDGE, JOHN D., *The Evangelicals: What They Believe, Who They Are, Where They Are Changing*, Baker House Books, Grand Rapids, Michigan 1977.

WHYTE, JOHN H., *Church and State in Modern Ireland 1923–1970*, Gill and MacMillan, Dublin 1971.

Relevant Government publications, Parliamentary Reports, newspapers, pamphlets, articles in academic journals, periodicals etc. were also consulted.

Alphabetical List of Persons Interviewed

ADAM, JOHN: Grand Secretary of the Grand Orange Lodge of Scotland. Mr Adam was the first to invite Rev. Ian Paisley to Scotland to address an Orange Rally in the early 1950s.

ANNESLEY, ALAN: Unsuccessful DUP candidate in the 1973 Northern Ireland Assembly election, and a member of South Antrim DUP constituency association.

BAIRD, ERNEST: Leader of the United Ulster Unionist Party.

BEGGS, ROY MP: DUP Mayor of Larne, later left the Party and became successful Official Unionist candidate in June 1983 Westminster general election for constituency of East Antrim.

BLEAKES, WILLIAM: Member of the DUP in North Down. Thereafter Official Unionist councillor in Lisburn and Member of the Northern Ireland Parliamentary Assembly.

BROWN, REV. JOHN: Lecturer at the New University of Ulster (retired); Grand Master of County Antrim Grand Orange Lodge.

CAMPBELL, JACK: DUP party activist South Antrim constituency.

CARSON, JOHN MP: Formerly Lord Mayor of Belfast and MP for North Belfast.

CLELLAND, ROBERT: One time Secretary of Ravenhill Road Free Presbyterian Church.

COULTER, MISS JEAN: Former Member of the Northern Ireland Assembly 1973 and the Northern Ireland Constitutional Convention 1975.

CRAIG, RT. HON. WILLIAM: Leader of the Vanguard Party. Formerly a Cabinet Minister in the Stormont Parliament. Later held Westminster Constituency of East Belfast for UUUC; lost seat to Peter Robinson in 1979.

DONACHIE, REV. TIM: Reformed Presbyterian minister, Cregagh Road Congregation, Belfast. Attended the Free Presbyterian theological hall as a trainee for the mission field.

EMPEY, REG: Unionist activist; served in the Young Unionists of the Ulster Unionist Party; left with William Craig and joined the Vanguard Party. Member of the Northern Ireland Constitutional Convention, later supported Ernest Baird and UUUP. Served as Official Unionist on the Assembly before that institution was dissolved in 1986.

GOWDY, MARVYN: Unionist activist; supported Craig and the Vanguard Party, and played an important role in the constituency of South Belfast.

GREEN, REV. NORMAN: Minister of Omagh Evangelical Presbyterian Church, formerly a Free Presbyterian minister.

HARVEY, CECIL: A leading lay figure in the Free Presbyterian Church of Ulster; supported Vanguard Party and elected to Northern Ireland Constitutional Convention; later joined the DUP.

HOLMES, WILLIAM: Now deceased; edited the monthly magazine 'Ulster Protestant'.

HORNE, REV. SINCLAIR: General Secretary, Scottish Reformation Society Edinburgh. Sinclair Horne has a detailed knowledge of Protestant political activists.

HUNTER, ALBERT: Loyalist activist, especially in the Orange Order in Belfast, and the DUP in South Antrim.

HUTTON, REV. GEORGE: Minister of Larne Bible Presbyterian Church, formerly minister of Larne Free Presbyterian Church.

LENNON, JOHN: Unionist activist in North Down.

LUCAS, ALAN: Appointed co-ordinating Secretary of the DUP in October 1971.

MACLEAN, J. G.: Leading Edinburgh Orangeman. Last Scottish Protestant Action candidate to contest a local government election (1972).

MCCUSKER, HAROLD MP: MP for Upper Bann.

MILLAR, FRANK SEN.: Secretary of Ulster Protestant Action; went on to establish himself as a highly successful Independent Unionist in North Belfast, being elected successively to the Northern Ireland Assembly, the Constitutional Convention and the new Northern Ireland Assembly.

MOLYNEAUX, RT. HON. JAMES MP JP: Leader of the Ulster Unionist Party and MP for South Antrim and, more recently, Lagan Valley.

PORTER, REV. NORMAN: Baptist minister, formerly leading figure in the Evangelical Protestant Society and associate of Rev. Ian Paisley in the early 1950s.

POWELL, RT. HON. J. ENOCH MP MBE: Member of Parliament for South Down.

SMYTH, REV. W. MARTIN MP: Member for South Belfast, Grand Master of the Grand Orange Lodge of Ireland.

THOMPSON, WALLACE BA: Former Finance Officer of the DUP.

TRIMBLE, DAVID LLB: Formerly Vanguard Party member elected to Northern Ireland Constitutional Convention; supported Craig over Voluntary Coalition proposal. Later joined Ulster Unionist Party.

WYLIE, GEORGE: Associate of Rev. George Hutton. Detailed knowledge of Free Presbyterianism in Ulster (father being Rev. John Wylie, a close associate of Rev. Ian Paisley and Protestant Unionist candidate in North Antrim in 1969).

Apart from a number of interviews which are non-attributable, there were conversations of considerable value with the following persons: William Black, Dr Steve Bruce, David Lyle, Charles McCullough, Charles McCreary, Frank Millar Jnr, Ed Moloney, Conor O'Clery, T. Johnson Reid and David Taylor.

Index of Names

Adams, Gerry, successful candidate for Sinn Fein in West Belfast, 1983 Westminster election, 185

Allen, David, warning regarding Action Council strike, 112

Allister, Jim, appointment to post as EEC adviser to Ian Paisley, 167

Ardill, Austin, initial involvement with Vanguard Party, 38
in 1973 Assembly election, 80
attitude to UUUC, 86
on three man negotiating team in 1975 Convention, 101
in secret talks with Paddy Devlin and John Hume of SDLP, 108

Arlow, Rev. William, role in setting up talks between church leaders and IRA, 94

Armstrong, Dr John, Paisley protest at enthronement as Archbishop, 170

Ashby, Ted, involvement in internal DUP dispute, 66

Atkins, Humphrey, appointment as Secretary of State, 166
initiation of constitutional talks, 167
replaced by Prior, 177

Baird, Ernest, on Free Presbyterian assistance for DUP in 1973 Border Poll, 37
leader of new movement which succeeded Vanguard, 104
formation of United Unionist Action Council in response to Direct Rule, 106
and Ulster Service Corps, 107
and demise of Vanguard, 155
invitation to Unionists for talks (1978), 156

Barry, Peter, implementation of Anglo-Irish Agreement, 191

Beattie, Rev. William, S. Antrim by-election, 1970, 25

N. Belfast general election, 1970, 25
Assembly candidature, 46
political career in DUP, 64
role in quashing controversial resolution, 65
on three man UUUC negotiating team in 1975 Convention, 100
setback as a result of initial attitude to Voluntary Coalition solution, 103
suggestion that he stand as second runner in EEC election, 160
and meeting of vigilantes at Ballymena on 5.2.81, 173
feud with William Belshaw, 186

Beggs, Rev. James, party position, 43
organisation of EEC election campaign, 164

Beggs, Roy MP, failure to conform to DUP norms, 136
win for Official Unionists in East Antrim in 1983 Westminster election, 185

Belshaw, William, involvement in internal DUP dispute, 66
resignation from DUP, 186

Bleakes, William, on leader's role in party sub-committees, 63

Boal, Desmond, and Ulster Protestant Action, 7
Constitution of UPA, 8
Shankill seat at Stormont, 10
W. Belfast 1966 Westminster election, 14
opposition to O'Neill, 19
increasing influence, 24
criticism of Callaghan–Chichester–Clark initiative, 24
part in formation of DUP, 28
and policy of total integration, 36
view of Roman Catholic influence in Northern Ireland politics, 36
resignation from DUP, 36, 77

199